Loire Valley

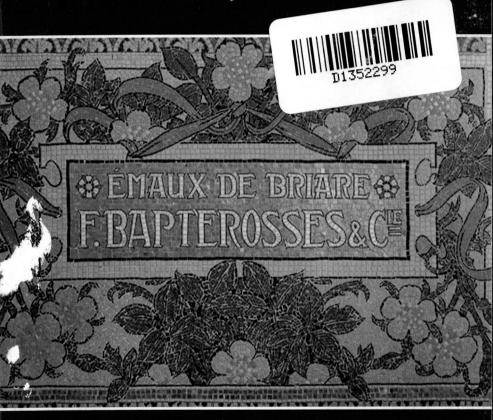

ÉMAUX DE BRIARE
F. BAPTEROSSES & Cᴵᴱ

...ger Moss

Introducing the region

About the region

Sancerre to the Orléanais

Blois & the Sologne

The Touraine

Anjou

Practicalities

The Nantais

Contents

About the author

Roger & Julia Moss

Roger Moss trained as a graphic designer before somehow managing to combine a career in advertising with that of professional guitarist, an activity which found him travelling the world. He soon developed a love for travel (and France in particular) and began using his creative abilities to share his experiences. He has since seen hundreds of illustrated magazine features published on France alone, and shot location photography to illustrate travel guides. Roger was Editor of *Everything France* Magazine and has been a member of the International Advisory Council of Atout France since its inception. An unexpected assignment in Quebec 'to learn to ski' fired a new passion which added 'ski journalist and photgrapher' to his expanding CV.

Roger has a daughter and lives in France with his wife Julia, whom he met while living in Cornwall. They now work and travel together, producing features on everything

Acknowledgements

The author would like to thank the enthusiastic tourism professionals who aided them during the various stages of their research. Particular thanks go to Hélène Haubois (Atout France, London), Hélène Ramsamy (Anjou Tourist Board, Angers), Katia Forêt (Nantes Metropole Tourist Office), Sarah Manser (Red Lemon PR, London), Frédérique Colin and Jean-Sebastian Mutschler (CRT Région Centre, Orléans), Samuel Buchwalder (CDT Touraine, Tours), Sandrine Goudeau (Domaine de Chaumont). 'Merci', too, to all those for whom we have insufficient space to name.

Most of all, though, I have to offer heartfelt thanks to Julia, who has a professional background in countryside management and sustainable tourism. Julia's unfailing ability to handle even the most deeply unappealing research tasks proved absolutely vital to the production of this book. Quite simply, I couldn't have done it without her.

About the book

The guide is divided into four sections: Introducing the region; About the region; Around the region and Practicalities.

Introducing the region comprises: At a glance, which explains how the region fits together by giving the reader a snapshot of what to look out for and what makes the region distinct from other parts of the country; **Best of Loire Valley** (top 20 highlights); **A year in Loire Valley**, which is a month-by-month guide to pros and cons of visiting at certain times of year; and **Screen & page**, which is a list of suggested books and films.

About the region comprises: History; Art & architecture; **Loire Valley today**, which present different aspects of life in the region today; **Nature & environment** (an overview of the landscape and wildlife); **Festivals & events; Sleeping** (an overview of accommodation options); **Eating & drinking** (an overview of the region's cuisine, as well as advice on eating out); **Entertainment** (an overview of the region's cultural credentials, explaining what entertainment is on offer); **Shopping** (what are the region's specialities and recommendations for the best buys); and **Activities & tours**.

Around the region is then broken down into five areas, each with its own chapter. Here you'll find all the main sights and at the end of each chapter is a listings section with all the best sleeping, eating & drinking, entertainment, shopping and activities & tours options plus a brief overview of public transport.

Sleeping price codes
€€€€ over €200 per night for a double room in high season
€€€ €100-200
€€ €60-100
€ under €60

Eating & drinking price codes
€€€€ over €40 per person for a 2-course meal with a drink, including service and cover charge
€€€ €30-40
€€ €20-30
€ under €20

Map symbols

	l'Information Information		Gare Train station
○	Endroit d'intérêt Place of interest	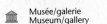	Gare routière Bus station
🏛	Musée/galerie Museum/gallery	Ⓜ	Station de métro Metro station
🎭	Théâtre Theatre	—●—	Ligne de tram Tram route
✉	Poste Post office		Marché Market
†	Eglise/cathédrale Church/cathedral	✚	Hôpital Hospital
	Mur de ville City wall	⊞	Pharmacie Pharmacy
P	Parking	🎓	Lycée College

Tuffeau stone townhouse, Loches.

Contents

Introducing the region

In the eyes and hearts of those who continue to fall under its spell, the Loire Valley represents the very soul of *la douce France*, a place of enchantment in which anything seems possible. And it's easy to see why, for where else can you find such a dazzling selection of extraordinary places in quite such an appealing package? No wonder a large proportion of the region is now classified by UNESCO as a World Heritage Site. The signs are everywhere, from world renowned vineyards, whose origins lie in the vines planted by the Romans, to elegant Renaissance chateaux created by kings and noblemen as places of pleasure and diversion. Gardens, too, are often exquisitely landscaped, creating an earthly paradise in what has long been aptly referred to as the Garden of France. It's also a realm of mysticism and spirituality, of holy sites dating from the dawn of Christianity, spectacular Gothic cathedrals reaching skywards and where a medieval abbey still resonates to the haunting chant of medieval plainsong. And, ever present, flowing among gentle landscapes shaped through millennia by the extraordinary people who have settled here, is the hypnotic presence of France's longest river.

At a glance

A whistle-stop tour of the Loire Valley

The birthplace of a mighty river.

The area we now refer to as the Loire Valley sits little more than a third of the way down the map of France. The river, although a constant presence, is often upstaged by the star attractions which lie along its banks, and by the more abstract concept of *l'art de vivre* – literally 'the art of living' – which underpin the privileged lifestyle on offer here. The Loire trickles into life far from the spotlight as three springs on the flanks of Mont Gerbier de Jonc (1551 m), a windswept volcanic pillar in the Ardèche region of southeastern France. Resisting the temptation to join the nearby Rhône, the infant river instead flows northwards, rapidly gathering strength as it bypasses Le Puy-en-Velay and St-Etienne en route for Roanne, and a subtle northwesterly progression. After broadening out near Nevers the river begins a gentle sweeping arc which finally tightens around Orléans, before relaxing into a pattern of gentle meanders which will take it, at last, through the fertile heartland and celebrated vineyards of the Loire Valley. The theory goes that in prehistoric times the river continued north to join the Seine, until a major geological or climatic event forced it westwards, where it formed an alliance with a stream surfacing near Gien. The result is the present course of the mighty Loire, which flows resolutely west and into the Atlantic beyond beyond Nantes at St-Nazaire.

Sancerre to the Orléanais

From the eastern edge of our area come two of the Loire Valley's most renowned wines: noble Pouilly Fumé, developed by monks during the 12th century, and crisp, fruity **Sancerre** – the perfect accompaniment for the local Crottin de Chavignol goat's cheese. A little further downstream is **Briare**, whose historic enamelled mosaic production is celebrated in a colourful museum. It's also the point at which the 17th-century Canal de Briare crosses the Loire on a spectacular belle époque aqueduct almost 700 m in length. You'll find another historic crossing, the 12-arched Vieux Pont, at nearby **Gien**, whose distinctive glazed earthenware is still produced by a company founded in 1821 by Englishman Thomas Hall. For a more spiritual experience visit St-Benoît-sur-Loire, where the ancient **Abbaye de Fleury** continues to resonate to the medieval chant of monks from the order of St Benedict, whose remains rest in the crypt. Across the river lies the moated chateau of **Sully-sur-Loire**, where Joan of Arc convinced Henry VII to accept the French crown in 1429. And if you like your history combined with city buzz then it's well worth exploring **Orléans**, gateway to 50,000 ha of protected ancient forest offering a peaceful haven for away-from-it-all activities.

Blois & the Sologne

We now enter the Valley of Kings, whose gentle landscapes were enriched beyond measure by the presence of the royal court and a love affair with the Italian Renaissance, which saw austere military fortresses transformed into showpiece chateaux. At Blois' sumptuous **Château Royal** you can see how powerful, visionary monarchs indulged their creative desires and began the wave of refinement which would inspire the great chateaux of the Loire Valley. Some, like family-owned **Cheverny** and François I's vast and ruinously extravagant **Chambord**, still function as hunting estates, while others like **Chaumont**, with its internationally renowned garden festivals, have found exciting

The lowdown

Money matters
If you visit two main attractions a day and enjoy restaurant meals, allow €50-70 each per day on top of what you pay for your accommodation.

Opening hours
Most major attractions open all year except public holidays. Many sites close at lunchtime during the winter, and smaller establishments may close completely after the end of October. If you want to visit somewhere specific outside the summer months it's always best to check before travelling. Cathedrals and churches welcome visitors all year round, but avoid Sunday mornings unless you wish to attend religious services.

Tourist passes
You can buy discount passes to some top sites and attractions. **Le Pass Châteaux**, from Blois, Cheverny, Chambord and Bracieux, for example, offers different combinations of visits, and the popular **Blois/ Chambord/Cheverny/Chaumont-sur-Loire** pass costs €26 – a saving of €5.90 on normal entrance fees. Free travel on public transport is included with the **Pass Nantes**.

Tourist information
For general information visit the Loire Valley Tourism site www.loirevalleytourism.com. The Blois and Chambord (bloispaysdechambord.com), Touraine (tourism-touraine.com), Anjou (anjou-tourisme. com) and Nantes (nantes-tourisme.com) websites (English versions available) are packed with ideas and information. Most towns and villages have their own tourist information offices, which are often a good place to start your visit.

Pick of the picnic spots

The riverside meadows at **Montrésor** with a fine view to the chateau.
At sunset during a boat trip from **Candes-St-Martin**.
On the vast lawns in front of the **Château de Chambord**.
In a shady spot overlooking the vineyards around **Sancerre**.
On a bench in the fragrant rose gardens of the **Parc de Richelieu**.

The Château de Montrésor.

new destinies. But the region also holds many surprises in store, not least historic towns like **Vendôme** and **Romorantin-Lanthenay**, where you'll discover the Espace Matra motor museum and the excellent Musée de la Sologne. There's no better introduction to this under-appreciated natural haven, whose man-made lakes and ancient forests have sustained the local people for centuries, and which today have become a paradise for walkers, cyclists and birdwatchers. The beauty of the Sologne has also attracted a new wave of potters and other creative talents who live and work in the village of **La Borne**, amid one of the most inspiring settings imaginable.

The Touraine
Here the river flows, apparently unconcerned, through a dazzling concentration of some of the Loire Valley's star attractions: exquisite jewel-like Renaissance creations such as **Azay-le-Rideau** and **Chenonceau** are set among mighty fortress chateaux like **Amboise**, **Chinon** and **Loches**. Some, like **Châtonnière** and **Villandry**, are celebrated for their inspirational gardens, while others such as **Langeais** and **Montrésor** rise proudly above the distinctive slate rooftops of the atmospheric villages which grew around them. So it is with **Tours**, whose symbolic role at the very heart of the Touraine adds a vibrant, upbeat city buzz to its formidable architectural heritage. Don't miss the exquisitely restored Flamboyant Gothic Cathédrale St-Gatien, or the medieval half-timbered and Renaissance stone façades around the famous place Plumereau, its market stalls now replaced by

sought-after bar and restaurant tables. There are few better places in which to meet, wander or enjoy a fine meal than in the historic heart of Tours – make a special point of looking for menus offering delicious, freshly caught river fish. And you can make your own discoveries while sampling some of the Touraine region's fine wines at vineyards around **Bourgeuil**, **Chinon**, **Montlouis** and **Vouvray**.

Anjou
The ancient former kingdom of Anjou today enjoys a certain cult status, qualifying it as one of the Loire Valley's great discoveries for curious visitors. Here the Loire is swelled by several other rivers, including the Maine, which slips beneath the watchful gaze of the mighty 800-year-old **Château d'Angers**. Inside is the world's longest hand-woven tapestry – the monumental Tenture de l'Apocalypse, created in 1375. The town itself has a fabulous wealth of architecture, many great bars and restaurants and is currently creating an efficient new tramway system. Nearby is Brissac-Quincé, highest of all the Loire Valley chateaux, whose estate vineyards were established five centuries ago. Further upriver lies Saumur, another historic town and a romantic setting for diners, with a fairy-tale medieval chateau plus its own fine wines. Not far away is the huge 12th-century Abbaye Royal de Fontevraud, where you'll find the ornate tombs of the great Plantagenêt King Henri II and his wife Aliénor (Eleanor) of Aquitaine. It's a far cry from the mysterious, subterranean world of Doué-la-Fontaine's former stone quarries and

trogolodytic dwellings. Alternatively, the natural richness and diversity of the world are revealed at Terra Botanica, a major new year-round family attraction close to Angers.

The Nantais

The Loire's long journey to the Atlantic brings the now-mighty river to the historic seaport of **Nantes**, birthplace of Jules Verne and for centuries the seat of the powerful Ducs de Bretagne. Standing in midstream is the Ile de Nantes, the fast-redeveloping site of the city's former naval dockyards, where you can ride a giant mechanical elephant and other fantastic *Machines de l'Ile*. Today the vibrant, forward-looking city's bold, modern architecture contrasts with its historic quarters, whose lost quays and waterways once made Nantes the 'Venice of France'. Similarly atmospheric are the palatial 19th-century salons of the legendary Brasserie la Cigale, and the Passage Pommeraye, a magnificent early 19th-century shopping arcade which became a classic French cinéma location. Alternatively, just below Nantes you can visit world-famous vineyards producing crisp, refreshing white wines including **Muscadet-Sèvre et Maine** which, in the hands of dedicated winemakers, are now achieving generous fruitiness. For a quieter mood, head upriver to historic villages like **Champtoceaux**, where you can enjoy one of the finest elevated panoramas of the river, find perfect peace in a woodland walk down to the riverbank, or look out for wildlife during a gentle summer river cruise.

The Grand Eléphant now roams the Ile de Nantes.

Best of the Loire Valley

Top 20 things to see & do

❶ Château & Domaine de Chambord

The greatest of all the Loire Valley chateaux, created with a royal hunting estate the size of Paris by François I, continues to stun all who see it. The genius behind its design remains a mystery – could it have been the King's protegé Leonardo da Vinci? Page 121.

❷ Puces de Montsoreau

Hunt for a bargain with a real French Country flavour at this monthly Sunday antique and flea market held in an incomparable setting on the banks of the Loire. It's the real thing, prices are reasonable and afterwards you can cool off with a refreshing drink in a nearby bar terrace. Page 247.

❸ Festival International des Parcs et Jardins

Each summer the estate of Château de Chaumont set high above the Loire hosts an unmissable event revealing the talents of contemporary designers from all over the world. On summer evenings the chateau (open to visitors) is transformed by candlelight and the show gardens are illuminated. Page 135.

2 Les Puces de Montsoreau antiques market.

4 King's bedchamber, Château de Cheverny.

❹ Château de Cheverny
One of the most elegant of all the great Renaissance country chateaux, Cheverny is still lived in by the descendants of the family for whom it was built. As a result, the sumptuous interiors are perfectly preserved and the historic hunting estate which surrounds this showpiece of the Sologne retains its natural splendour. Page 126.

❺ *Son et lumière*
When dusk falls, great chateaux like Azay-le-Rideau, Chambord and Chenonceau undergo a miraculous transformation, courtesy of state-of-the-art sound and lighting effects. Add to this the dazzling reflections which sparkle and flash from the surrounding waters and you have a spectacular summer experience you'll never forget. Pages 121, 182 and 260.

❻ Château Royal de Blois
Several French kings resided and indulged their passions for art, and much more, right here. The lovingly restored medieval jewel box interiors will dazzle you, and there's no better introduction to the architecture of the Loire Valley than the chateau itself. And don't miss the historic town at its feet. Page 114.

❼ Château et Jardins de Villandry
It takes a lot to upstage this sensitively restored Renaissance chateau, but its vast formal gardens have no problem doing just that. Finally seeing for yourself their exquisitely maintained *parterres*, avenues and ornamental lake is something you'll never forget. Page 178.

❽ Teinture de l'Apocalypse
The mighty fortress-like Château d'Angers guards one of the Loire Valley's most precious treasures: the legendary Apocalypse Tapestry, created over six centuries ago by order of Louis I. In the dimly lit, hushed stillness of its specially constructed gallery the startling imagery of 74 huge, hand-stitched panels will leave you awestruck. Page 228.

❾ A hot-air balloon ride
Lose the crowds by heading up and away. The great chateaux and their surrounding landscapes look even more magical when seen from above, in the cool of early morning or while the evening sun sinks and shadows lengthen. Page 69.

Introducing the region

10 The restored Château des Ducs de Bretagne, Nantes.

12 Plantgenet tomb, Abbaye de Fontevraud.

⑩ Château des Ducs de Bretagne
The truly remarkable story of the Loire's greatest port is told in the vast and beautifully restored 15th-century Renaissance chateau built by François II and Anne de Bretagne. The very best modern multimedia techniques are sure to entertain visitors of all ages. Page 265.

⑪ Pont-Canal, Briare
Gaze in wonderment as canal boats following the 17th-century Canal de Briare, one of France's oldest waterways, are carried high above the Loire on a spectacular 700-m-long belle époque aqueduct opened in 1876. You can walk or cycle across, too. Page 78.

⑫ Abbaye Royale de Fontevraud
Since it was built during the 12th century, France's largest and most perfectly preserved medieval abbey has also served as a nunnery, leper colony and even a prison. It was a favoured haunt of Eleanor of Aquitaine, who lies buried here alongside her husband Henry II. Page 219.

⑬ Château d'Azay-le-Rideau
The beauty of its setting, amid the waters of the river Indre, provides the perfect complement for the measured elegance of this world-famous Renaissance jewel. Page 183.

⑭ La Cave des Roches, Bourré
Here's where the finest pale *tuffeau* limestone, used to build the great chateaux of the Loire, actually originated. Visit the underground quarries and see for yourself how the stone was extracted by hand by generations of quarrymen. Page 137.

⑮ Machines de l'Ile
The spirit of Jules Verne is reborn in his birthplace of Nantes, whose former naval dockyard workshops now construct fantastic mechanical creatures. See things differently while riding the giant elephant which is attracting visitors from all over the world. Page 261.

⑯ Château de La Ferté-St-Aubin
While this chateau and its estate undergo long and patient restoration, the interiors remain frozen in time. But that's not all; nearby you'll discover a steam locomotive and a set of Orient Express carriages. Page 90.

⑰ A river cruise
Take the road less travelled – by taking to the river. Sections of the Loire and Cher are still navigable, and offer cruises from places like Amboise, Angers, Champtoceaux, Candes St-Martin and Montsoreau. It's a great way to see wildlife, too. Page 68.

⑱ Château de Chenonceau
Audacious in its ambition, the exquisite chateau of Catherine de' Medici began beside the River Cher, and then continued across to the opposite bank. It then added not one but two huge Renaissance gardens. Page 158.

⑲ Clos Lucé
When François I encountered Leonardo da Vinci he invited the great artist, inventor and military engineer to live as his guest in this elegant manor house, close to the royal court in the Château d'Amboise. See his rooms, his beloved gardens, models of his designs and much more. Page 156.

⑳ Montrésor
La Belle France as you've always imagined it: wander along the streets of one of the most beautiful villages in France (yes, it's official), visit the historic chateau which overlooks it and then select the perfect picnic spot along a peaceful riverside walk. Page 166.

19 Leonardo da Vinci's works celebrated in his final home at Clos Lucé, Amboise

Month by month

A year in the Loire Valley

The Parc Floral de La Source, Orléans.

January & February

Not surprisingly, the weather is likely to be cold and frosty for long periods, the upside of which is the chance of clear, steely blue skies which really lift the spirits. New Year is a bigger event in France than Christmas, and celebrations continue to be as lively as ever – particularly in cities, where the atmosphere becomes electric as the magic hour approaches. In situations like this you're unlikely to feel left out.

The post-New Year lull brings cheaper accommodation, but you'll find that many attractions will be closed. This is often the time when owners and staff take off on their own holidays. On the other hand, there are no crowds at major sites which do remain open all year, and which will be particularly pleased to see you, and in the evenings you can enjoy long, cosy fireside suppers.

March & April

Days can often be mild, but don't be surprised if you get some rain, particularly near the coast, where the Breton climate can make its influence felt. Equally, the variable weather means there's every chance of surprisingly warm, sunny days. In the countryside, spring flowers inject fresh colour and the landscape softens as trees come into leaf. Low season (*basse saison*) accommodation prices offer added value, and there's plenty of capacity as long as you avoid the Easter (*Pâques*) period. Towns and cities start to blossom with extravagant plantings of flowers which tell you that summer isn't too far away.

May & June

With spring coming early here, summer can be long. May and particularly June are often characterized by plenty of sun but without excessive heat. It's therefore the ideal time to explore the countryside, take a woodland walk or make use of the Loire Valley's large (and still growing) network of cycle paths. The former towpaths are a particularly attractive option. Long, sunny days which are pleasantly warm allow you to pack a lot in, although in May you'll find that evenings can still be chilly. Visitor-wise, things will be uncrowded except during French May bank holiday periods (*jours fériés*), and during well-supported events like the annual jazz festivals of Cheverny, Loches, Orléans, etc. The markets will be selling mounds of asparagus, strawberries and other fresh local produce, which you'll also see on seasonal menus. Finally, rose gardens start their first flowering, and all gardens will be starting to look their very best.

July & August

Temperatures will be at their highest, and weather can be unpredictable in August. Prolonged dry periods can be followed by summer thunderstorms, which are often spectacular but soon pass, leaving things noticeably cooler and fresher. However, you should still be able to enjoy long, relaxing evenings sitting outside, and take in one of the state-of-the-art *son et lumière* events at major sites like the chateaux of Azay-le-Rideau, Chambord and Chenonceau. In addition, you'll find lots of extra events which are staged specifically for the peak French holiday season, such as Montrichard's evening historical re-enactment shows. But bear in mind also that major tourist sites will be at their most crowded, and gardens will be past their best. Accommodation is also more expensive and vacancies harder to find; the same story applies in popular restaurants, which will also be extra busy. If you've set your heart on experiencing one in particular during your stay, you're advised to book a table in advance to avoid being disappointed.

September & October

Days can still be warm even though evenings are drawing in noticeably and dinners *en terrasse* are no longer a certainty – although perfectly possible in more sheltered settings. The countryside becomes more colourful, with ever-richer foliage colours, including the famous vines. October usually brings the perfect grape picking time, the *vendange* producing an infectious flurry of activity in and around wine-producing villages. If that's simply too late, you can get a taste of the local wines throughout the year by visiting producers, or Saumur's annual wine market, which unfolds

during the first week in September. There are also more festivals for harvests, food and wines, and you can visit historic and other important sites not normally open to the public during the annual *Journées du Patrimoine* weekend, normally around the 18-19 September.

November & December

Days are now short, and can also be cold and damp. Winter, though, brings people together in France, so you'll come across various seasonal events including the famous traditional Christmas markets, which usually begin in late November. There's a great atmosphere in cities like Angers, Nantes, Orléans and Tours, whose street illuminations add a welcome sparkle to winter evenings.

Some chateaux, like Brissac and La Ferté-St-Aubin, host special Christmas events including shows, markets and even candlelit tours during December. When it finally arrives Christmas is a one-day affair – but manages to pack a lot in.

Snowfall transforms the Château de Brézé.

Screen & page

The Loire Valley in film & literature

Films

Fanfan la Tulipe
Gérard Krawczyk, 2003
Both the original classic from 1952 (Christian-Jaque) and this remake starring Penelope Cruz feature the Château du Plessis-Bourré, whose appearance has remained largely unchanged for 500 years. The historical plot shouldn't be taken too seriously, of course.

Fahrenheit 451
François Truffaut, 1966
The monorail which appears in this sci-fi classic was actually a French test track constructed in 1960 at Châteauneuf-sur-Loire. The Metro Aérienne was roughly 2 km in length, and the Renault-designed cars travelled at around 100 kph beneath an elevated concrete track.

Lola
Jacques Demy, 1961
Demy's romantic tale stars Anouk Aimée as cabaret dancer Lola and Marc Michel as Roland, who falls in love with her. Set in Nantes, numerous vividly portrayed characters are woven into the story.

Quentin Durward
Richard Thorpe, 1955
An historical film set in the 15th century, with Robert Morley playing the devious Louis XI and Robert Taylor as Quentin Durward. Filmed almost entirely in the Loire valley, with magnificent background scenes from the chateaux of Chambord and Chenonceau (as Louis XI's castle).

Peau d'Ane
Jacques Demy, 1970
Catherine Deneuve stars as a princess who enlists the help of her fairy godmother to disguise her, thereby avoiding marriage to a man she doesn't love. Also known as *Donkey Skin* and *Once Upon a Time*, the fairy tale was partly filmed at Chambord, but the main location was the chateau at Plessis-Bourré.

Un Homme et Une Femme
Claude Lelouch, 1966
A beautiful film by Claude Lelouch starring Anouk Aimée and Jean-Louis Trintignant. The award-winning romantic drama follows the love kindled between a widowed man and a woman, and features the Passage de Pommeraye in Nantes.

Books

Fiction
Le Lys dans la Vallée
Honoré de Balzac, 1836
Balzac drew inspiration for his novels from local characters and the landscape. This was especially the case in the *Lily of the Valley*, in which he describes the valley of the Indre between Azay-le-Rideau and Pont-de-Ruan, and the first time he set eyes on the Château de Saché.

Five Quarters of the Orange
Joanne Harris, 2002
Set in a small village near Angers, this is the last of the 'food' trilogy, the other titles being *Chocolat* and *Blackberry Wine*. *Five Quarters* follows the

fortunes of a widow and her three children during the German occupation of France, and was inspired by the wartime experiences of the author's maternal grandfather.

Selected Poems
Pierre de Ronsard (Penguin Classics, 2002)
An introduction (in English) to the poetry of Ronsard, including translations of some of both his political and erotic work, with the original Renaissance French versions alongside. Regarded as one of the greatest poets of his time, he lived and worked at the Prieuré de St-Cosme, near Tours. His great love was Cassandre, whose father owned the Château de Talcy, and about whom he wrote the odes Amours de Cassandre, published in 1552.

Gargantua and Pantagruel
François Rabelais (Penguin Classics, 2006)
Born in Chinon at the end of the 15th century, Rabelais is known for his satire and mischievous works of fantasy, still notorious today for their vulgar and obscene humour. Gargantua and Pantagruel is the comical story of two giants, father and son, with some serious passages describing contemporary humanistic ideals.

The Adventures of Tintin
Hergé, 1929-1986
The Château de Cheverny was the inspiration behind Hergé's Marlinspike Hall (Moulinsart for French readers), where it was home to Tintin and his friends in the adventures The Secret of the Unicorn (1942) and Red Rackham's Treasure (1943). Visitors can see a permanent exhibition dedicated to Tintin at Cheverny.

Non-fiction
A Chateau of One's Own: Restoration Misadventures in France
Sam Juneau, 2007
Another from the myriad of tales about restoring property in France. Juneau's amusing story tells of the trials and tribulations when he took on a chateau in the Loire.

Alastair Sawday's Special Places to Stay: French Vineyards
Patrick Hilyer, 2009
A guide for those thirsting for a taste of French culture. The author describes over 70 wine-growers who offer accommodation in a variety of properties, from simple B&Bs to grand chateaux.

French Cheeses
Eyewitness Companions, 2006
A comprehensive and fully illustrated directory of French cheeses, with history and tasting notes that will improve your knowledge and tempt you into trying local delicacies.

French Wine
Robert Joseph, Eyewitness Companions, 2006
An essential and authoritative companion on your wine tours in the Loire Valley and throughout France.

Gardens of the Loire Valley
Marie-Francoise Valéry, 2008
Produced with the support of the Loire Valley region and UNESCO, it takes the reader on a trip to the fabulous gardens of the Loire.

The Most Beautiful Villages of The Loire
Hugh Palmer and James Bentley, 2001
A gentle meander through the region's villages (and towns) with historical insight and a tangible sense of place.

The Traveller's Key to Medieval France: A Guide to the Sacred Architecture of Medieval France
John James, 1987 (British Edition)
There's no better travelling companion to help decode the mysteries of France's oldest buildings, and why they're still able to affect us so profoundly.

Contents

About the region

1950s Renault 4CV, Chinon.

History

A little knowledge of the key events and personalities in the turbulent and convoluted history of France will add a whole new dimension to your visits here in the Valley of Kings.

Prehistory

At the dawn of mankind, during the Middle Palaeolithic period (90,000-40,000 BC), much of the area of what now constitutes the Loire Valley would have been inhabited by Neanderthal hunter-gatherers, who led a nomadic existence and fashioned primitive stone hand tools. Their successor, 'modern' man, endured the Ice Age about 20,000 years ago, witnessed the disappearance of mammoth, reindeer and rhinoceros from the area, refined hunting techniques and began to settle, herd animals and sow crops. As cultivation became widespread, settlements grew and areas of forest began to be cleared. The presence of numerous menhirs, dolmens and other megalithic monuments dating from around 3500 BC indicates that the southern banks of the Loire were settled extensively by Neolithic man. The establishment of a regional identity came a significant stage closer during the first century BC with the arrival – probably from the Celtic lands – of what are generally referred to as the Gallic tribes. The Cenomani people, for example, developed into a highly organized society and traded in its own currency. They would also fight fiercely when threatened by outside forces, as the Barbarians, and even the Roman legions, discovered. Other tribes existing in this area at about the same time included the Namnetes around Nantes, the Andes (or Andecavi) from the Anjou area, the Pictones from northern Poitou, the Turones from Tours and the Bituriges and Carnutes around Orléans. Subjugating their combined resistance would prove to be a protracted and tiresome affair for the Romans.

Prehistoric remains

The Dolmen de Bagneux, near Saumur, is the largest in all France, with a length of 23 m by 5 m wide, while you'll find what is quite possibly the smallest tucked away in the Landes-le-Gaulois just north of Blois. To find some of the less obvious and wooded sites, you'll have to refer to detailed IGN maps and be prepared to walk, but a fine menhir is visible at the roadside (D751) north of Gennes.

Neolithic burial-chamber, Gennes.

Gallo-Roman vessel, Collégiale Saint-Ours, Loches.

Roman occupation – a modest local legacy

The Roman conquest of what they referred to as Gaul was eventually completed in AD 52, although not without a final indignant revolt the following year by Dumnacos, commander of the Andes. Then began a long period of occupation during which the familiar model of Roman refinement was systematically applied to this new territory. Not surprisingly, it wasn't long before centres of trade and authority were established – one of the first was the former Carnute stronghold of Cenabum, on which Orléans now stands. It was rebuilt from its post-battle ruined state and renamed Aurelianis, its surrounding territories becoming civitatis Aurelianorum. The process continued along the Loire (which they referred to as the Liger), the Turone settlement of what is now Tours becoming Caesarodunum and the present site of Angers developed as Juliomagus. With the establishment of trade and commerce, estates also appeared, centred around villas, thus promoting a period of stability and prosperity that lasted until the late third century – by which time it was deemed necessary to fortify much of what had been created. It was an early but ominous indicator of a changing world order; the occupation ended with an urgent return to a very different Rome during the late fifth century.

Today there's relatively little in the way of visible evidence of the Roman presence. But although you won't find the great, well preserved arenas of Provence, you are likely to stumble upon more modest traces of early construction when and where you least expect them. The city of Tours, for example, preserves parts of the original fortified castrum walls, traces of a huge arena and private baths. A little further west near Luynes you'll find an arched section of a Gallo-Roman aqueduct, along with a curious brick-built tower from the second century at Cinq-Mars-la-Pile. Its purpose (possibly a burial monument) is now unknown, unlike the forlorn coursed limestone walls and trenches which are all that remain of Tasciaca, an early centre of pottery and ceramics production. You'll find it at Thésée-la-Romaine, south of Montrichard. Discoveries from these and nearby excavations are displayed in the village Musée Archéologique, and you can visit the site of a Gallo-Roman temple and thermal baths at nearby Pouillé.

Elsewhere you'll have occasional chance encounters with Roman artefacts in churches, either in the form of fonts and other stone objects (see Collégiale St-Ours in Loches) or in sections of early masonry incorporated in later rebuilding. Of course, for the most potent visual legacy of the Roman presence in the Loire Valley you need look no further than the great vineyards which drape the landscape like giant candlewick bedspreads, and which continue a tradition of viticulture dating back to the first vines transported here and planted in the Pays Nantais by the occupying forces of Rome.

About the region

The coming of Christianity

According to fifth-century St Gregory (Gregorius) of Tours, Pope Fabian's emissary Gatianus began preaching the gospel locally in 250, possibly from a hermit-like cave close to Vouvray. At first he was met with great hostility, but he persevered and during the course of 50 years of constant and dedicated toil he gathered many converts, some of whom he then dispatched to establish churches in other areas of France. He became first Evêque (Bishop) of Tours in AD 304 and the city's Cathédrale St-Gatien (see page 171) is still dedicated to him. On his death things entered a period of instability until the appointment of St-Martin (a former Roman officer who had converted to Christianity) as Bishop of Tours in 371. Two years later he founded the nearby abbey of Marmoutiers. He died in 397 and lies in the Basilique St-Martin (see page 174).

The fifth century was a difficult period, with invasions by Visigoths (who took Tours in 476) and Huns, who attacked Orléans in 451, but were successfully resisted by forces led by Bishop (later St) Aignan. The invaders were finally routed, further south in Poitou, by Frankish King Clovis in 507. The following year Clovis, reformer of the Merovingian dynasty of Franks, celebrated his own coronation in the Basilica in Tours. The greatest documenter of this era was Gregory, sixth-century Bishop of Tours, who created his *Decem Libri Historiarum* (Ten Historic Chronicles), which later became known as *l'Historia Francorum* (A History of the Franks).

Another key event in western history took place between Tours and Poitiers in 732 when the Saracens were vanquished by the forces of Charles Martel in the Battle of Poitiers – the prisoners were held in or around Véron, west of Chinon, and many later settled in the area. Martel's descendant Charlemagne (768-814) unified the Carolingian dynasty, which endured until the 10th century.

Medieval era & the Renaissance

In 987 Hugues Capet (the first Capetian King) was elected ruler in the Cathédrale St-Croix d'Orléans (see page 89), heralding a period of relative stability for the Franks. However, bitter rivalries flared over Touraine, which was eyed covetously by the counts of both Anjou and Blois. The victor proved to be feared warrior Foulques III, count of Anjou, who was dubbed *'le Noir'* (the Black) and became known as Foulques Nerra. With his son Geoffroi Martel he then expanded his territories by seizing Maine and the Vendômois, and constructed a series of impressive fortresses, including the donjons of Langeais (see page 177), Loches (see page 162) and Montrichard (see page 136). In 1110 one of his descendants, Geoffroi V d'Anjou, married Mathilde, daughter of Henry I of England, beginning a train of events which eventually saw his son Henri Plantagenêt becoming King Henry II of England after his marriage to Aliénore (Eleanor) d'Aquitaine in 1152. Her previous annulled marriage to Louis VII only added to the bitterness of the subsequent power struggle between the Capetian and Plantagenêt empires which ended with Henri accepting defeat (and dying shortly afterwards) at Chinon (see page 191) in 1189. He and Aliénor lie buried in the Abbaye de Fontevraud (see page 219).

Cathédrale Sainte-Croix, Orléans.

The last of the Capetian Kings, Charles I, died in 1328, leaving no male heir. Soon afterwards pretender to the throne Philippe de Valois was crowned Philippe VI of France. Already heir to Anjou, Maine and Valois, he had a fondness for the Loire Valley, and established a royal presence here which would last for two centuries. Philippe's thwarted rival for the French throne was Edward III of England, who began what was eventually to become known as the Hundred Years' War between the two nations in 1337. By 1369 Aquitaine had fallen under English rule, and in 1415 Henry V defeated the French armies in the Battle of Agincourt. Within five years Charles VI had reluctantly signed the Treaty of Troyes, disinheriting his son the Dauphin Charles, who escaped to the Loire, staying in the chateaux of both Chinon (see page 191) and Loches (see page 162). However, in 1421 the English forces were routed at Baugé near Saumur (see page 215), encouraging Charles to reclaim the French throne. The Loire soon became a battle zone, English troops famously laying siege to Orléans in 1428. Against all odds, and with Joan of Arc's encouragement and spiritual leadership, the French forces triumphed and the Dauphin

The grand escalier of the Château Royal de Blois.

The enduring legacy of Foulques Nerra

Throughout the Loire Valley you'll come across the name of Foulques (Foulque or Fulk) Nerra. This powerful Count of Anjou (987-1040) proved himself both a formidable warrior in battle and a similarly unforgiving adversary in everyday life – it is said, for example, that after suspecting her of adultery he had his wife burnt alive. He also eyed Touraine covetously, as did his counterpart Eudes (or Odo) de Blois, whom he defeated at Pontlevoy (between Tours and Blois) in 1016. As his territories continued to expand he defended them by constructing a series of fortresses at strategic locations such as Langeais (see page 177), Loches, (see page 162) and Montrichard (see page 136). Of the many such structures he originally built only foundations and other less-visible portions now remain, underpinning later and more sophisticated reconstructions. At Langeais, however, you can still see a substantial part of the donjon

he created around 990 (the earliest stone fortress in France), standing on a hill behind the present chateau. Nerra's aggressive qualities were obviously only part of a complex personality, for he undertook four pilgrimages to the Holy Lands in penance for his actions, and was also responsible for establishing the abbey of St-Nicolas d'Angers and another at Beaulieu-les-Loches, where he was buried.

Not that all his monuments are confined to early architecture. During a violent storm at sea during one of his voyages, Nerra prayed for deliverance to the Patron Saint of mariners. In gratitude for his prayers apparently having been answered, he created the Etang St-Nicolas, a large lake just to the east of Angers. Completed around 1000, the works yielded huge quantities of slate which were then used in the construction of the vast chateau of Angers (see page 228).

became Charles VII. Joan, on the other hand, was tried for heresy and burnt at the stake in 1431 when she was just 19 years old. After driving the English from most of France, Charles settled into an easier life in Loches with his wife Marie d'Anjou and his mistress Agnès Sorel.

The Loire power base shifted to Tours, which assumed great prosperity after Louis XI came to power in 1461 and saw powerful families flexing their economic muscle by constructing showpiece townhouses and chateaux. The Court moved again to Gien (see page 79) when his successor, 13-year-old Charles VIII, inherited the throne. Six years later, he married Anne de Bretagne in the Château de Langeais (see page 177), thereby uniting France and Brittany. He was also persuaded to re-launch Anjou's longstanding claim on Italy, his artillery proving victorious at the Battle of Naples in early 1495. Within months, though, his troops were in retreat and the campaign proved a costly mistake. The King had, however, developed an admiration for Italian architecture which blossomed into a passion (shared by his successor François I) and produced the Loire Valley's first Renaissance expressions at Amboise (see page 154) and Blois (see page 114). Soon the effect would inspire Chambord (see page 121), Cheverny (see page 126) and many other chateaux which have come to define architectural splendours of the Loire Valley.

Revolution & beyond

Despite (or perhaps because of) the visible power and privilege of the monarchy and ruling classes, for the remainder of the population prosperity and equality for all remained a distant dream. In 1562 tensions between Catholics and Huguenot Protestants gave rise to the Wars of Religion, during which great symbolic monuments including the Cathédrale St-Croix d'Orléans (see page 89), the Basilique St-Martin de Tours (see page 174) and Blois' Benedictine Abbaye St-Nicolas (see page 119) were decimated. (The Edict of Nantes, signed by Henri IV in 1598, offered tolerance to non-Catholic sects within France.) In the 18th-century Age of Enlightenment, powerful literary figures such as Rousseau and Voltaire reflected a shift in public mood, as spiralling debts and taxation sat uneasily beside barely concealed displays of decadence by those in positions of power. Things came to a head in 1789 with the convening of 'les Etats-Généraux' – a People's National Assembly, which proved to be a pivotal moment in France's history. The subsequent Révolution Française replaced the monarchy with a democratic republic (whose founding principles of *Liberté, Egalité et Fraternité* still adorn the façades of French official buildings), abolished feudalism and saw the break up and

Cathédrale Saint-Gatien de Tours.

dispersal of vast Church-owned estates representing around 10% of mainland France. Many chateaux were stripped of their furnishings, the best of the spoils being stored and entered into the inventories which eventually formed the basis of fine-art museums like those of Tours (see page 172) and Orléans (see page 87). In some cases grand showpiece chateaux like those of Chanteloup (see page 157), Châteauneuf-sur-Loire (see page 82) and Richelieu (see page 195), were so badly damaged that they were eventually deemed beyond economic repair and demolished.

The early 19th century saw la République replaced by the first Empire, ruled by Napoléon I, whose expansionist policies brought much of western Europe under French control. After his defeat by allied forces of England, Austria, Prussia and Russia in 1814, power passed through various hands via Restoration, a second Revolution, two further Empires and Républiques. Through it all life continued much as it always had for most people, despite such memorable events as Napoléon III's Interior Minister Léon Gambetta landing in Tours after having fled Paris in a hot-air balloon. It was the arrival of the Industrial Revolution, however, with its effects on manufacturing, communications and trade, which finally shaped the society we see today.

Brasserie La Cigale, Nantes.

Troubled times

First & Second World Wars & the post-war 20th century

The dawn of a new century found the whole of France in a celebratory mood, as the nation hosted the Olympic Games during the Exposition Universelle in Paris, which welcomed 50 million visitors between April and November 1900. Among the more enduring repercussions of this was the adoption elsewhere of the art nouveau style which caused such a stir in decorative displays at the show. The movement soon filtered down to the cities and towns of the Loire Valley, where you can still find examples of both the pure form and an interesting hybrid which fused elements of the new art with those of the belle époque. Orléans, for example, has large-scale architectural landmarks in each style – La Rotonde and the Hôtel Moderne (see page 87) – plus several art nouveau private home façades. The real gem, however, is the time-warp brasserie interior of La Cigale in Nantes (see page 267), which is simply impossible to ignore. The confident (and perhaps naïve) exuberance expressed in the movement persisted until a troubled Europe fell under the dark shadow of the First World War, in which France soon found itself hopelessly entangled. Several chateaux were commandeered for military use, even the exquisite 16th-century Grande Galerie of Chenonceau (see page 158) being adapted to serve as a hospital to care for some of the huge numbers wounded on the battlefields further north. In 1917 a US command centre was established in Tours and American troops were spreading themselves along the Loire, after disembarking beyond Nantes at St-Nazaire. By the end of the conflict France had been

Mounted cavalry war memorial, Saumur.

decimated by an estimated 1.4 million military and civilian casualties.

A failure to resolve the underlying causes of the conflict made it inevitable that a period of considerable unrest would follow. As the people of the Loire shared the sombre mood of a nation in mourning and began repairing the ravages of battle, France suffered economic depression and became divided politically. It was thus poorly prepared for the outbreak in 1939 of the Second World War, the speed of the German advance forcing the Government to flee Paris and once again commandeer several chateaux in the Touraine before heading further south to Bordeaux. As Tours suffered aerial bombardments several bridges along the Loire were partially destroyed in an attempt to stem the flow of refugees fleeing across the river. An uneasy armistice signed in June 1939 divided the region in two, Chinon and the west falling under German occupation, while the remainder was controlled by the French Vichy regime, whose collaboration with Germany was agreed by Hitler and Pétain in

the station of Montoire-sur-Loire in October. The period which followed found countless agricultural workers shipped off to labour in Germany, while those who remained suffered the ignominy of their situation until allied troops reached the area in August 1944. However, the lead up to the liberation produced some of the worst conflict of the war, with riverside towns like Gien suffering devastation from both sides, and more river crossings being attacked.

The euphoria which accompanied the allied forces' liberation of France was followed by a prolonged period of post-war austerity, as the nation struggled to get back on its feet. A US aid scheme saw tractors and agricultural equipment shipped in, starting the process of modernisation which would make France a leader in farming efficiency. As mechanisation cut the need for such a vast labour force, the region's towns and cities began to attract those leaving the land, in turn fuelling their economic development. Later, new opportunities for university education also drew more young people to the cities, and revealed a lifestyle which many were reluctant to leave after their graduation.

Considerable controversy still surrounds the nuclear power plants (*centrales nucléaires*) that the government decided during the early 1960s to site at key points along the Loire, at Belleville, Chinon, Dampierre and St-Laurent. The main inducement, of course, was a ready source of water for cooling, but this was one of many factors in a less-than-glorious period of the river's management. After protracted wrangling, however, UNESCO was sufficiently reassured that the Loire had successfully recovered to grant its coveted World Heritage status to the valley in December 2000.

Clearly they're not the only ones who are reassured, judging by the resident population who seem content to remain in the land of their birth. Joining them in steadily increasing numbers are those who come to put down roots of their own. The process was kick-started during the late 1980s by the arrival in of the LGV (Ligne à Grande Vitesse) Atlantique which brought Tours-St-Pierre-des-Corps within a mere 70-minute train journey from Paris, and Vendôme closer still. Nantes followed, with similar benefits, both practical and economic. The region's present dynamism, coupled with an enviable international image as a tourism destination, have made the area a popular centre for conferences.

In terms of leisure tourism, the Loire Valley remains perhaps the most desirable of all locations in France, a country renowned as one of the world's most popular holiday destinations. Mindful of their still-powerful historical resonance, tourism marketing has revived the names of the old Provinces – welcome back Anjou, Brétagne, Poitou, l'Orléanais and Touraine. In addition to new construction, heavy (and continuing) investment has transformed traditional accommodation enjoyed by the majority of visitors, while private chateaux offer ever-higher levels of comfort and services for the most demanding guests.

United by the mother tongue

With such a startling diversity of architecture, climate, culture, landscape and geology, it's hardly surprising that France can sometimes look and feel more like a continent than a mere country. If making sense of it all can take a lifetime (a pleasurable prospect in itself) at least here in the Loire Valley you somehow sense that you're getting to the heart of things. For one thing, it's in and around Tours that you'll hear what is generally agreed to be the purest spoken French, uncoloured by the multitude of regional variations which at their most extreme can make things almost incomprehensible to outsiders. Yet for all its elegance, the definitive French of Touraine now has little to do with class; it's just the way things sound in everyday life here in the gentle, unchanging rural world of *la douce France*.

The common accent also unites a population whose individual identities are rooted in the pre-Revolutionary provinces of Anjou, Maine and Touraine, not to mention the Celtic former Duchy of Bretagne. You'll also hear the term *ligérien* ('Loire' is thought to be a corruption of 'Liger') used when referring to all manner of things from the region, including the people themselves.

Nuclear power: an uneasy truce, Chinon.

Art & architecture

Romanesque

Today's visitors mainly come to see the Gothic and Renaissance architectural jewels which have made the Loire Valley world-famous, but the area also preserves some extraordinary examples of the Romanesque ecclesiastical buildings which generally pre-date them. Instantly identifiable for its use of round-arched windows, doors and stone vaults, this form of construction's reliance on the thick masonry of its walls for structural stability limited the ambitions of both architects and masons. As a result, windows and doorways tended to be small and to admit relatively little daylight compared to those of later Gothic buildings. Larger early structures were often roofed in timber, which was lighter than vaulted stone but inherently flammable. (As the highest features in the landscape, countless important buildings were destroyed by fire after lightning strikes.) Those which did employ stone were limited in size by the weight of the vaults forcing walls outwards, so side aisles were often added to help share the loading. So much for the theory. But for all their limitations, early Romanesque buildings often have a serene (and occasionally mysterious) beauty and their carved or painted decorative features make them truly fascinating.

Five of the best

Romanesque creations

❶ **Abbaye de Fleury**, St-Benoît-sur-Loire, for the abbey, crypt and tomb of St-Benoît (Benedict). Page 81.

❷ **Abbaye de Fontevraud** for the abbey church, Plantagenêt tombs and abbey kitchen. Page 219.

❸ **Eglise Notre-Dame**, Cunault, for the clocher, capitals and interior. Page 224.

❹ **Chapelle St-Gilloes**, Montoire-sur-le-Loir, for its 11th-century wall paintings.

❺ **Germigny-des-Prés** for its Carolingian oratory and apse mosaic c.806. Page 82.

Gothic North portal tympanum, Abbaye de Fleury, Saint-Benoît-sur-Loire.

Romanesque (beneath a Gothic vault), Abbaye de Fleury, Saint-Benoît-sur-Loire.

About the region

For all its beauty and eventual refinement, the Gothic Revolution in France began as a practical response to the structural and stylistic limitations of Romanesque. What changed everything was the arrival, after the Crusades, of the *ogival* (pointed) arch, whose dramatically improved load-bearing abilities allowed windows to be much larger (important, since stained glass imagery communicated the messages of the Holy Scriptures to a largely illiterate population). In religious buildings the arrival of flying buttress (external arched props which resist the outward force of the heavy stone vaults inside) allowed walls to become lighter and to rise ever higher. In the 12th century the cathedral of St-Maurice d'Angers (see page 230) used huge Gothic arches and higher dome-like diagonal ribs to span the nave, in what became known as Angevin, or Plantagenet, vaulting. Later, intersecting arches of uniform height created the lightweight rib vaults seen to great effect in vast cathedrals like St-Gatien de Tours (see page 171).

This new freedom of expression liberated the architects and masons to explore decorative embellishments for their creations. By the 14th century the potential was expanding dramatically as ecclesiastical construction projects like cathedrals and abbeys were joined by more decadent secular architecture – initially manor houses for wealthy traders and eventually the new chateaux. Military fortresses like Loches and Saumur underpinned their military muscle with Gothic influences, but it was in the Château Royal de Blois (see page 116) that things really took off, employing the full-blown Flamboyant French Gothic which marked the apogee of the great medieval cathedrals. Even Chambord (see page 121), the greatest of all the Loire chateaux, is essentially a Gothic building in Renaissance clothing.

François I's Royal salamander emblem, Château de Chambord.

Charles VIII's ill-fated invasion of Italy in 1494 had one positive outcome: it heightened awareness of Italian style in French high society. Some 20 years later, François I returned to France from a resounding victory at the Battle of Marignano (near Milan) and enjoyed a chance meeting with Leonardo da Vinci, his artistic sensibilities dazzled by the elegance of the Italian Renaissance. The young French king, at the height of the monarchy's wealth and power, sought to express his passion by transforming the previously severe Château d'Amboise (see page 154) into an elegant Renaissance palace for pleasure and luxury. Soon influential artistic figures like Celini, Rosso and Primaticcio were enticed to leave Italy but, while eminently capable of applying their talents to architectural styling, they were not trained in construction techniques. Unsurprisingly, the French master masons were unimpressed, but were persuaded to adapt the new designs into a workable, structurally sound format. The resulting fusion of French and Italian creativity established an architectural style which would come to define the Renaissance chateaux of the Loire Valley.

François eventually tired of life in Amboise and transferred his court to the new Renaissance wing which he had created in the Château de Blois (see page 116). As the French chateau's raison d'être shifted from fortress to fashionable pleasure retreat, so attention turned to the wealth of opportunities presented by beautiful and secluded locations (with hunting terrain) along the Loire. Classic early examples like Azay-le-Rideau, Chenonceau and Chambord inspired numerous others, as the spirit of the Renaissance fired the imaginations of those with the means to indulge their fantasies. Soon the defensive corner towers of medieval donjons evolved into decorative *tourelles* with slated spires, while previously unusable roof spaces were freed for habitation by the addition of dormer windows.

Five of the best

Renaissance masterpieces

❶ François I's monumental **Château de Chambord**. Page 121.

❷ The François I wing of the **Château Royal de Blois**. Page 116.

❸ Catherine de' Medici's Grande Galerie in the **Château d'Azay-le-Rideau**. Page 183.

❹ **Château de Chenonceau**. Page 158.

❺ **Musée des Beaux Artes**, Angers. Page 232.

Patterns and mouldings preserved in the Château de Chambord.

Trogolodyte

The construction of the architectural treasures of the Loire Valley consumed vast quantities of pale *tuffeau* and other forms of limestone, all of which had to be extracted from beneath the region's apparently undisturbed green and pleasant landscapes. Around all the great construction sites were quarries created by countless former peasant farmers who now spent their lives hand-cutting stone in near-darkness, as they worked their way ever further from daylight. The resourceful stone cutters then began to add walls, windows and doors to sections of the caves they had created, providing a secure refuge for themselves and their precious grain supplies during troubled times, and establishing a pattern of troglodytic architecture which is surprisingly widespread along the Loire Valley. In the past, it was not uncommon for whole communes to live this way: as recently as the 19th century around half of the population of the Saumur region, for example, was still living in 'troglo' homes. From the mid-20th century, though, a more prosperous society viewed the dwellings with mounting disenchantment, and many were abandoned during this period. More recently, however, they have been rediscovered by a new generation which values their low environmental impact, sense of tradition and potential for providing characterful tourist accommodation. Add modern heating and ventilation systems, and you see why the expression 'troglo' now carries a certain cachet in the Loire Valley.

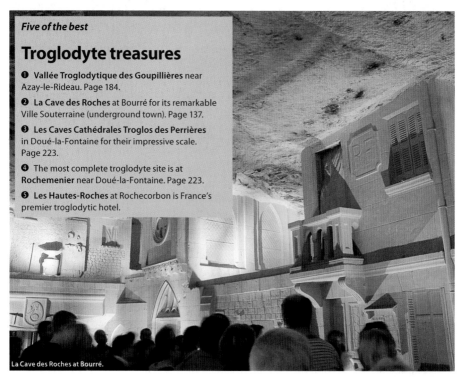

Five of the best

Troglodyte treasures

❶ **Vallée Troglodytique des Goupillières** near Azay-le-Rideau. Page 184.

❷ **La Cave des Roches** at Bourré for its remarkable Ville Souterraine (underground town). Page 137.

❸ **Les Caves Cathédrales Troglos des Perrières** in Doué-la-Fontaine for their impressive scale. Page 223.

❹ The most complete troglodyte site is at **Rochemenier** near Doué-la-Fontaine. Page 223.

❺ **Les Hautes-Roches** at Rochecorbon is France's premier troglodytic hotel.

La Cave des Roches at Bourré.

The Musée des Beaux-Arts, Orléans.

Contemporary gardening, at the Domaine de Chaumont-sur-Loire.

Loire Valley today

Fresh blood

The Loire Valley's allure continues to attract not only seasonal visitors but also higher profile personalities who elect to settle in the Garden of France. Since the 1980s Rolling Stone Mick Jagger has been raising a few eyebrows among his neighbours at the Château de Fourchette, just across the river from Amboise. His presence in the otherwise peaceful commune of Pocé-sur-Cisse, which has also glimpsed occasional guests such as Paul McCartney, David Bowie and Roman Polanski, added a newly hip note to the staid blend of local cultures more generally allied to centuries' old traditions. Apparently the influences work both ways, for Jagger was soon passionately immersed in the creation of formal landscaped gardens for his 18th-century Renaissance chateau. In 1989 French actor Gérard Depardieu went a substantial step further when he bought the Château de Tigné, west of Doué-la-Fontaine, with the intention of indulging a longstanding dream of becoming a successful wine producer. Apparently he's never happier than when he's away from it all, among his 27 ha of vines, nurturing the wines' progress to maturity in the chateau's vaulted caves or sampling for himself the end results – the flagship, naturally, is 'Anjou Rouge AOC Cuvée Cyrano'. He's not the

only Hollywood habitué to have developed a taste for the alternative lifestyle on offer in the Loire Valley. At every opportunity, actor Jude Law spends time at the home which he and his parents Peter and Maggie purchased near Saumur (see page 215), and where for the past 15 years they have run a theatre school. Despite his preference for a vegetarian diet, Law declares himself a great lover of the region's fine foods and wines. In 2007 his well-known enthusiasm for France was rewarded when he received the prestigious 'Chevalier des Arts et des Lettres' medal.

A change of climate

While it's true to say that the greater part of what attracted the nobility of France to the Loire Valley centuries ago is still very much alive and well today, it's hard to ignore the potential for change posed by a shift in global climate patterns. Already the region's wine producers have had to adapt to the effects of higher summer temperatures, which have seen grapes ripening early. Will the wines of the Loire Valley, as some are wondering, begin to take on some of the personality traits of their counterparts further south in the Rhône Valley or even the Languedoc? Only time will tell, but you can be sure that the Loire's resourceful wine

Buying property in the Loire Valley

If you are seduced by the region and considering buying property here, it's worth bearing a few things in mind before you take the plunge.

The property

Second-home buyers planning to offset their investment by letting their property when they're not using it will need to look in an area close to key tourist sights. While this improves letting potential, it also increases the purchase price, particularly as you'll be in competition with French buyers (and commuters, if you're within easy driving distance of cities like Tours, Angers and Nantes).

If you're buying to live here, you'll get a lot more for your money in rural areas away from the river, which can still turn up some surprisingly cheap property. This approach also puts you further from nuclear power stations, sited at various points on the banks of the Loire.

Think carefully before committing to properties requiring major restoration, particularly any with local *tuffeau* stonework in poor repair. Yes, it's beautiful, but fragile and susceptible to frost damage (and unless you own a listed Monument Historique it's now virtually unobtainable). If you're tempted to stretch things to a chateau, you need to be aware that ownership has its price, not merely in restoration but also in ongoing maintenance.

At the other end of the scale, an often overlooked sector is the traditional townhouse or apartment, which can offer convenience and full-on French atmosphere, although usually at the expense of a meaningful garden. Worthwhile hunting grounds include the old town of Blois, although it's debatable how much longer this will remain an affordable option.

The purchase

Properties can be advertised privately, sold through an *agence immobilier* or a *notaire* (a legal specialist similar to a solicitor, but representing both parties' interests). If you choose an agent make sure they are registered with a body such as FNAIM (fnaim.fr) and visit their office.

Don't get carried away too quickly. Study the plans of the house and land and check that there are no proposals to build nearby. If the boundaries aren't clear, employ a *Géometre* (who establishes such things for formal land registration) to confirm and mark them on the ground. Study the technical reports (*Dossier de Diagnostic Technique* or DDT) for lead, asbestos, termites and energy – they are required by law and if any work needs doing the seller will be held responsible.

If you're still happy to go ahead you'll be asked to sign two documents. The first, a *Compromis de Vente*, sets out the main terms of the agreement and once signed is legally binding. At this point the buyer pays 10% of the purchase price as a deposit, after which the notaire will start the conveyancing process. Buyers have a seven-day cooling off period, after which the deposit is usually lost; the seller cannot withdraw. The document will also contain the date when both parties will sign the final full contract (*Acte de Vente*), usually only three or four months later.

The total fees payable for older properties are between 7 and 10% of the purchase price. New properties under five years old are about half this figure but TVA (VAT) is also payable.

Riverside tranquility, Montrésor.

Bike-hire on the Ile de Nantes.

producers, like *vignerons* the world over, always relish a challenge and will waste no time finding ways of turning things to their advantage.

For tourism, too, prospects of climate change are not without their up side, particularly as the popularity of outdoor activity holidays shows no sign of diminishing among French visitors and those from overseas. Already 52 million euros have been committed to the *Loire à Vélo* initiative, which will soon offer 800 km of dedicated cycle routes throughout the length of the Loire Valley. Big cities like Nantes, Tours and Orléans, too, have embraced the convenience, flexibility and greener advantages of cycling as a means of personal transport with their own bike rental schemes. And now Angers is following the lead of Nantes and Orléans by adding a state-of-the-art tramway system; transport-wise things are changing fast,

and for the better. But perhaps the most intriguing response to the opportunities for creative lateral thinking in the Loire Valley's offer to visitors is the brand new Terra Botanica nature park (page 234), which opens its doors in 2010. Billing itself as Europe's very first theme park entirely dedicated to plant life, and spread across a massive 11 ha on the outskirts of Angers, this new initiative looks set to update the world's perception of the Loire Valley, and particularly the Anjou region. But take a wider view and you'll see that the park's 'eco-responsible' credentials are merely logical developments of the more enlightened approach to environmental management which in recent years have had a major impact on the River Loire and its tributaries – which is great news for residents and visitors alike.

Getting married in the Loire Valley

Understandably, many people are attracted to the idea of getting married in a romantic chateau setting in the Loire Valley. The reality is that you can't actually tie the knot in a private location in France; this has to be done at a Mairie (Town Hall), although you can exchange vows in a symbolic ceremony at any location and complete the legal requirements afterwards. A religious ceremony can also only be performed after having completed the civil ceremony either in France or the couple's home country. The minister will require the Certificate of Civil Marriage (translated into French if necessary).

Many Loire Valley hotels offer splendid accommodation and wedding reception venues – for example Le Choiseul in Amboise (hotel-le-choiseul-amboise.federal-hotel.com), which has river views. It's also possible to hire reception halls in some of the major chateaux. The Orangerie at Cheverny (see page 126) has views of the chateau, and at the Château du Rivau (www.chateaudurivau.com) not far from Chinon, guests can enjoy illuminated gardens.

Getting married in France can be dauntingly bureaucratic, however, so make sure you are organized. Among the documentation required are passports, birth certificates, certificate of non-impediment (known as a *Certificat de Célibat*), the divorce judgment for divorcees, the death certificate of a former spouse for a widow or widower, and a pre-nuptial medical certificate. All the documents must be translated into French. One of the parties to be married must be resident where the marriage is due to take place for at least 40 days before the ceremony and be able to provide proof via receipts for rent or a utility bill. This is the absolute minimum of time required and consists of a month's residence followed by 10 days for the banns to be posted. For a civil ceremony you will require an interpreter if either of you don't speak French and two witnesses, who must provide full names, addresses and occupations. The marriage is legal worldwide but you will need to have the certificate translated into English (contact your nearest British Embassy). You can request the certificate be forwarded by the British Consular to the General Register Office in the UK, where it will be deposited.

Various agencies can organize your wedding in France for you. They will do as much or as little as you wish, from helping with documentation to finding a venue and organizing the reception. Websites such as Wedding Chaos (weddingchaos.co.uk) give plenty of advice and help you weigh up the pros and cons of getting married in your chosen location.

Same sex couples can celebrate commitment ceremonies and receptions with the help of Rainbow Star, an agency dedicated to gay weddings (rainbow-star-events.com).

Useful websites
Chateaux Story (chateaux-story.com)
France Guide (uk.franceguide.com)
French Embassy in London (ambafrance-uk.org)
Grandes Etapes Françaises (grandesetapes.fr)
Oui & You (ouiandyou.com)
Pièce Montée (piecemontee.com

Nature & environment

Throughout its journey from source to sea the waters of the Loire will cover over 1000 km, and change beyond recognition from a gentle trickle to a broad navigable waterway. Not surprisingly, as it does so the river also passes through the pronounced variations in landscape, climate and geology.

Flood management

By the time it reaches the Atlantic at St-Nazaire after a marathon 1013-km journey (the longest of any French river) the Loire has been joined by around 80 tributaries, among them such important watercourses as the Allier (which receives rainfall run-off and winter melt-water from the mountainous Massif Central), Cher, Creuse and Vienne. Low-lying areas along the Loire have lived with the constant threat of flooding (*crues*), which man has attempted to prevent by creating *levées* (dykes) – not always successfully. In June 1856, for example, the waters rose over 7 m at Orléans, rapidly inundating an area of over 100,000 ha. (In a cruel coincidence, the years 1846 and 1866 were almost as catastrophic.) Here and there, on the walls of older homes you'll still come across major flood dates recorded on commemorative stone plaques from the mid-19th century.

The occasional violent mood swings of what is often referred to as 'the last wild river in western Europe' have prompted a complex system of management, whose science continues to evolve with the stimulus of Plan Loire Grandeur Nature, a government initiative established in 1994, and Mission Val de Loire, which manages the UNESCO World Heritage Site area. The World Wildlife Fund has also been active, campaigning successfully against the construction of new dams, founding the Loire Vivante (Living Loire) committee and launching the Loire Nature project, which aims to secure ownership and sustainable management of 4500 ha of land in the Loire Basin. Such collective muscle underlines the fact that assuring the security of those who live and work in an area with an irreplaceable architectural heritage is no easy task, especially when coupled with the challenge of preserving the delicate ecological balance of various important natural habitats.

Shady canal bank, Château de Chenonceau.

About the region

The landscape

South of Orléans, the moors and lakes of the Sologne date back to the Middle Ages, when man was forced to drain useless marshland formed in the wake of intense deforestation. Traditions of crop cultivation and hunting for game continue and much of the Sologne remains a mysterious and secretive landscape of shimmering, reed-fringed pools and dark forest. The area is dotted with magnificent chateaux, many slumbering amid forests, while others such as Chambord were constructed deep in the heart of huge tracts of hunting forest.

In Touraine the landscape is characterized by limestone, vineyards and troglodytic dwellings. The gentle contours are punctuated with peaceful villages and wide open spaces now given over to intensive agriculture. Climb the hillsides behind riverside settlements like Vouvray and Rochecorbon to discover the broad limestone plateaux on which the famous Chenin grape vines thrive. From Montsoreau to Saumur the limestone escarpments are pitted with troglodytic houses and wine cellars and pale *tuffeau* stone is in evidence in more refined local architecture. South of Saumur the town of Doué-la-Fontaine is situated on the only occurrence of the soft shell-filled limestone known as *falun*. Ideal for growing roses, it has contributed to the enormous flower industry which exists here today. Unusual geology led to an industrial past in the area west of Angers known as the Corniche Angevine. Coal mining and lime kilns once dominated the hillsides, which were also dotted with windmills. Today the area is well-known for its stunning views of the Loire, and numerous walking and mountain bike trails. The Loire flows through both the landscape and lives off the valley communities.

Autumn cyclamen, Château de La Chatonnière.

It's a fact...

The Loire was the first river in the world to be recognized as a World Heritage Site by UNESCO in 2000. The designation extends from Sully-sur-Loire to Chalonnes, and recognizes its outstanding cultural landscape, historic towns and great architectural monuments.

The source of the Loire is in the Massif Central region at the foot of Mont-Gerbier-de-Jonc at an altitude of 1408 m.

The Loire is 1013 km long. The river basin extends over one-fifth of the land surface of France.

Depending upon their size, traditional flat-bottomed boats used on the river are called *chaland*, *gabarre*, *toue* or *futreau*.

The river has long been a migration route for aquatic species. Enlightened environmental management efforts (including a total ban of sand and gravel extraction) have seen increased numbers of eels, sea trout, shad, lampreys and Atlantic salmon returning upstream to spawn in various tributaries, while rare molluscs including pearl mussels and white-footed crayfish are reliable indicators of water quality. As you'd expect, fishing is popular, both from the riverbank and from small boats moored mid-stream. The resident fish population includes white bream, catfish, eel, silver carp, loach, pike and sturgeon, tench and (in the estuary) flounder.

The river, whose diverse habitats include shingle banks, wetlands and dense hardwood forests, is also an important route for bird migration. Among the regular breeding species are corncrake, stone curlew, black and middle-spotted woodpeckers, and you may be lucky enough to encounter black kite or Bonelli's warbler. The vast Forêt d'Orléans provides a breeding ground for booted and short-toed eagles, honey-buzzards, ospreys and woodlarks plus golden orioles, nightjars, nightingales and wrynecks. The lakes and wetlands of the Sologne and Brenne also attract bitterns, goshawks, grebes, herons and kingfishers. In summer terns are a familiar sight just about anywhere along the river itself.

Not surprisingly, the area is also a haven for countless varieties of butterfly and dragonfly, while pond tortoises are well-established in the Brenne wetlands. River mammals include beaver, muskrat and otter, plus the rather less universally welcomed coypu, whose excavations began to destabilise riverbanks and whose numbers are now controlled. The area's forests are home to larger mammals such as wild boar, pine marten, wild cat and deer and include long-established hunting reserves like Cheverny and Chambord.

Sandbank activity near Saint-Benoît-sur-Loire.

Festivals & events

Outside entertainment, Indre et Loire.

True to a nation whose climate favours outdoor life, the Loire Valley has a long tradition of mounting festivals and other events for the sheer enjoyment of it. It makes no difference whether you're resident or just visiting; everyone is welcome. Some are grand affairs attracting thousands celebrating, for example, regional food and fine wines. Others are more modest, convivial get-togethers with a charm of their own. Along the way you'll find enthusiastic gardeners opening their gates to all, local actors working together to re-enact important historical events, dancers and musicians taking to the stage before equally passionate audiences, and much more. Mixing like this offers much more than mere entertainment; you'll be rubbing shoulders with local people (and those from other nations) and gaining a real sense of being part of the area you're visiting. After all, the landscapes, architecture, food and drink with which you fell in love were all created by the skill, passion and spirit of the local people. And their traditions are alive and well, as you'll soon discover.

January

La Folle Journée
T08 92 70 52 05 (€0.34 /mn), follejournee.fr.
Nearly 300 short classical music concerts spanning five days at the end of January in Nantes.

February

La Fête des Vins d'Anjou
Chalonnes-sur-Loire, T06 60 34 36 26, chalonnes-sur-loire.fr.
An annual event in the last weekend in February showcasing the wines of Anjou and Saumur, with wine-tasting classes, walks through the vineyards and more.

March

Printemps Musical de St-Cosme Symphonia
La Riche (5 mins from the centre of Tours), T02 47 32 07 11, lesmusicales.fr.
A chamber music festival dedicated to the promotion of young musicians which takes place in the Priory of St-Cosme, last residence of the famous poet Pierre de Ronsard.

April

Festival International de Guitare de Vendôme
T02 54 89 44 00, vendomeguitarfest.com.
The festival features all of the available genres of guitar music, from traditional to Celtic to mariachi to Argentinian tango. The event also includes the opportunity to take a masterclass with performers.

Fêtes de Jeanne d'Arc
T02 38 24 05 05 (tourist office), fetesjeannedarc.com.
There's plenty to see and do in Orléans at the end of April and beginning of May, including a medieval festival and market, concerts, exhibitions, *son et lumière* at the cathedral and parades.

May

Le Printemps des Arts de Nantes
T02 40 20 69 70, printempsdesarts.fr.
European baroque music festival with concerts throughout the spring and early summer at venues in Nantes and heritage sites in Pays de la Loire.

June

Chinon en Jazz
T02 47 38 67 62.
Free music events at locations all round the town in early June.

Festival Aucard de Tours
T02 47 51 11 33, radiobeton.com.
Rock festival held in early June in the parc de la Gloriette in Tours plus live music in the streets and bars around the city.

Festival du Sully et du Loiret
T02 38 25 43 43, festival-sully.com.
Held at various venues in the Loiret, this international festival held in the first two weeks in June presents classical and choral music.

Foire aux Fromages et Gastronomie
Sainte-Maure-de-Touraine, T02 47 72 00 13, sainte-maure-de-touraine.fr.
A celebration in the first weekend in June of regional foods, with the distinctive goat's cheese from Ste-Maure-de-Touraine taking pride of place. The streets of the town come alive with performances from wonderful French musicians and artists.

Les Courants
T02 47 30 43 05, lescourants.com.
Amboise hosts a week (end June) of contemporary music combined with a strip cartoon (*bandes dessinnées* or BD) festival – a huge craze in France.

Rendez-vous aux jardins
rendezvousauxjardins.culture.fr.
A national event in the first weekend in June when famous and not so well-known gardens are

About the region

opened to the public. A detailed brochure on the parks and gardens in the Loire Valley in English can be downloaded from the Loire Valley Tourist Board website (visaloire.com).

July

Avoine Zone Blues
T02 47 98 11 15, avoine-zone-blues.com.
The Touraine blues festival held annually at the beginning of July in Avoine, between Chinon and Saumur.

Garlic and Basil Festival
T02 47 21 60 00.
Gastronomic sights and smells of summer in Tours at the end of July.

Nuits des Mille Feux (The Night of a Thousand Candles)
T02 47 50 02 09, chateauvillandry.com.
For two consecutive evenings in early July the gardens at Villandry are candlelit and animated by players and acrobats. The night ends with an extraordinary fireworks display – very different to traditional sound and light shows.

Tous sur le Pont
T02 54 58 84 56, toussurlepont.com.
Annual music festival held over five days in

Tradition celebrated: Festival de Loire, Orléans.

mid-July with concerts staged in the courtyard of the Château Royal in Blois, free live music in the town centre, dancing and fireworks.

August

Blues in Chédigny y Musicas de Cuba
T02 47 92 51 43, blues-in-chedigny.com.
International artists perform blues and Cuban music in the heart of this Touraine village (mid-month).

Les Grandes Tablées du Saumur Champigny
Reserve on T02 41 40 20 60 (tourist office).
For two nights in early August, the centre of Saumur is filled with tables and 10,000 diners enjoy good food from the region and plenty of Saumur Champigny wine. Advance bookings for dining (€10 per person) are essential but you can buy a glass (€4) to taste wine on the night.

September

Festival de Loire
festivaldeloire.com.
Five-day festival at the end of September on the quays in Orléans, with hundreds of traditional boats from the Loire and its tributaries, music and entertainment.

Festival Européen de Musique Renaissance
T02-47 57 00 73, vinci-closluce.com.
Amboise hosts three days of Renaissance music around the third weekend of the month. Internationally renowned musicians grace the wonderful surroundings of Leonardo da Vinci's home at the Château du Clos Lucé.

Fête du Vélo
T02 54 79 95 63 (Blois tourist office).
Join hundreds of others in a day of cycling in chateau country around Blois in early September. (There are shorter trails for families.) Competitions and surprises along the route.

Jazz en Touraine

T02 47 45 85 10 (tourist office), jazzentouraine.com.
Even though it's called a jazz festival, you can expect various musical styles like salsa, electro, gypsy jazz and blues in this well-established late summer revelry. Official and fringe events are staged at Montlouis-sur-Loire and venues nearby during mid-September.

Journées du Patrimoine (European heritage days)

journeesdupatrimoine.culture.fr.
On the third weekend in September, thousands of historic sites (from a modest *pigeonnier* to private chateaux) open their doors to the public.

La Fête de la Citrouille (Pumpkin Feast)

T02 47 95 77 47, chateaudurivau.com.
In mid-September, the remarkable gardens at the Château du Rivau come alive with activities and performers celebrating the pumpkin and other unusual vegetables.

Les Journées du Potager

T02 47 50 02 09, chateauvillandry.com.
On the last weekend of the month, Villandry gardeners share their knowledge in demonstrations, workshops and guided tours with special activities for children.

Tomato Festival

T02 47 45 16 31.
Discover hundreds of varieties of tomatoes for sale at the Château de la Bourdaisière in mid-Septemer.

Journées Gastronomiques de Sologne

T02 54 96 99 88, romorantin.fr/jgs/.
In the last weekend in October, Romorantin-Lanthenay hosts producers and artisans from the region all competing for one of various prestigious trophies.

Euro Gusto

T02 47 64 24 38, eurogusto.org.
European gathering of the international Slow Food movement that takes place every two years in Tours' Parc des Expositions. You can sample over 1000 wines, taste regional foods, take part in workshops or watch demonstrations. The next Euro Gusto takes place in 2011.

Grand Marché Animé de Noël au Château de Brissac

T02 41 91 22 21, chateau-brissac.fr.
The last weekend in November finds France's tallest chateau enlivened by a traditional Christmas market with all the trimmings, lots of stalls and of course Père Noël.

Marché aux Truffes & Produits de Terroir

T02 47 58 31 11.
As the festive season approaches, visit the traditional truffle market at Marigny-Marmande. The markets take place on the Saturdays before and after Christmas, second and fourth Saturdays in January, and second Saturday in February.

Noël au Château de La Ferté St-Aubin

T02 38 76 52 72, chateau-ferte-st-aubin.com.
For three weekends before Christmas (and from 26-30 December) the chateau (about 20 km south of Orléans) is open 1400-1800 for a traditional Noël au Château.

Sleeping

There's no shortage of high-quality character accommodation.

The region offers an enormous range of different places to stay. You can choose from historic chateaux, family-run hotels, charming *chambres d'hôtes* (B&Bs), unusual troglodytic dwellings, self-catering cottages and campsites amidst vineyards or on the banks of the Loire and its many tributaries. Whether you are looking for peace and quiet in idyllic countryside or a city-based break with plenty to see and lots of nightlife, the chances are that the area can provide it for you somewhere. A note of caution, though: if you don't like crowds, come outside the peak season. You'll sometimes feel as if you have the place to yourself – and you'll have a huge choice of accommodation.

Prices

Prices and quality are fairly standard throughout the region, although there's a high proportion of luxury accommodation (with higher than average prices). City centre hotels cost slightly more than elsewhere, although France has a huge number of cheap chain hotels placed strategically around the edge of cities, ensuring that budget rooms, too, are available. Most hotel bills will include an additional modest sum called a *taxe de sejour* – a tourist tax.

A double room in most hotels graded three-star and above cost from €110-150, though this can exceed €400 for the most luxurious rooms in outstanding hotels and chateaux. The Loire Valley also has a large number of small two-star hotels typically costing €60-80 for a double room. Single occupancy will cost a little more.

Hotel breakfasts are regarded as optional in France and are hardly ever included in the price. They cost anything from around €8 per person, substantially more in expensive hotels. Half-board options in hotels with restaurants can offer a considerable saving on dining bills.

Self-catering rural *gite* accommodation first appeared in 1951. The National Federation of Gîtes de France now has over 56,000 properties to rent (including 'Charmance' B&Bs and 'Pre Vert'

campsites). The average price for a gîte is around €400 per week in high season and €270 in low season. Gîtes are normally let for a minimum of one week during the summer months but at other times it's possible to rent them for a weekend or a few days. Other self-catering properties are available through property directories or by booking direct with private owners – always check what services are included in the price, as there may be extras like end-of-stay cleaning and electricity. Prices vary considerably according to the season, the highest being at Easter and during July and August.

The best value accommodation is often in B&B-style *chambres d'hôtes*, rooms in a family home or annexe that cost from around €50-100 per night for two people sharing. Rooms usually come with a private bathroom, and breakfast is generally included in the price.

There are good deals for short breaks outside the peak season – tourism websites are a good place to start looking. Tours, for example, offers rooms and entry to tourist sites at a 50% discount over 6 weekends in November and December through the annual Plus de Touraine scheme. It's a great opportunity to whisk your partner away at short notice and indulge in a luxury hotel at an affordable price. City tourist offices encourage low season travellers by offering attractive short-break packages; in Angers you can get a hotel room and a 24-hour City Pass (worth €14 each) through the central reservation service for as little as €50 per night, based on two people sharing.

Booking

If you are visiting during peak periods, book your accommodation well in advance. Sought-after self-catering accommodation is often booked almost a year in advance, and the most charming chambres d'hôtes can disappoint those trying to book at short notice.

Prices quoted on hotel websites will depend on your arrival date and the levels of occupancy. You can often get a great deal if you are flexible on dates. If you book by phone, always make sure you get written confirmation. This is especially true if you have requested a particular room or adapted accommodation. Let your accommodation provider know what time you'll be arriving – some hotels state they will let the room to someone else if you don't show up by a specified time, whereas in chambres d'hôtes you are usually expected to turn up *after* 1600-1700 on the first day of your stay.

Some hotels and B&Bs close during winter, normally November-March. Most gîtes are only booked for an average of 16 weeks annually and may close for most of the autumn and winter unless they can be adequately heated (expect to pay extra for this).

If you want a room with a view, overlooking the Loire or a chateau for instance, specify this when you book, confirming how much extra it will cost. It's also worth checking whether rooms are on a busy or noisy road. Review websites such as tripadvisor.com can be helpful in deciding whether a hotel is suitable. Don't assume that small hotels, chambres d'hôtes, gîte owners or campsites are able to accept payment by credit card – check this when booking.

Chateaux

Central to the Loire Valley's reputation as a premium tourist destination is its selection of luxury chateau-hotels and manor houses in superb settings. Expect antique furniture, stone staircases, tapestries and even a four-poster bed, plus high levels of comfort and modern facilities. Of course, they vary enormously, but depending on what sort of experience you want, you should be able to find something suitable. You can get away from it all in a small manor house offering B&B or do it in style in one of the larger chateaux with gastronomic restaurants, spa facilities, or even a golf course. Chateau-hotels can also provide an unforgettable venue for wedding celebrations, and you can even rent an entire chateau for a family holiday.

Traditional family-run hotels are alive and well.

Hotels

Hotels are graded on a star system, with five stars being the highest grade possible in France. Most, though, are two-star and above but you'll find considerable variations, especially in three-star hotels, where the decor and furnishings can at worst be tired and dated, and at best offer high quality contemporary rooms with seductive en suite bathrooms, flat screen TVs and Wi-Fi as standard. Many now provide facilities to prepare hot drinks in the rooms.

If you are booking a hotel on the internet you'll generally be able to see pictures of the rooms. If you haven't booked in advance and just turn up looking for a room, you'll be shown what is available so you can choose. If this isn't offered you should ask – it's normal practice.

Chambres d'hôtes

Staying with local people is one of the nicest ways to really get to know your surroundings. Guests are welcomed into the family home, which can be anything from a quite ordinary house to a troglodyte dwelling, farm or manor house, or even a chateau. Chambres d'hôtes can have up to five guest rooms and breakfast is included in the price. This is often served with home-made jams, fresh bread and pastries, local cheeses, dairy products and cold meats (*charcuterie*). If you really want to immerse yourself in the local culture, take advantage of the evening meals (*tables d'hôtes*) offered by some owners, usually for around €20 per person.

Self-catering/gîtes

There is an almost overwhelming choice of rural *gîtes* and other self-catering accommodation throughout the region. The Gîtes de France label ensures that certain standards and levels of comfort are met through their rating system, which awards between 1 and 5 *épis* (ears of corn) – one being the most basic. Other organizations

Useful websites

Chateaux
relaischateaux.fr
chateauxhotels.com
bienvenue-au-chateau.com
simplychateau.com

Hotels
logisdefrance.com
hotel-bb.com
accorhotels.com

Chambres d'hôtes
guest-garden.com
guidesdecharme.com
likhom.com
ownersdirect.co.uk
sawdays.co.uk

Self-catering/gîtes
cheznous.co.uk
clevacances.com
cottages4you.com
gites-de-france.com
frenchconnections.co.uk

Campsites & hostels
camping.fr
france-auberges-de-jeunesse-gaf.com

such as Clévacances have a similar system. Expect accommodation to be self-contained, with some private outside space. It should be satisfactorily furnished and equipped for the requisite number of guests. Make sure that you confirm whether bed linen and towels are supplied and take your own beach towels for swimming, etc. The owner may not necessarily live on-site, so make sure you have a way of contacting them if there is a problem. Quite a few campsites have chalet-style cabins for those who like the camaraderie of camping but enjoy some home comforts. Alternatively, hire a boat and gently cruise the canals and rivers.

Eating & drinking

H ere in the Garden of France fine food and wines are part of daily life, a simple pleasure for all to enjoy rather than a luxury reserved for the privileged few. Not that you can't dine in considerable style (and expense) if you so wish. After all, indulging your every desire is a local tradition which stretches back to the days when kings and nobles built their chateaux with just that in mind. But, to our mind, nothing surpasses the down-to-earth enjoyment of visiting a local market, preparing a picnic and savouring the results in the perfect spot, whether it be a shady riverbank, within sight of a noble landmark or even in a lively city square.

Practical information

You'll find a huge range of *auberges*, restaurants and hotels at every price, and gastronomic, level. Most larger towns have particular squares or streets dedicated to restaurants, where you will be able to browse and compare menus. Tourist offices can give you information about restaurants, particularly those specializing in local cuisine. Restaurants generally only serve lunch between 1200 and 1400. During the afternoon, unless you are in a city or at a major sight, it's hard to find anything more than a sandwich in a bar or *boulangerie*. Evening meals are served from around

The Rabelaisian table

From the game-filled forests of the Sologne to the natural landscapes of the Touraine, the cuisine of the Loire Valley is predominantly one of meats and sausages. This dates back centuries; writer and well-known local bon viveur Rabelais would have enjoyed the same hearty dishes as people do today. In fact, modern menus, particularly around his birthplace in Chinon, will often refer to Rabelaisian-style food.

In Touraine pork products such as the *rillons de Tours* (large pieces of lean pork belly, seasoned and preserved in fat) are survivors from the days when whole animals needed to be processed and preserved for the larder. *Pâté de Chartres* looks, to our eyes, something like a pork pie. Traditionally made from the once-abundant dotterel (a now-protected member of the plover family), it now mainly consists of game such as partridge and duck. Autumn is the season not just for wild game – notably venison, often married to wild mushrooms gathered from the forest floor – but you may also come across wild boar, which proliferate throughout much of France.

Another survivor from the Middle Ages, and mentioned in Rabelais' novel *Gargantua*, are *fouaces* – small breads rather like pitta. The name comes from the Roman *'focus'* meaning 'hearth', and the time when bread would have been baked among hot ashes. Now something of a novelty, they have been revived and are served with a choice of fillings such as *rillettes*, beans or goat's cheese. There's nowhere better to sample them than in a troglodytic restaurant with a blazing fire.

1900, and many finish taking orders at around 2130 (even earlier in smaller places). Two courses plus a drink typically cost around €20-30 per person, and in most French restaurants a service charge is included (see Tipping, page 285). The menu reader on page 58 gives further explanations of the various French terms for foods and dishes mentioned here.

Entrées

You'll find sometimes *foie gras de canard* served with a fruit chutney, savoury tarts such as *Tourte Tourangelle aux rillons et Ste-Maure de Touraine*, assorted *fromages de chèvres*, fresh vegetables and salads. There is often a vegetable soup (*potage de légumes*), although vegetarians should be wary, as it is likely to incorporate a meat stock. The entrée is sometimes preceded by an appetizer called *amuse bouches*, examples of which could be *rillettes* or a few mouthfuls of an intensely flavoured seasonal soup. They are normally complimentary. Look for seasonal starters such as *asperge* or *primeurs* (new, young vegetables) in late spring, and come late summer, you'll find wild mushrooms, local tomatoes or dishes using varieties of pumpkin (*citrouille*, *potiron*, etc).

Plats

The main course is usually meat or fish accompanied by a wine-based sauce, and can be roasted, baked or sautéed. Surprisingly, main dishes rarely come with many vegetables – sometimes nothing other than *frites*, another potato side dish, pasta or rice. (The French, doubtless anxious to reach their 'five-a-day', will often start with a salad or eat one after the main course and before launching into the cheese board.)

It is more common now for restaurants to offer a vegetarian main course, but always check ingredients, as many French chefs regard *lardons* (diced bacon pieces), anchovies or tinned tuna as perfectly acceptable vegetarian fare. Always let

restaurants or *tables d'hôtes* hosts know in advance if you have any particular dietary requirements.

Poissons

The Loire is the main source of wild fish. They are caught by a handful of professional fishermen who brave the occasionally wild river in order to fill their nets. Carp, pike, trout and pike-perch (the ubiquitous *sandre*) are often served with *beurre blanc* – a delicious sauce made with butter, shallots, garlic and white wine. Small deep-fried fish served like whitebait are known as *la friture* and are excellent with a glass of crisp white wine. Fresh eel (*angouille*), simply grilled, is worth sampling in a riverside restaurant, or when cooked in red wine in a dish called *matelote*.

Viandes

Prior to the 19th century, sheep were principally reared for wool, but farmers soon realized that *l'agneau de Touraine* lamb raised in the Maine-Touraine area produced a tender and sweet meat. Its quality is recognized by the coveted Label Rouge (see Menu reader page 58). The *Géline de Touraine* chicken, another Label Rouge holder, was originally bred in the 19th century from a farmyard hen from Touraine and a Langshan from Asia. The resulting *Dame Noire* is so called because of its black feathers, and is highly prized for its tender meat. You will often see *coq au vin rouge* (chicken cooked in red wine), sometimes with a local twist such as *à l'angevin* (with onion and bacon). In Touraine, and particularly in Tours itself, pork dishes predominate but a French classic – *pièce de boeuf* – is given a local touch when served with a Ste-Maure de Touraine goat's cheese sauce. As you travel further upriver wild game, rabbit and veal appear regularly on the menu.

Fromages

Most good restaurants will have a selection of regional cheeses and will be able to assist you in making your choice. You can ask for several different types, perhaps starting with a delicately flavoured fresh goat's cheese and working up to a tasty (demi-sec) *Crottin de Chavignol* (try it with a Sancerre wine). The flavour and character of the cheese changes markedly according to its age. South of Tours the cylindrical *Ste-Maure de Touraine*, whose crust is coated in ash, has a straw running through the centre – look carefully and you'll find the maker's identification etched onto it. It partners very well with a Sauvignon de Touraine. Both the *Pouligny-St-Pierre* and the *Valançay* are shaped like a pyramid. Finally, the *Selles-sur-Cher* has a nutty flavour and a fine texture; its blue mould the result of at least 10 days maturation.

There are also two cow's milk cheeses to note. *Cendré d'Olivet* is made when the cows graze on the banks of the Loire in early spring, when the grass has most flavour. *Feuille de Dreux* is a soft-centred, mild cheese wrapped in a chestnut leaf, which adds to its flavour.

Desserts

French classics feature on every dessert menu. The most well-known native of the Loire Valley is the *tarte Tatin*, an upside-down apple tart. Apples and pears from the local orchards feature strongly, and cherries are a popular fruit for a *clafoutis*. Also look out for strawberries and melons; either is just as likely to appear as a starter or as a dessert. The French also adore rich and creamy chocolate desserts, so there is always a large choice of ice cream and sorbets. If all this sounds too sweet, try *fromage blanc* (sometimes called *faiselle*), an unsweetened dairy product a bit like a light fromage frais often served plain or with sugar, honey or a berry *coulis*.

Also striking is the infinite selection of cakes, biscuits and confectionery, either offered at the end of a meal or on sale in *pâtisseries* throughout the region. Tours has its *nougat de Tours* (in fact more of a cake), Angers tempts you with the *quernon d'ardoise* (a square of chocolate stuffed with nougat and resembling a roofing slate) and

there are *cotignacs d'Orléans* made from a highly concentrated quince jelly and sold in tiny round boxes. And many, many more.

Wine

Despite being among the most northerly of France's vineyards, Loire Valley wines have real personality. They're versatile, too, with something for every taste and occasion. In the east lies the AOC growth area of **Sancerre** covering some 2457 ha, three-quarters of it planted with Sauvignon Blanc vines which produce the classy white wines for which the area is renowned. Much less well-known outside the region are the reds and rosés produced from local Pinot Noir plantings. But what ultimately separates the drinking qualities of one region's produce from another's is the complex combination of climate and *terroir* – the soil and underlying geology of the very land itself. Subtly different drinking qualities in the wines of individual communes – tiny areas like Bannay, Bué, Crézancy, Menetou-Ratel, Montigny and Verdigny, for instance – each have their aficionados.

You can discover some of the best red and white AOC Sancerre wines on the family estate of father and son Emmanuel and Jean-Paul Fleuriet (Cave de la Petite Fontaine, rue de la Petite Fontaine, Chaudoux, Verdigny, T02 48 79 40 49, scev-fleuriet.fr, open throughout the year during variable working hours) who work the family's 12-ha vineyards. They also carry out the entire wine-making process in traditional stone vaulted cellars constructed by their ancestors in 1735.

Further west, both Anjou and Touraine also offer tremendous choice, and far more variety than is generally understood: a full-bodied Bourgueil, Chinon or Saumur are well able to counter those who still equate the region with crisp whites and gentle rosés. For an insight into more complex qualities, take a look at **Vouvray**, a few kilometres upstream from Tours. The appellation now comprises 1800 ha, with 300 estates in and around eight villages, and the *vendanges* (harvest) are typically among the latest in all France. Like both

Local hero

The late Gaston Huet became something of a celebrity in 1990, when the route of a new LGV high-speed rail line threatened to carve through the heart of the vineyards of Vouvray. His high-profile, impassioned protests resulted in tunnels being cut, at great expense, deep beneath them instead.

Muscadet and Sancerre, production is founded upon a single *cépage* or grape variety – Chenin Blanc, also known locally as Pineau d'Anjou, Pineau de la Loire or simply 'Chenin'.

An acknowledged master is the Domaine Huet l'Echansonne (11/13 rue de la Croix-Buisée, Vouvray, T02 47 52 78 87, huet-echansonne.com, Mon-Sat 0900-1200 and 1400-1800, closed bank holidays, tastings by appointment), founded in 1928 just above Vouvray on a family estate totalling 35 ha, and now with a total commitment to 'bio-dynamic' management. The estate's *mousseux* (sparkling) wines – whites only – are characterized by fruity sweetness balanced with fresh acidity. The results, · whether *demi-sec* (medium dry) or *moelleux* (sweet) can be sublime.

Dramatically higher in their annual output are the Loire Valley's most westerly **Muscadet** AOC vineyards – Muscadet des Cotteaux de la Loire, Muscadet Côtes de Grandlieu and Muscadet de Sèvre-et-Maine – centred around Nantes. Uniting them is a single grape variety, the Melon de

Bourgogne (known to Californians as Pinot Blanc). When the spectacularly harsh winter of 1709 decimated the Nantes wine industry, only the Melon de Bourgogne vines survived. It requires careful handling, to overcome a susceptibility to both mildew and botrytis, but in skilled hands magical things can happen and today endless rows cloak the shallow undulations of the Sèvre-et-Maine hills. For many years Muscadet, France's most exported wine, was seen merely as a light, refreshing and affordable 'dry white', best drunk young and, for the most part, informally. Now, though, 'new' Muscadets are being created, adding real fruitiness for modern wine drinkers. Some of the region's best AOC wines, both 'new' and classic, come from the Château de Cléray-Savion en Eolie (Vallet, T02 40 36 22 55, sauvion.fr, Mon-Fri 0900-1200 and 1330-1630, visits preferably by appointment), where Jean-Ernest Sauvion is one of the great emissaries for Muscadet de Sèvre-et-Maine. Some are designed to be drunk young, while the Château du Cléray Sauvion Cuvée de Garde, produced exclusively from old vines, has complex aromas and peppery, nutty undertones, combined with ageing potential up to (and beyond) 20 years.

Tip...

When selecting Muscadets look for the words 'Sur Lie', which denote fermentation on the lees, achieving a rounder, fuller fruitiness.

The first overnight chills colour the vine-leaves to fiery crimson.

Menu reader

General

Agriculture Biologique (AB) organically produced product.

à la carte individually priced menu items.

Appellation d'Origine Contrôlée (AOC) label of regulated origin.

biologique or *bio* organic

carte des vins wine list

déjeuner lunch

dîner dinner or supper

entrées starters

fait(e) maison home-made

hors d'oeuvre appetisers

Label Rouge often applied to poultry, label indicates premium quality and standards in production.

les plats main courses

menu/formule set menu

petit déjeuner breakfast

plat du jour dish of the day

plat principal main course

Drinks (*boissons*)

apéritif drink taken before dinner

bière a beer

café coffee (black espresso) / *grand crème* a large white coffee

chocolat chaud hot chocolate

cidre cider

dégustation tasting

demi small beer (33cl)

demi-sec medium dry – or slightly sweet when referring to Champagne.

digestif after-dinner drink, usually a liqueur or spirit.

doux the sweetest Champagne or cider.

eau gazeuse/pétillante sparkling/slightly sparkling mineral water.

eau plate/minérale still/mineral water

grand(e) big, large

jus de fruit fruit juice

kir apéritif made with white wine and a fruit liqueur usually cassis (blackcurrant).

lait milk

noisette espresso with a dash of milk.

panaché beer/lemonade shandy

petit(e) small

pichet jug, used to serve water, wine or cider.

pression a glass of draught beer

sec dry

thé tea, usually served with a slice of lemon (*au citron*).

une tisane/infusion herbal tea, *tisane de menthe* (mint tea), *tisane de camomille* (camomile tea) and *tisane de tilleul* (lime blossom) are the most popular.

verre a glass

vin rouge/blanc/rosé red/white/rosé wine

Signs of an enduring love affair with le chocolat.

Fruit (*fruits*) & vegetables (*légumes*)

artichaut artichoke
asperge asparagus
cassis blackcurrants
céleri-rave celeriac, usually served grated in mayonnaise.
champignons de paris button mushrooms
châtaignes chestnuts
choux cabbage
citron lemon
citrouille or *potiron* pumpkin
courge marrow or squash
épinard spinach
fenouil fennel
fraises strawberries
framboises raspberries
gratin Dauphinois potato slices layered with cream, garlic and butter and baked in the oven.
haricots verts green beans
lentilles vertes green lentils
mesclun a mixture of young salad leaves
mirabelles small golden plums
myrtilles blueberries
noix walnuts
oseille sorrel
pêches peaches
petits pois peas
poireaux leeks
poires pears
pomme de terre potato (*primeurs* are new potatoes and *frites* are chips)
pommes apples (*Reinette d'Orléans* and *Reine des Reinettes* are local varieties)
prunes plums

Meat (*viande*) & poultry (*volaille*)

agneau lamb
andouillette soft sausage made from pig's small intestines.
blanquette de veau veal stew in white sauce with cream, vegetables and mushrooms.
boeuf beef
boudin blanc smooth white sausage, made from various white meats.
boudin noir blood sausage or black pudding made with pig's blood, onions and spices.
canard duck
charcuterie encompasses sausages, hams and cured or salted meats.

Catching up on street gossip, Tours.

chevreuil venison, roe deer
confit process used to preserve meat, usually duck, goose or pork.
cuisse de grenouille frog's leg
dinde turkey
escalope thin, boneless slice of meat.
faux-filet beef sirloin
foie gras fattened goose or duck liver
fumé(e) smoked
géline de Touraine or *la Dame Noire* grain-fed chicken prized by restaurateurs.
gigot d'agneau leg of lamb
jambon ham
lapin rabbit
médaillon small, round cut of meat or fish.
mouton mutton
pâté au biquion puff pastry filled with minced pork, veal and cheese; a speciality of Tours.
pavé thickly cut steak
pintade guinea-fowl
porc pork
pot-au-feu du braconnier a stew of rabbit and diced bacon, slow-cooked with vegetables and served with poached liver.
poulet chicken
rillettes a coarse pork pâté.
rillons chunks of pork cooked in pork fat.
ris de veau sweetbreads
sanglier wild boar
saucisse small sausage
saucisson salami, eaten cold
saucisson sec air-dried salami
soupe Tourangelle a vegetable soup (leek, new turnips and fresh peas) with salt pork.
veau veal

Fish (*poisson*) & seafood (*fruits de mer*)

aiglefin or *églefin* haddock
alose shad
anchois anchovies
anguille eel
brème bream
brochet pike
cabillaud cod
coquillage shellfish
colin hake
crevettes prawns
dorade sea bream
friture de la Loire small fish such as smelt and gudgeon deep-fried like whitebait.
homard lobster
huîtres oysters
lotte monkfish
loup de mer sea bass
matelote fish stew (often eel) cooked in red wine
moules mussels
poissons de rivière river fish
sandre zander or pike-perch
saumon salmon
thon tuna
truite trout

Useful phrases

I'd like to reserve a table... *Je voudrais réserver une table...*

... for two people at eight o'clock ... *pour deux personnes, à vingt heures.*

What do you recommend? *Qu'est-ce que vous me conseillez?*

Does it come with salad? *Est-ce que c'est servi avec de la salade?*

I'd like something to drink. *Je voudrais quelque chose à boire.*

I'm a vegetarian. *Je suis végétarien/végétarienne.*

I don't eat... *Je ne mange pas de...*

Where are the toilets? *Où sont les toilettes?*

The bill, please. *L'addition, s'il vous plait.*

Desserts (*desserts*)

chantilly whipped, sweetened cream
clafoutis a fruit tart (usually cherries) covered in a custard-style filling, served hot or cold.
compôte stewed fruit, often as a purée.
crème anglaise thin custard normally served cold.
fromage blanc unsweetened dairy product with a refreshing flavour served on its own or with a fruit coulis.
glace ice cream
coupe glacée cold dessert with ice cream, fruit or nuts, chocolate or chantilly.
le parfum flavour, when referring to ice cream or yoghurt
île flottante soft meringue floating on custard, topped with caramel sauce.
liègeois chilled chocolate or coffee ice cream-based dessert topped with chantilly.
nougat de Tours a cake made with preserved fruits on a bed of *Reine des Reinettes* apples
pâtisserie pastries, cakes and tarts (also the place where they are sold).
quernon d'ardoise a crunchy nougatine square enrobed in chocolate.
sabayon creamy dessert made with beaten eggs, sugar and wine or liqueur.
tarte Tatin a celebrated upside-down apple tart.

Seafood, fresh from the Atlantic Coast.

Other

assiette plate (eg *assiette de charcuterie*)

beurre butter

beurre blanc buttery white wine sauce often served with fish.

Bordelaise red wine sauce served with steak.

brioche a soft, sweet bread made with eggs and butter.

crêpe large pancake served with various fillings as a dessert or snack.

croque-monsieur grilled ham and cheese sandwich.

croissant rich and flaky crescent-shaped roll usually served at breakfast.

crudités raw vegetables served sliced or diced with a dressing, as a starter or sandwich filling.

en croûte literally 'in crust'; food cooked in a pastry parcel.

escargots snails

forestière generally sautéed with mushrooms.

fouée or *fouace* a flat bread, baked in a wood oven, often filled with *rillettes*, beans, mushrooms, bacon pieces or pâté.

fromage cheese

fromage de chèvre goat's cheese

galette savoury filled pancake made with buckwheat flour, served as a starter or main course.

garniture garnish, side dish

gaufre waffle, usually served with chocolate sauce.

oeuf egg

pain bread

pain au chocolat similar to a croissant, but pillow-shaped and filled with chocolate.

pâte pastry or dough, not to be confused with *pâtes*, which is pasta or *pâté*, the meat terrine.

riz rice

salade verte simple green salad with vinaigrette dressing.

soupe/potage soup

viennoiserie baked items such as croissants and *brioches*.

For every event, there's the perfect viewpoint for diners (Festival de Loire, Orléans).

Entertainment

A glance at the extravagantly styled theatres and opera houses in some of the larger towns and cities will leave you in no doubt about the enduring French passion for the performing arts. Sculpted into the more extravagant façades are names like Racine, Molière, Hugo and Voltaire, evoking the great age of theatre-going which happily persists in modern-day France. Bigger venues host impressively staged touring shows from dance and theatre companies, orchestras and contemporary music acts, so if you have a taste for the bright lights, being on holiday here needn't mean being completely away from it all. Club-goers will find lively night spots (especially in Nantes), while anyone visiting in summer will find a whole host of festivals and other special events (many of them free of charge). Out of town things are different, of course, but in peak season the range of options can be surprising. If you've never seen one of the big French firework displays which accompany major events (including Bastille Day, 14th July) then you're in for a real treat – and you'll be equally amazed by the state-of-the-art effects employed in spectacular *son et lumière* performances at major visitor attractions.

It's sometimes hard not to join in.

Traditional meeting place.

An alternative style.

Bars & clubs

In cities it's generally possible at most times of day to find a bar, café or brasserie in which you can get a drink or something to eat. Despite large numbers of bars closing throughout France, there are still considerably more than there are pubs in the UK. Bars may not open until late afternoon but in cities will often stay open until the early hours. Rural bars tend to rely on locals calling in for a coffee or a drink before dinner and will usually close early. Most places close at least one day a week, often Sunday or Monday.

In rural areas you may be surprised to find a discotheque in the middle of nowhere, or at least away from any towns or public transport. They often open at weekends only. City centre clubs open their doors around 2200 and continue until the early morning (generally closing between 0400 and 0600). There is normally an entrance fee or a requirement to buy a drink. Music-wise, the style varies from hip-hop, rap and techno to R&B, disco and 80s retro. One of the most lively bar and club scenes is in Nantes, followed closely by Angers, which has a huge student population.

Gay & lesbian

There are active gay communities in cities, with social events and welcoming bars and restaurants. Nantes has the largest selection of gay-friendly venues, the best place to start being rue Kervégan and rue du Maréchal-Joffre, where you'll find Le Petit Marais (lepetitmarais.fr) and L'Hypnotik (hypnotik-cafe.com). Gay 41 (grlc.ifrance.com) has all sorts of information for those visiting the Blois and Tours areas, including organized cycling, walking and canoeing activities. The Gay Guide (leguidegay.com) has entertainment and accommodation listings (by department) for France. *FranceGuide for the Gay Traveller* is a useful magazine available by ordering online at franceguide.com. The website also has general information for gay visitors to France, and some useful relevant links.

Shopping

Gifts & souvenirs

There are the usual gift shops in all the chateaux and visitor attractions, which offer some interesting, high quality items alongside the mugs, T-shirts and keyrings. Both the **Château d'Azay-le-Rideau** and the **Château Royal d'Amboise** boutiques sell a good range of tapestries if you fancy introducing a medieval theme to your home. The Festival des Jardins at **Chaumont** sells a wide range of books on French gardens, garden design and wildlife, plus some lovely eco-friendly gifts. If you're feeling inspired after visiting the gardens at **Villandry**, there is a super little shop selling must-have garden accessories and plants. Rose lovers should visit **Doué-la-Fontaine**, a centre of European rose production near Saumur. Each year the growers put on a fabulous mid-July spectacle, but you can visit and buy plants at any time of year. Still on a scented theme, the Savonnerie Artisanale Martin de Candre at **Fontévraud** produces fine traditional soaps.

At the **Château de Cheverny**, the Orangerie has a collection of Gien tableware, full settings being beautifully displayed on tables around the shop – especially interesting if you can't visit the celebrated Faïencerie in **Gien**. Notable ceramicists in the region include Charles Hair, who works from his studio in **Thizay**, near Chinon, and whose work is displayed in the Musée Pincé in Angers and several galleries in Paris. He produces unique contemporary items and particularly beautiful Celadons. The village of **La Borne** near Henrichement has evolved into an artistic centre with a community of working potters selling their creations direct from individual studios. You can stroll around the village, visit the potters and discover their work.

For another lasting memory of your trip to the Loire Valley, there's an amazing range of wickerwork products for just about any use or decoration at the basketwork cooperative in **Villaines-les-Rochers**, near Azay-le-Rideau. The village is home to the largest number of basket workers in France. Artisan studios are dotted around the village and visitors can buy individual pieces direct from the makers.

It would be hard to resist buying some of the confectionery and chocolate produced by artisan *pâtissiers* and *chocolatiers* throughout the region. **Orléans** has a wonderful selection of food shops in and around the Châtelet indoor market, although you must see Les Musardises on rue République for its fine display of local specialities like the *cotignac d'Orléans*, a quince-based fruit confection. **Blois** is host to master chocolatier Max Vauché, who also has a large shop near Chambord in **Bracieux**, where visitors can watch chocolates being made.

In **Angers**, visit rue des Lices, where you can find the famous *quernon d'Ardoise*, small chocolates stuffed with nougat and made to represent the slate roof tiles. You'll also be tempted by the delicious hand-made chocolates and macarons; beautifully wrapped, they make an ideal gift. In **Nantes**, look out for colourful sweets known as *berlingots* and *rigollettes*, produced from the sugar which helped bring wealth to this Atlantic port. Visit Débotté Gautier on rue de la Fosse – the interior is as stunning as the chocolates. Specialties include *le Muscadet Nantais*, a wonderful marriage of wine and chocolate which they recommend you simply allow to melt in your mouth. For something less sweet, the *sel de Guérande* salt goes down well with cooks and foodies.

Import/export

Travellers who want to send home or take back any food products or wine into the UK from France can do so if they are for personal consumption; however, both fish and honey are restricted items, so check with the Food Standards Agency (T+44 20-7238 6951 from France) before you travel. Visitors returning to the US from Europe should avoid taking fresh meat, fruit or vegetables and plants. Chocolate, hard cheeses, preserved or tinned foods and condiments are generally admissible. Details about bringing in goods from abroad are available online (hmrc.gov.uk/customs for UK; cbp.gov for US). Visitors who live outside the EU can reclaim tax paid on purchases above a certain amount. Look out for shops displaying a 'tax free shopping' sign – they will sell you goods with the tax already deducted (remember to have your passport with you).

Quality souvenirs, courtesy of the Domaine de Chambord.

About the city

Food is one of the main reasons that people love to visit France. Feast your eyes on the magnificent displays of fresh and regional produce on sale in the regular markets throughout the Loire Valley region and you'll soon realize why it's called the 'Garden of France'. Best buys are seasonal fresh produce such as asparagus (in spring), cherries and strawberries (in early summer) and apples, pears and pumpkins (in the autumn). At the height of summer expect to find tasty local tomatoes, cucumbers and beetroot, with a range of different varieties to try. Visit **Chateau de la Bourdaisière** in Montlouis-sur-Loire which grows all the old varieties of tomato and holds an annual tomato festival in September. Similarly, the **Château de Rivau** has a pumpkin festival around the same time, where you'll discover pumpkins in all shapes,

sizes and colours, plus other ancient vegetables.

Some apple and pear orchards sell direct to the public; others will take huge crates to market and sell them freshly harvested and very cheap. One apple variety to look out for is the Reine des Reinettes, said to be best for the famous *tarte Tatin*. A really interesting local product is the Poire- or Pomme-Tapée. Visit the artisan producers at **Rivarennes** (pears) or **Turquant** (apples) and discover the traditional method of preserving the fruit by slow drying and 'tapping' to verify removal of the moisture. The end product is deliciously sweet dried fruit which, when preserved in wine, can be added to sweet or savoury dishes (and is often seen on restaurant menus).

Autumn also brings wild mushrooms to market, although visit one of the troglodyte mushroom growers at any time and you can buy more unusual varieties of mushroom as well as the ubiquitous

Local produce still has real meaning here.

The best boulangeries have loyal and devoted customers.

Champignon de Paris button mushroom sold in French supermarkets. Covered market halls like Châtelet in **Orléans**, Talensac in **Nantes** or Les Halles in **Tours** present the very best from the region's producers. If you are shopping for a picnic, look out for traditional *charcuterie* and pork products – Hardouin in **Vouvray** and **Tours** are particularly renowned. They also sell a huge range of preserved meats. Alternatively, try any of the five AOC *fromages de chèvres* (goat's cheeses) from the region, which you will find at any market.

For details of recommended wine producers see page 56; for information on wine tours, see respective listings sections.

Shopping hours

The French shopping week is generally Monday to Saturday. The restrictions on Sunday trading have been relaxed in Paris, Lille and Marseille, but elsewhere you'll only find *boulangeries*, some supermarkets and florists opening on Sunday mornings. The traditional two-hour closure between 1200 and 1400 is still observed, although in recent years larger supermarkets and many independent shops in towns have started to remain open. Some *boulangeries* open until 1300 for the lunchtime trade but may not re-open until 1500. If you need anything for a picnic buy it before midday. Many clothes shops and small traders are closed on Mondays.

Activities & tours

Rivers make entertaining travelling companions, and with not one major river but several, you're spoilt for choice. Take to the water on a gentle cruise and you'll add a whole new dimension to your understanding of the landscape and its natural riches, not to mention the way of life of those who work on the region's waterways. If you're fit and experienced (or would like to be) you can hire a kayak or a self-drive cruiser. Or you could simply enjoy it from dry land by walking or cycling on the countless dedicated routes along banks and former towpaths, or deep within vast tracts of forests which just beg to be explored. Either way you'll be away from it all, with perfect picnic spots and a good chance of meeting some of the plentiful wildlife that made the Loire Valley a natural choice for the great hunting estates of kings and noblemen. Add to this world-class golf-courses, balloon flights, chateau visits and, of course, wine tours, and you'll find more than enough to inspire you, however long your stay.

Boat trips

There is a growing number of sightseeing trips available on large cruise boats such as the *Saint-Martin-de-Tours* (naviloire.com). You can board this at **Rochecorbon** to discover the wild river, the limestone cliffs and troglodytic dwellings (plus occasional birdwatching trips with an expert on board). Similar trips leave from the quay in the centre of **Saumur** (bateaux-nantais.fr), where you can also take a picturesque sunset cruise. Traditional-style boats *La Belle Adèle* and the

Amarante (loireterroir.com) sail from **Candes-St-Martin** near the confluence of the Loire and Vienne rivers and are a great way to discover the river and encounter its wildlife and scenery. You can choose a themed trip such as wine, cooking, fish or birds, sunrise or sunset picnics or even rent the whole boat and its crew for an overnight adventure. Some trips on the Cher and departing from Chisseaux (labelandre.com) pass beside or even under the arches of the **Château de Chenonceau**.

At **Nantes**, Les Bateaux Nantais (bateaux-nantais.fr) offer Loire and Erdre river cruises combined with lunch or dinner aboard. With a fascinating historical commentary, it's interesting to nose around the port of Nantes with Marine & Loire Cruises (marineetloire.fr). You'll pass the Béghin Say sugar cane refinery, the Island's Machine Warehouse and the former ship-building yards.

From the little port of **La Doutre** in the heart of Angers, birdwatching trips on the *Hirondelle* (maine-anjou-rivieres.com) or the *Union* (bateau-croisiere-union.com) offer sightings of crested herons and egrets on the Mayenne and Sarthe rivers.

Those who want to take the helm and navigate themselves might consider hiring a boat and cruising 250 km of **Anjou waterways** (anjou-navigation.fr). If the gentle pace of canal cruising appeals, the best place to start is **Briare**, where Charmes Nautiques (charmes-nautiques.com) offers a choice of self-drive cabin cruisers for hire. Glide across Eiffel's famous Pont-Canal and continue south on the Canal Latéral or head north on the Canal de Briare towards Montargis.

Balloon flights

There's nothing quite like floating over the landscape in a balloon and seeing the magnificent chateaux of the Loire Valley from above. Flights are at dawn or dusk and are highly weather-dependent – make sure your ticket price can be fully refunded if your trip doesn't go ahead. If you wish to re-book, tickets are normally valid for 12 months. The flights themselves usually last around an hour. There are various companies offering flights (see relevant Activities sections throughout the book) – you can choose to take a standard trip and fly over one or two chateaux or indulge in a lavishly expensive personalized package.

Cycling

The long-distance cycling route *Loire à Vélo* (loire-a-velo.fr, in French only) offers around 800 km of gentle cycling through the Pays de la Loire and Loire Valley regions, including the Loire-Anjou-Touraine Regional Natural Park. The route helps you discover the Loire and its surroundings, often following river banks on dedicated cycle paths. It will take you to gardens, interesting towns, chateaux and other remarkable sites, as well as through unspoilt countryside and vineyards. The Loire route is well signposted and there are leaflets (available in English) detailing the route and adjoining circuits in most tourist offices. Most

Tip...

Look for the **Accueil Vélo** signs on accommodation close to the cycle trail. These offer a special welcome to cyclists, secure bike storage, an energizing breakfast and other services such as quick repairs.
Travel with your bike on the **TER regional trains** free of charge (except in peak periods).
Explore the countryside around Chambord on a 300-km network of secure cycle paths known as **Les Châteaux à Vélo** (chateauxavelo.com). You can even download 40 free MP3 audio commentaries.
Pack light – remember that many cycle hire points offer baggage transfers.

cycle hire shops will be able to help you plan an itinerary, and Detours de Loire (locationdevelos. com) has a chain of partners throughout the region where you can either pick up or leave your cycles, so you won't have to retrace your tracks at the end of your holiday.

For independent travellers **Loire Valley Travel** (randovelo.fr) organizes self-guided cycling and walking tour packages. It includes the provision of suitable bikes, hotel accommodation and baggage transport, detailed route maps and suggested visits. If you want your itinerary meticulously planned and accommodation and restaurants specially selected, companies such as Headwater (headwater.com) or Backroads (backroads.com) for visitors from the US both offer all-inclusive Loire Valley cycling packages.

Golf

The Loire Valley region is often described as being a golfers' paradise, not only for the number of courses, but also because the quality and variety on offer is likely to satisfy players of every level. It is usually possible to turn up and get tee-time during quiet periods. Those new to golfing in France will find that the courses are generally uncrowded and beautifully maintained. Some of the most natural environments are to be found in the Sologne (golf. tourismloiret.com), with natural lakes and forest incorporated into the course. Many of the famous chateaux have courses nearby, such as at the Golf du Château de Cheverny (golf-cheverny.com). The very best, Les Bordes (lesbordes.com), lies between Blois and Beaugency.

Expect to pay from around €30-55 in green fees for 18 holes, although this will vary according to season, and some clubs (such as Les Bordes) will be considerably more costly.

Horse riding

There are plenty of varied routes throughout the Loire Valley for riders to enjoy. The banks of the Loire are perfect for gentle canters and the woods

About the region

and ponds of the **Sologne**, or the forests of **Chambord** and **Amboise**, offer long trots amid beautiful scenery, plus visits to some magnificent chateaux. There are companies which provide all inclusive holiday packages for experienced riders (look at cheval-et-chateaux.com or rideinfrance. com) – expect to ride for up to five hours each day. Alternatively, if you want to enjoy a day's ride as part of your holiday, tourist offices can supply details of stables offering trail rides for both beginners and advanced riders. Look out for the Centre de Tourisme Equestre quality label for riding centres in France (label-tourisme-equestre.com lists members).

Kayaking

The Loire is navigable by canoe and there are many opportunities to hire one and take to the water either on the Loire or one of its tributaries. Canoe clubs offer a range of guided trips and welcome beginners. Experienced canoeists can enjoy the river with or without a guide, although a series of useful river cards are available from the Maison du Parc at **Montsoreau** (see page 220) or through canoe-regioncentre.org, which has detailed maps and essential safety advice. They also recommend heritage sites to see and detail wildlife you might encounter. Tourist offices can supply a list of canoe clubs.

Swimming

For safety reasons swimming is forbidden in the Loire river and in the Cher below Tours. If you want a dip in a river, there are designated swimming areas in some riverside leisure locations such as the *plage* at **Pouzay** and the Parc Capitaine in **Bourgueil**, each of which has supervised river bathing during July and August. You can bathe in a lake (*étang* or *base nautique*) dedicated to leisure and water sports, for example at **Brissac-Quincé**, Lac du Maine in **Angers** or the Lac du Val Joyeux at **Château la Vallière**. There is a public swimming pool in most major towns, one of the best being

the Centre Aquatic du Lac in **Tours**, which has a 50-m outdoor heated pool and an exciting whirlpool area.

Walking

Relatively few people travel to the Loire Valley specifically for a walking holiday. However, the region's gentle routes along river valleys, woodland paths, among well-tended vineyards and open parkland are all there waiting for you to discover. Tourist offices produce a collection of self-guided walks which you can enjoy as part of your holiday. The *Strolls in Touraine* series of leaflets, available in English, is free from tourist offices in the area.

If you'd like to do a walk of several days' duration, the **GR3** (long distance route) follows the Loire river and takes in prestigious chateaux such as Chambord, Cheverny, Blois and Chaumont-sur-Loire. You should equip yourself with the appropriate IGN blue series maps at 1:25 000 which show footpaths. The Fédération Française de la Randonnée Pédestre (ffrandonnee.fr) produces a series of *Topo Guides* including 'Chateaux de la Loire' on the GR3 (in French only). Some all-inclusive, self-guided walking holidays include detailed routes, baggage transfer, accommodation and meals (see bellefrance.co.uk or sherpa-walking-holidays.co.uk).

Wine tours

Wine enthusiasts may like to follow a signposted wine route (Route des Vignobles). Routes throughout the region are generally through picturesque scenery, and will pass many wine producers who welcome visitors for tastings and purchases. You can also take advantage of the many personalized wine tours from companies such as loire-valley-tours.com or loireuncorked.com. Your guide will pick you up at your accommodation and take you to visit several vineyards.

A vine romance

You'll search in vain for 'Eolie' on the map, however detailed. But I'm here, all the same, according to wine producer Jean-Ernest Sauvion. He should know, since he declared it so (in homage to the ancient island home of Greek goddesses Alcée and Sappho) some years ago, as if having seceded from the rest of France. But 'Eolie', it turns out, is the land of wine, and its founder is one of the great ambassadors for the Pays-Nantais area's speciality: the world-famous Muscadet de Sèvre-et-Maine. The Sauvion family has been producing some of the finest examples at the Château du Cléray near Vallet, southwest of Nantes, since purchasing the estate in 1935. Most of its 38 ha of vineyards are planted with Melon de Bourgogne vines (so called because of their rounded leaves, and known to Californians as Pinot Blanc). It's said that this early ripening, frost resistant variety (the sole grape permissible for Muscadet wines under French Appellation d'Origine Contrôlée regulations) was planted by 17th-century Dutch merchants seeking a dependable source of white wine for distillation to supply the lucrative Brandy trade. Another version has it that Louis XIV ordered the vineyards to be re-planted with the present vines following the decimation of previous red varieties during prolonged frosts in 1709. Either way, the vines thrived here, with Muscadet becoming France's most exported wine.

The chateau itself has a graceful elegance which elsewhere would pass for classic English Georgian, and sits on huge stone-vaulted cellars (*caves*). I'm welcomed by Jean-Ernest's associate Roselyne Delaunay, who underlines her shared passion for the estate and its wines by describing herself on her business card as 'Ambassadrice d'Eolie'. After briefly outlining the estate's mission to give a certain *noblesse* to the often underrated Muscadet, it's time for the wines to take up the conversation and speak for themselves. We begin with 'Fildefere', an accessible, everyday Muscadet vinified in stainless steel vats. Even at this level the characteristic dry crispness is balanced with a refreshing citrus fruitiness. Next comes 'Hermines du Cardinal', an even drier experience, with 0% sugar, and which adds mint and apple to the citrus hints. Its companion, the 'Baronne du Cléray', is subtitled 'Sur Lie' and, as expected, provides an eloquent demonstration of the effect of ageing wines in the presence of exhausted yeast cells known as 'lees', with a more rounded fruitiness prized by many

modern wine drinkers. Again, it's bottled direct from the vat, complete with a natural slightly effervescent quality which lightens things. A subtly different variant, 'Le Chemin d'Eolie', adds more finesse and complexity to its Sur Lie credentials.

By now I find my taste buds beginning to tune in to the more obvious, yet surprising, variations; however as I'm about to discover, the estate's reputation is founded on its own distinctive interpretations of the style and drinking qualities which have come to define Muscadet. For that we now move on to what the chateau terms its 'Haute Culture' range, which employ classic methods to exploit the effects of *terroir* – the combined qualities of climate and geology which are unique to every estate and which underpin the personalities of its wines. Sure enough, the resulting full-bodied, ripe fruitiness will be a revelation to anyone expecting the bone dryness of Muscadet's bad old days, as will the wine's potential for ageing up to (and perhaps considerably beyond) 20 years. We follow this with 'Cardinal Richard', Sauvion's flagship wine, selected each year by a panel of independent tasters and named after Cardinal Richard de la Vergne, who owned the estate during the 19th century. Should a vintage prove to have been less than generous, there is no Cardinal Richard for that year, maintaining the very highest standards for discerning wine drinkers. Amazingly, for connoisseurs Jean-Ernest's brother Pierre creates an even more eclectic blend – the 'Jardins Secrets brut 00', combining grapes from old vines from up to six different *terroirs* on the estate. The results are sublime, bursting with complex citrus, pear and dried fruit flavours and with a rich, golden hue. Before leaving the Château du Cléray I spend a few minutes among the vines, to see for myself where the magic begins in the Land of Eolie.

The fruits of summer, Loire Valley style.

Contents

Maisons à Colombages, Vieux Orléans.

Introduction

Our journey begins in a hilly landscape described by Balzac as "a chain of small mountains" – an appropriately romantic setting for a love affair with the Loire to begin. Climb the steep ramparts of the town of Sancerre to see the surrounding contours draped with the productive vines which have made this ancient hilltop settlement and its wine-producing neighbours world-famous. In past times the little port of St-Thibault shipped the wines and unloaded timber for local barrel-makers. Today you can take to the water by cruising on the nearby Canal Latéral à la Loire – while you enjoy the landscapes you'll never be far from the river. In fact, you'll eventually pass high above it on the spectacular 19th-century Pont-Canal aqueduct at Briare, a perfect place to moor and meet other boating types or relax at a quayside restaurant.

The Loire, meanwhile, continues through gentle landscapes, passing chateau towns such as Gien and Sully-sur-Loire on its way towards Orléans. Joan of Arc's town has become a vibrant, elegant city and nearby are over 35,000 ha of ancient forests and lakes of the Fôret d'Orléans, where you might chance upon eagles, ospreys and, of course, deer and wild boar. Beyond Orléans lies historic Beaugency, whose 26-arch former toll-bridge across the Loire dates from the 14th century.

The Château de Sully-sur-Loire.

What to see in…

…one day
Wake up in the cheerful riverside town of **Sully-sur-Loire**, visit the moated chateau then follow the river to **St-Benoît-sur-Loire** to see the sculpted tomb figure of **King Philippe I** in the magnificent medieval abbey of **Fleury**. Picnic on the riverbank then visit the fascinating **Musée de la Marine de Loire** in nearby **Châteauneuf-sur-Loire**. Pause at the old river port of **Combleux** before ending your day in style with a meal and a stroll around the historic heart of **Orléans**.

…a weekend or more
After an overnight stay in **Orléans** visit the vast **Cathédrale Ste-Croix**, right beside which you'll see the dazzling treasures of the city's **Musée des Beaux-Arts**. Then simply cross the road to the 16th-century Renaissance **Hôtel Groslot**, which once played host to the several kings of France. After lunch in the **old town**, head south to **La Ferté-St-Aubin's** time-warp chateau (with an **Orient Express** train in its grounds), before crossing the Loire on a 14th-century bridge to discover the medieval heart of **Beaugency**.

Sancerre & downstream to Châteauneuf

While Sancerre attracts many visitors, drawn by the allure of some of the region's most prestigious wines, this is an otherwise quiet and often overlooked corner of the Loire Valley. But the river landscapes are perhaps at their most beautiful here and offer plenty of opportunities for relaxed picnicking, walking and birdwatching as the Loire flows past historic towns and villages towards Châteauneuf-sur-Loire. During your own journey find time to pause, too, at the great Benedictine abbey of Fleury in St-Benoît-sur-Loire, as travellers and pilgrims have done for a thousand years.

The hilltop town of Sancerre, beyond the River Loire.

Sancerre

Sancerre looks and feels like a major centre of wine production. And it smells like one, too, during the annual *vendange* period when freshly picked grapes are being crushed in and around this ancient hilltop town. Short of transporting it to Provence, the setting couldn't be better, with productive vineyards draped over the surrounding hills and valleys as far as the eye can see. The town's medieval layout converges on place du Befroi and the Eglise Notre-Dame, near which the **Maison des Sancerre** (maison-des-sancerre.com, daily end March to mid-November), a beautifully restored townhouse dating from the 14th century, offers plenty of information and insight into local wine production. There are plenty of options for wine tastings (and purchases) in and around the town, whose visitor focus has shifted towards the Nouvelle Place, an agreeable spot for a cool drink or an evening meal. Explore the streets which rise behind the square and you'll find the **Tour des Fiefs**, an early 16th-century circular tower, which now has a viewing platform at the summit offering definitive panoramas of the town and the surrounding landscapes.

Before leaving the Sancerre area it's worth sampling the local Crottin de Chavignol goat's cheeses and visiting the nearby slightly sleepy pleasure port of **St-Thibault St-Satur**, nestled between the Loire and its Lateral Canal.

Châtillon-sur-Loire

Châtillon's spidery suspension bridges across the Lateral Canal and the Loire itself are much better known than the historic town, which therefore counts as something of a discovery. Its name comes from the 10th-12th-century *castello* known locally as Château Gaillard, a few ruined sections of which survive high above the town. After parking near the tourist office (see opposite) in the town centre (which you'll probably have all to yourself around midday) follow rue des Prés then take rue Haute, which climbs to the most ancient part of

Façades from various eras in Sancerre.

Essentials

➐ Getting around Most people will choose the convenience of the car to get around this region; however, thanks to the *Loire à Vélo* cycle route and the network of canals, it is possible to visit the area at a slower pace. Gien is the largest town and is about half way between Sancerre and Orléans. Bus services throughout the Loiret region are operated by Ulys. Lines 3 and 7 from Orléans serve this area as far as Châtillon-sur-Loire. There are regular trains to Gien, Briare and Tracy-sur-Loire (for Sancerre) from Paris Bercy (about 1½ hours journey time).

➌ Bus station Buses to Gien stop at various locations in the town, place Leclerc is the most central stop.

➏ Train station Place de la Gare, Gien, T08-36 35 35 35.

➒ ATMs You'll find ATMs in Gien town centre just north of the old bridge.

⊕ Hospital 2 avenue Jean Villejean, Gien, T02 38 29 38 29, ch-gien.com.

✛ Pharmacies Pharmacie du Centre, quai Lenoir, Gien, T02 38 67 21 63. Other towns and large villages will all have at least one pharmacy.

➐ Post office Quai Lenoir, Gien, T02-38 29 54 80.

➊ Tourist information offices 1 place de Gaulle, Briare, T02 38 31 24 51; 3 place Aristide Briand, Châteauneuf-sur-Loire, T02 38 58 44 79; 47 rue Franche, Châtillon-sur-Loire, T02 38 31 42 88; place Jean Jaurés, Gien, T02 38 67 25 28; 44 rue Orléanaise, St Benoît-sur-Loire, T02 38 35 79 00; Esplanade Porte César, Sancerre, T02 48 54 08 21; place de Gaulle, Sully-sur-Loire, T02 38 36 23 703.

Vendange

For more full-on exposure to wine production you can't do better than to head for nearby **Chavignol**, a normally peaceful village which erupts into frenzied activity during the annual *vendange*, typically around early to mid-October. In the hills above the village are footpaths leading into the very heart of the vineyards, where you can see the picking process first hand (an experience which will bring a new dimension to your subsequent wine enjoyment).

Vendange time above the village of Chavignol.

the town. On either side are stone façades, one of which retains a four-storey, half-timbered *escalier* (an external spiral staircase) accessed by a further set of stone steps. A little further on you'll reach the surprisingly large **Eglise St-Maurice**, whose 19th-century neo-Gothic interior is beautifully proportioned. There's also some rich stained glass in the choir windows and an ornate Gothic altarpiece. Just beyond the church you'll find a footpath leading to the chateau ruins and a bird's-eye view of the valley. After returning to the lower town, turn left before the tourist office into rue Franche, where a tall bell tower denotes a former **Protestant Temple** (only the third to be built in France and dating from 1596) which alternated between destruction and rebuilding amid attacks on the fiercely Protestant town during the Wars of Religion.

As you leave Châtillon it's worth turning right off rue Martial Vuidet onto rue du Port, which has a bar/restaurant and leads to a small pleasure port on the canal. The port begins just above the gardens to your left and there's an up-market restaurant (Le Lafayette, T02 38 38 18 63) on one of the barges moored along the quayside.

Briare

Pont-Canal de Briare

Access via the Port de Commerce, Briare or St-Firmin-sur-Loire on the left bank of the Loire. Information from the Office de Tourisme, 1 place de Gaulle, Briare, T02 38 31 24 51, briare-le-canal.com or the Musée des Deux Marines et du Pont-Canal, 58 bd Buyser, Briare, T02 38 31 28 27.

The 17th-century Canal de Briare, one of France's oldest waterways, flows beside the *rive gauche* (left bank) of the river, while the Lateral Canal sits on the *rive droite* (right bank). Linking the two would open up the lucrative Parisian market to businesses below the Loire, but was always going to be technically challenging. The solution, achieved with the help of Gustave Eiffel's engineers, was the sensational Pont-Canal de Briare, a 663-m-long aqueduct whose 3000 tonne water channel of structural steel is carried on rugged stone piers. It took seven years to complete and opened in 1876, carrying barges and other waterway traffic across the Loire in belle époque style. It's still in use and is particularly appreciated by river cruisers, for whom Briare's Port de Plaisance (leisure port) has expanded its facilities in recent years. Alternatively, you can cross on foot, or see things differently from the leafy riverbank footpaths below.

Musée de la Mosaïque et des Emaux

1 bd Loreau, T02 38 31 20 51, musee.mosaique@wanadoo.fr. 1 Jun-30 Sep daily 1000-1830, 1 Oct-31 Dec and 1 Feb-31 May daily 1400-1800. €4.

The story of how Briare became world-famous during the 19th and early 20th centuries for its buttons, beads, costume pearls and enamel-glazed mosaic tiles is recounted in this stylish collection, housed in the former factory building of the company which produced them. Period examples of Emaux de Briare's mainstream products are ultimately less inspiring, however, than the important collection of decorative mosaic panels spanning art nouveau and art deco periods, plus work by today's contemporary designers. Production of newly fashionable ceramic mosaic tiles continues and there's a small factory shop behind the museum building.

Gien

Château de Gien & Musée de la Chasse et de la Nature

Entry by rue du Château (parking in front of the church) or climb the Escalier des Degrés from the town, T02 38 67 69 69, tourismeloiret.com. Jul-Aug daily 1000-1800, Apr-Jun and Sep Wed-Mon 1000-1800, Feb-Mar and Oct-Dec Wed-Mon 1000-1200 and 1400-1700. €5, €2.50 children (6-17), €12.50 family (2 adults, 2 children).

Cross Gien's 16th-century *dos d'âne* (donkey-back) stone bridge to admire classic views of the town rising from the right bank of the Loire. Notice how the red-brick Eglise Ste-Jeanne-d'Arc blends almost seamlessly into the main body of the château. Like the church, the château's oldest feature is a stone tower (the **Tour Charlemagne**, retained from a much earlier structure), although the remainder of the building is hardly youthful, its construction

having started in the late 15th century. This places it among the very earliest of all the Loire Valley chateaux, comfortably pre-dating the wave of building which would elsewhere be fuelled by the Renaissance. Not that it remained untouched by the arrival of the new stylistic influences, however, notably in the romantic-looking wing rising from the opposite (eastern) end of the building. For a closer look recross the bridge to the town centre and climb the steps of l'Escalier des Degrés which ascend to the chateau from avenue du Maréchal Leclerc. Today it's hard to appreciate the scale of destruction which the site endured during the Second World War, thanks to the long campaign of skillful and patient reconstruction which has restored the building to its former glory. Note the intricate brickwork – diamond patterns for the Renaissance wing and individual motifs (including a crossbow) for the main body of the building. The site was long a meeting place for hunters, a theme developed in the museum within the chateau. The exhibits may fail to convert you to the pursuit and killing of assorted wildlife for pleasure, but they present a pretty definitive overview (with works by great animal painters) of a historically important activity which for centuries helped feed the people of the region.

The Château de Gien and the Tour Charlemagne, beyond the town's 16th-century stone bridge.

Around the region

Eglise Ste-Jeanne d'Arc

Rue du Château, information available from tourist office, T02 38 67 25 28.

With its commanding position high above the town, there's no mistaking the heavily buttressed Gothic tower of the early 16th-century royal collegiate church of St-Etienne, damaged during the Revolution and effectively abandoned in 1828. The church's baroque successor was dedicated to St-Pierre in 1832, but was virtually destroyed by the aerial bombardments in June 1940 which claimed much of the town. The tower's massive structure, however, enabled it to survive. The present neo-Romanesque church, completed in 1954 and dedicated to St Joan, was constructed in reinforced concrete, which was then entirely clad in red brickwork. The style is curious, to say the least, and becomes a lot more so when you enter the other-worldly interior. As your eyes acclimatize to the low light levels, notice the nave and side aisles divided by circular columns (drum piers) whose round-arched arcades sit on simple terracotta capitals depicting the life of the Patron Saint. These in turn support plain barrel vaults, of which the central arch, hanging 22 m above the 12-m wide nave, represents an impressive architectural achievement. The pencil-like diamond-arched lancet windows, on the other hand, are neither Gothic nor Romanesque, but those of the nave do at least contain vibrant stained glass panels by master glassmaker Max Ingrand, who also worked nearby in Azay-le-Rideau, Blois, Chenonceau and Tours. (The altar, hewn from solid Vosges marble – red, naturally – is decorated with further panels by Ingrand.) Sadly the eastern Ste-Jeanne windows by François Bertrand were partly obscured following the bizarre decision in 1986 to install a giant organ (manufactured by Roethinger of Strasbourg) in front of them. The remaining interior decoration is mainly confined to tall Orléans ceramic figures of the Virgin and Saints adorning the piers, along with the Stations of The Cross in glazed ceramic panels by Jean Bertholle and manufactured in Gien.

Musée de la Faïencerie

78 place de la Victoire, T02 38 05 21 06, gien.com. Jan-Feb Mon-Fri 1400-1800, Sat 0900-1200 and 1400-1800, Mar-Dec Mon-Sat 0900-1200 and 1400-1800, Sun 1000-1200 and 1400-1800. Closed 1 Jan, 1 May, 1 and 11 Nov, 25 Dec. The adjacent factory shop is closed Sun.

France has something of a reputation for fine *faïence*, and the Musée de la Faïencerie in Gien (glazed earthenware, or majolica) and the company (which is also called Gien) ranks among the very finest and most highly prized of all producers. The business was established in 1821 by Englishman Thomas Hall who was attracted to Gien because of its proximity to substantial deposits of the high quality clay and sand on which the manufacturing process depended. Better still, the local forests would provide timber to fire the kilns, while the finished goods could then be shipped direct from Gien's quays. He purchased a former convent dating from the 16th century and set about establishing his new factory. Using production techniques popularized in England, the company went on to develop a steadily broadening range of tableware and other domestic items. Much of Gien's success was due to the decision to base its designs on (and even convincingly replicate) the forms and decorative styles from other renowned centres of production including Rouen, Marseille and Delft, plus the Italian designs of Faenza, from which the French product takes its name. The whole story is recounted in the company's museum, which is housed in a former clay store cellar dating from the 16th century. The displays show examples of work from 180 years of production, including several large showpieces created for important exhibitions. There's also a faithful recreation of a 19th-century dining room, the table laid with colourful Gien *faïencerie* tableware. Should you be tempted, there's a factory shop adjacent to the museum.

Château de Sully-sur-Loire

*About 50 km southeast of Orléans, T02 38 36 36 86,
tourismeloiret.com.*
Feb-Dec daily. €6, €3 children, small supplement
for guided visits.

On a warm summer evening, when the sinking
sun turns Sully's pale grey stones to fiery gold,
the chateau appears to float on the mirror-like
surface of its wide moat. Most of what you see
was constructed before 1360, at which time the
scene would have looked very different. The
chateau originally stood right beside the Loire,
defending Sully's important river crossing with a
square keep flanked by massive rounded corner
towers and equipped with crenelated sentry walks
plus numerous *meurtrier* openings for bows or
crossbows. It was conceived by royal architect
Raymond du Temple (creator of the Palais du
Louvre) for Guy de la Trémoille, a close friend of
Charles VII. The king, a frequent guest, received
Joan of Arc at Sully in 1429 and 1430. To increase
accommodation, the eastern Pétit Château wing
was added around 1524, and in 1602 the chateau
passed to Henri IV's treasurer Maximilien de
Béthune, first Duc de Sully. After the river burst its
banks in 1608 he made the improvements to flood
defences which created the present moat-style
canals, then set about establishing gardens and
landscaped parkland. He also began the process
of restyling, which would determine the chateau's
present appearance, including lowering the towers
and adding their distinctive slate roofs. More
recent extensive restoration work included a 19th-
century study and three 18th-century apartments,
the Salle d'Honneur (in which the young Voltaire
performed his plays with his friends), the royal bed

Tip...

When planning your visit, try to be here for one of
Sully's lively Monday markets.

The Château de Sully-sur-Loire at dusk.

chamber used by Louis XIV and the famous and
extraordinary roof space, whose timbers resemble
those of a vast, upturned boat.

Abbaye de Fleury

*St-Benoît-sur-Loire, T02 38 35 72 43,
abbaye-fleury.com.*
Individual visits are welcome between 0630
and 2200, guided visits are only given between
Easter and All Saints (1 Nov). Daily mass is held
at 1200 (1100 on Sun) and is accompanied by
Gregorian chant (duration about 1 hr). You can
attend the service, or quietly observe and listen.
Visits are discouraged until after services end.

The unassuming village of St-Benoît-sur-Loire
would pass largely unnoticed by the outside world
but for the presence of its Benedictine abbey,
founded in the seventh century near one of the
wilder sections of the Loire. Around 673 a group of
monks travelled to Italy, disinterred the remains of
St Benoît (or Benedict) from the ruined abbey of
Monte Casino and brought them here. As the
resting place of the patriarch of western
monasticism, Fleury immediately became a major
place of pilgrimage, and eventually transformed its
abbey into the immense structure we see today.
The massive entry portal (named the Tour de
Gauzlin after the abbot who conceived it) had its
upper storey removed after the monks refused to
accept an externally appointed abbot in 1527. The
capitals of the supporting piers are a dazzling
showcase for the skills of the 11th-century masons

Around the region

who carved them – one capital is inscribed UNBERTUS ME FECIT (*'Unbertus made me'*). Compare the work here with the bas-reliefs in the left-hand wall of the tower, the nearby Gothic portal of the main body of the church, and the countless other decorated capitals inside.

The subtly magnificent 12th-century nave is late Romanesque beneath a later Gothic rib vault. The choir, though, is pure 11th-century and the Sanctuary retains the Roman polychrome marble mosaic floor of the previous fifth-sixth-century abbey. Here you'll find the sculpted tomb figure of King Philippe I, close to a flight of steps descending to the dimly lit and rather melancholy crypt containing St-Benoît's remains. A much more uplifting experience is provided each day in the church above by the monks, whose Gregorian plainsong will haunt you long after your visit.

L'Oratoire de Germigny-des-Prés

Place du Bourg, Germigny-des-Prés (on D60 about 30 km southeast of Orléans), tourist office T02 38 35 79 00, tourisme-loire-foret.com. **Oratory open to visitors all year round. Free. Museum, T02 38 58 27 97, and souvenir shop Feb-Dec. €2, €1 children.**

The area has no shortage of historic architecture, but this is in a league of its own. Over 1200 years ago (in 806) Théodulphe, Abbot of Fleury, Bishop of Orléans and a key advisor at the court of Charlemagne, built a Gallo-Roman villa complex here in what the Romans referred to as *Germanicus*, including a private chapel. A century or so later

Mosaic in the Oratoire de Germigny-des-Près.

pillaging destroyed the remainder of the site, but the little stone oratory survived the flames to become one of the earliest religious structures in France. The nave was enlarged around the 15th century, and major renovation between 1867 and 1876 produced a deceptively youthful appearance inside, but look beyond immaculate paintwork and almost surreal light fittings and you'll begin to notice details such as the horseshoe-shaped arches of the apse, which have more of the spirit of the Orient than of early France. Other important surviving features include a 12th-century reliquary decorated with Limoges enamels, a 14th-century carved figure of the Virgin and a beautiful Pietà from the same period. Lighting it all is a tall, airy lantern tower poised above the transept crossing arches. What makes this place really important, however, is the celebrated Ravenna School mosaic which was applied to the ceiling of the apse during the 11th century. Around 130,000 tiny squares of gilded glass and richly enamelled stones provide a startling vision of the Ark of The Covenant descending from heaven beneath the outstretched hands of God. Probably unique in the world, the presence of the priceless image was concealed by layers of applied limewash, and only came to light when unsuspecting 19th-century restorers uncovered it. A coin-in-the-slot box illuminates things further and supplies a descriptive commentary in your preferred language.

Eglise St-Martial

Grand' Rue, Châteauneuf-sur-Loire.

The assertive 50-m high bell tower looks promising but, as you'll soon see, Châteauneuf's occasionally troubled history has left its mark on this once noble church (which has also suffered more visibly than most at the hands of insensitive restorers). Completed in 1154 with a square lantern tower above the transept crossing, it survived more or less intact until the Wars of Religion, which left it in ruin. By 1627, however, the nave had been rebuilt and the present tower was added shortly afterwards. Blame the Revolution, and particularly the bombardments of June 1940, for the worst of what followed. Subsequent rebuilding ran out of steam some way short of replacing the full nave, which is now linked to the tower by a curious long, arched porch. But the church remains worth visiting, if only to see one treasure which has somehow survived – the magnificently over-the-top monument of Marquise Louis-Phélypeaux de la Vrillière, Secretary of State to Louis XIV and owner of the nearby chateau. Attributed to virtuoso Italian sculptor Guidi, who also worked at Versailles, the centrepiece of his spectacular creation is the Marquess gazing heavenwards while an angel prepares to bear him aloft. Caryatid figures on either side in skeleton form add a macabre touch, and are replicas of those destroyed during 1940.

Musée de la Marine de Loire

Ecuries du Château, 1 place Aristide Briand, Châteauneuf-sur-Loire, T02 38 46 84 46, musees.regioncentre.fr.
1 Apr-31 Oct Wed-Mon 1000-1800, 1 Nov-31 Mar Wed-Mon 1400-1800. Closed 1 Jan, 1 May, 25 Dec. €3.50, €2 concessions. An interesting and well-written English translation of exhibits and related information is available at reception.

Little remains of the town's 'new chateau' and its grand estate (which once rivalled Versailles) apart from some modest but pleasantly landscaped gardens and the elegant former stables. Inside is the Loire Marine Museum filled with memorabilia recounting not only the long history of navigation on the river but also the town's related activities. You'll discover, for example, that the famous transporter bridges of great ports like Marseille, Rochefort, Nantes and even Newport, were designed and built here in Châteauneuf – the documentation is all there, along with an impressively detailed scale model. Everything is very stylishly presented in a beautifully restored historic setting, and the visit will give you real insight into many of the things you'll see during your visits along the Loire.

Musée Campanaire Bollée

56 Faubourg Bourgogne, St-Jean-de-Braye (a few km east of Orléans centre on N152), T02 38 86 29 47, visaloire.com.
All year, Fri-Sun for self-guided or guided tours. €4, €2 children. To park, turn right by the Courtepaille restaurant.

You'll barely notice the suburban village of St-Jean-de-Braye straggling anonymously along the road, much less a grimy old workshop set well back from it behind iron railings. But look a little closer and you'll see a modest Musée Campanaire sign pointing towards an unlikely looking alleyway. Follow it and you'll be rewarded with something extraordinary. Since 1715 eight generations of the Bollé family have been *maîtres-saintiers* (master bellmakers), at first travelling to cast their creations close to the sites where they were required but from 1838 based here in a cavernous foundry on the outskirts of Orléans. They've since produced 45,000 bells, and today the workshop (one of only three remaining bell foundries in France) is very much a working museum, which in a typical year still consumes around 30 tonnes of bronze. During a visit you'll learn about the whole process, including how each bell's tonal purity depends on precise mathematical calculation – and that, having established its personality, each bell is given a name. You might also see some of the bells being made to fulfil orders from throughout the world.

If, by the time you leave, you're ready for a stroll, turn right and right again to reach the towpath of the nearby river, a popular haunt for local fishermen. A little further upstream the Loire is joined by the Canal d'Orléans and the Canal de Briare in the charming old port of **Combleux**, whose iron swing bridge once permitted cattle to reach fertile grazing on the river banks. Today you can dine in some style at the elegant Restaurant de la Marine (see page 104) beside the old lock gates, while enjoying views of unspoilt landscapes designated as a nature reserve.

Orléans

If Joan of Arc were to return today she wouldn't believe her eyes. But the city in whose destiny the Maid of Orléans played such a pivotal part continues to pursue its role as a dynamic centre of commerce and trade, and looks just as unstoppable as it proved to be back in 1429 – or in 451, when its inhabitants succeeded in fending off the army of Attila the Hun. The city's formidable defences may have long since vanished but their trace is still followed by the modern road system, within whose occasionally gridlocked embrace lies evidence of a long and eventful history. Dominating the skyline is the Cathédrale Ste-Croix, a huge and grandiose 18th- and 19th-century homage to the great Gothic cathedrals. Nearby is the Renaissance Hôtel Groslot, which accommodated François II, Charles IX, Henri III and Henri IV during state visits. Meanwhile, below wide boulevards and narrow streets lined with medieval half-timbered houses, lie old quays from which goods and travellers once departed for Nantes and the coast, a journey which could take six days or more. It's here, too, that the history and traditions of the river are celebrated in style during the annual Festival de Loire.

Old Orléans

Map: Orléans, p86.

The legendary spirit of old Orléans has been much diluted by events in its turbulent past, but what remains is scattered around a relatively compact area between the cathedral and the river. Tracking it down can take time, so you might prefer to follow the 'Orléans & The Middle Ages' itinerary, one of nine themed walks created by the city tourist office. The route takes you first to the grandiose and much-reconstructed **Eglise St-Aignan** begun in 1439 by Charles VII (and currently closed for long-overdue restoration). Its complex crypt, a remarkable survivor from the previous 11th-century church, contains one of the earliest-known Gallo-Roman carved capitals. Next comes the **Tour Blanche**, a 15th-century watchtower, followed by **rue des Tanneurs**, a medieval leather tanning area whose by-products

The neo-Gothic western towers of the Cathédrale Sainte-Croix, Orléans.

Essentials

❶ **Getting around** It's cheaper and easier to park your car at the edge of the city in one of the designated P+R (*Parcs Relais*) sites and use the tramway. The north-south line is fully operational and the east-west line is due to be completed in 2012 (for information visit cleo.agglo-orleans.fr). The tram will transport you quickly between most of the city centre sights.

❷ **Bus station** Gare routière behind the rail station, in place d'Arc; you can join the tram or catch a local bus to access other parts of the city from here.

❸ **Train station** Gare SNCF, avenue de Paris, behind a striking modern façade. It is served by TER regional trains, which include regular services to Paris and stops along the western Loire Valley. Visit gares-en-mouvement.com for all station information and services. There is a shuttle service between Orléans central station and Les Aubrais Orléans, 3 km north of the city, from which some train services depart. Ligne A tramway services also stop there.

❹ **ATMs** Around place du Martroi and the main shopping street, rue de la République.

❺ **Hospital** Hôpital de La Source, 14 avenue de l'Hôpital, about 10 km from the centre, T02 38 51 44 44, deals with emergencies and is accessible via the Ligne A tram.

❻ **Pharmacies** Several on rue des Carmes and near the market hall in the Châtelet area of Orléans, also on rue de la République.

❼ **Post office** At the entrance to the place d'Arc shopping centre near the rail station and at 9 rue Ste-Catherine, near the market hall and the medieval quarter.

❽ **Tourist offices** 111 rue du Maréchal Foch, Cléry-St-André, T02 38 45 94 33; Moulin Massot, 7 rue des Mauves, Meung-sur-Loire, T02 38 44 32 28; 2 place de l'Etape, Orléans, T02 38 24 05 05, tourisme-orleans.com.

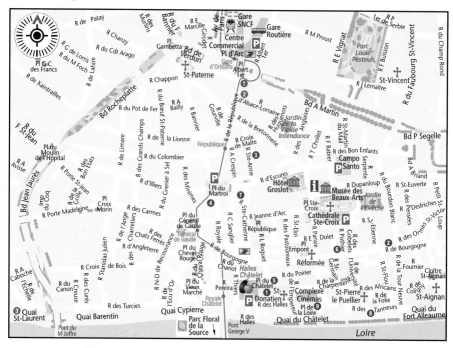

once discharged into the nearby Loire. In rue de la Tour is the Gothic residence of a wealthy merchant, indicated by a crest above the doorway, while a few steps away lies the 12th-century Romanesque **Eglise St-Pierre-le-Peullier**, now beautifully restored and used as an exhibition space. Notice the humorous carved corbel heads on the exterior of the apse. The route passes more half-timbered houses en route for place des Halles, where a single forlorn tower survives (in rue du Lin) from the Châtelet fortress which guarded the main river crossing. More medieval houses follow from time to time as the route returns to place St-Croix and the cathedral. The handsome **Maison Jeanne d'Arc** (3 place de Gaulle, T02 38 52 99 89, jeannedarc.com.fr; 2 May-31 Oct Tue-Sun 1000-1230 and 1330-1830, 2 Nov-30 Apr 1330-1800; €2, €1 students and over 65 years, children under 16 years free) is actually a total reconstruction (completed in 1965) of a medieval building

destroyed during the Second World War. Inside you'll find a wealth of information relating to the Maid of Orléans, including a large model of the fortified town under attack by the English forces in 1429.

More city character

In addition to the precious fragments of its illustrious history, Orléans has much to reward those with a more eclectic eye. A good starting point is the **place du Martroi**, where an arresting bronze figure of Joan of Arc, on horseback with sword in hand, surveys the scene from a huge plinth of pink granite. Look closer and you'll find a bronze bas-relief depiction of her in the thick of the celebrated battle to defend Orléans. Across the square, on the corner of rue de la République, is the belle époque (with added Renaissance touches) **La Rotonde**. Opened in 1898, its once grand café

Orléans listings

was for years the most fashionable meeting place in town. Further up rue de la République is an even more assertive period piece: the towering **Hôtel Moderne**, in full-blown, swirling art nouveau and designed by Louis Duthoit in 1902. Bizarrely, the interior decoration installed by the present owners combines Louis XVI with art deco. You'll find further art nouveau façades at 46 rue Saint-Marc, 7 bis route d'Olivet and 10 quai Barentin. As for the surviving Renaissance architecture, among the best is the **Hôtel Euverte Hatte** (11 rue de Tabour), whose three Italianate façades around a courtyard were created in 1524 for a wealthy merchant. More in the French style, with red brick and pale stone, are the four elegant residences constructed opposite the gardens of the Hôtel Groslot (see below) in rue d'Escures. Intended from the outset for letting, they represent an early piece of property speculation on the part of Henri IV's chief military commander Pierre Fougeu Escures.

Ultimately, though, it's grand vistas like the view towards the cathedral from rue Jeanne d'Arc which create the most enduring impressions of the city.

Musée des Beaux Arts

Place Ste-Croix, T02 38 79 21 55, musees.regioncentre.fr.
Tue-Sun 1000-1800. Closed 1 Jan, 1 and 8 May, 14 July, 1 and 11 Nov, 25 Dec. Audio guides in English available free. €3 entry fee also gives access to the History and Archaeological Museum of Orléans.
Map: Orléans, p86.

Spread across five floors of a light and elegant modern building designed by Christian Langlois, it's worth taking your time to immerse yourself in one of the finest art collections to be found outside Paris. The setting, beside the cathedral, is also near-perfect. Like Tours, Orléans' Fine Art Museum was founded on the spoils of the Revolution, and began displaying the substantial cache of possessions plundered from both church and aristocracy in 1797. Subsequent donations from wealthy traders, wine merchants and other art collectors added many Flemish and Dutch canvasses, while the state financed the acquisition of important Italian School works. The visit begins on the second floor, with 15th-18th-century Dutch, Flemish, Spanish, Italian and Scandinavian works. Here you'll find *Madonna and Child* by Sienese School painter Matteo di Giovanni, plus *Holy Family* by Correggio, from Parma. Other heavyweights include Brueghel, Tintoretto, Velázquez and van Dyck. The floor below counters with the full force of what 17th- and 18th-century France had to offer – particularly interesting are canvasses by Deruet and Fréminet from the lost Château de Richelieu

Tip...

Visit on a Sunday morning and you'll have the fabulous collections virtually to yourself – the nearby cathedral bells only heighten the sense of occasion.

The interior splendours of the Hôtel Groslot, Orléans.

(see page 195). Eighteenth-century works include portraits by Tocque, Drouais and Perronneau, along with sculptures by Houdon and Pigalle. Descend to two mezzanine floors to see how things evolved during the 19th century. One of the most haunting images, *Scène d'Incendie* by Orléans' own Alexandre Antigna, is a graphic portrayal of a family attempting to flee from a fire raging in their home. Rather underwhelming in comparison, the museum's collection of 20th-century works is consigned to the basement.

Hôtel Groslot

3 place de l'Etape.
Mon-Fri 0900-1200 and 1400-1800, Sun 1000-1200 and 1400-1800 (without interruption during summer). Closed Sat for marriage ceremonies. Free.
Map: Orléans, p86.

This subtly magnificent creation was completed around 1552 by town bailiff Jacques Groslot. Its Renaissance style is reminiscent of the Château de Blois (see page 116), combining diamond pattern black-and-pink brickwork with pale stone detailing.

The effect is complemented by a pair of elegantly styled stone staircases which unite at their mid-point before going their separate ways to first-floor level. Set between them is a bronze statue of Joan of Arc (calmly contemplating the bullet holes she acquired during the Second World War) by Princess Marie d'Orléans, daughter of Louis Philippe. In its heyday the roll call of vistors here included François II (who died here in his teens during a meeting of the French General Council in 1560), Catherine de' Medici, Charles IX, Henri III and Henri IV. Everything changed abruptly when the Revolution found the *hôtel particulier* (gentleman's mansion) a new role as the Hôtel de Ville(town hall). It then underwent major alterations, including the addition of two outer wings. Fortunately the architectural style was retained, leaving the underlying spirit largely intact. The city council eventually outgrew its surroundings and moved out, leaving the sumptuous interiors to stun unsuspecting visitors with a sizzling tour de force of 19th-century neo-Gothic splendour. Every surface is painted, papered, panelled or gilded and the whole thing is set off with vast crystal chandeliers which would not look out of place in

Versailles. Detail touches include a wooden chest given by Louis XI to the canons of St-Aignan, plus stirring bas-relief panels above the largest of the fireplaces. Their theme takes the exploits of Joan of Arc, who also appears in stained glass form in the windows. Intriguingly, the city's Salle de Mariage is the very room in which Charles IX met his future mistress Marie Touchet in 1569.

Cathédrale Ste-Croix

Place Ste-Croix.
Oct-Apr daily 0915-1200 and 1400-1800,
May-Sep 0915-1800.
Map: Orléans, p86.

The Cathedral of the Holy Cross is built on the site of a fourth-century basilica. Construction began with the choir in the early 12th century but over-hasty construction resulted in the nave collapsing in 1227. Work recommenced in 1288 and was completed with the patronage of Charles VII and Louis XI. In 1568 Protestants pillaged the cathedral, destabilising the crossing piers and causing the nave and transepts to collapse. The subsequent long campaign of rebuilding, with contributions from Henri III, Henri IV, Louis XIII, Louis XIV and Louis XV, was not completed until 1829. The styling of the later work has divided opinion ever since, Marcel Proust declaring it the ugliest church in France. But ignore the slightly kitsch, Miss World-style crowns of the 113-m-high towers and look instead at the scene round at the eastern *chevet* (apse) and you might feel very differently. It's the same inside, particularly when the nave fills with multicoloured light from the wealth of stained glass. Many windows depict the life and trial of St Joan – look closely and you'll see that some of the characters have a distinctly 19th-century appearance. The geometric rose windows of the transepts look a little undersized, unlike the magnificent panelling of the choir, designed by Jules Hardouin-Mansart. The medallions above the 95 stalls were executed between 1680-1708 by Louis XIV's most skilled artists. Notice also the magnificent organ mounted above the western

Plan-Vélo

Orléans is one of a growing number of French towns that has signed up to the Plan-Vélo bike-hire scheme (for details, including online subscription and an instruction video, visit agglo-veloplus.fr). In Orléans the system is called Vélo+ and provides 300 bikes at 32 stations, ready and waiting for anyone to use. To start using the service go to the tourist office (or the train station), provide some personal details and you'll be given a user card and a pin number. Subscriptions (*'abonnements'*) work on a pay-as-you-go basis, either weekly (€3) or by the day (€1). Once you have your card you can go to the information post at any of the bike stations (you'll see eye-catching racks of cheerful bicycles positioned throughout the city centre), pass your card over a reader, enter your pin number and the number of the bike you wish to use. The bike (which can be adjusted to suit your height) is then released for use. When you've finished your journey, simply plug it back into a vacant slot at any other station. Your first 30 minutes of use are free of charge, so your subscription could be all you pay, and charges for longer periods are modest.

Vélo + bike-hire pick-up point, Orléans.

portals of the nave. It was built in 1631 for the Abbaye de Fleury in St-Benoît-sur-Loire (see page 81), where it remained until being sold during the Revolution. Construction work on the cathedral meant that it would not finally be transported down the Loire by boat, reassembled and installed in Orléans until 1821.

Around Orléans

Château de La Ferté St-Aubin

About 20 km south of Orléans via the N20 (direction Vierzon), T02-38 76 52 72, chateau-ferte-st-aubin.com.
Mid-Feb to Easter 1400-1600, Easter to end Sep 1000-1900, Oct to mid-Nov 1400-1800. €8.50, €5.50 children (4-16). Allow 2-3 hrs for a visit with young children, picnics welcomed. Special events include a plant fair at the beginning of May and a *Grande Brocante* (bric-a-brac market) at the end of Sep. For three weekends before Christmas (and 26-30 Dec) the chateau is open 1400-1800 for a traditional *Noël au Château.*

Whatever your image of Loire Valley chateaux, this is something else – a classic Sologne estate with 350 years of history behind it, but which fell on such prolonged hard times that visiting it is like opening a time capsule. Its present owners (since 1987) have made steady progress with their heroic rescue plan, but there's still so much to do that the interior looks and feels as if the last occupants had simply left one day and never returned. Visitors can explore virtually everything at their own pace, from comfortable family apartments to the below-stairs world of estate staff. The kitchens in particular retain all the daily clutter of their working past, putting firmly into perspective the manicured presentation of showpiece attractions elsewhere. When you climb the stairs to explore the upper floors you'll be equally surprised to stumble upon perfect reconstructions of a village post office, an *épicerie* (grocer) and a school classroom, all *c.*1930. You can even enter the forest of roof timbers supporting the slate roof, over

300,000 of which have already been replaced, thanks to visitor revenue.

Outside, the stables have been restored and are once again occupied (the horses' names appear above their respective stalls) while the former orangery now houses a vast collection of dolls and other childhood toys from chateau life. But what lies just across the moat in a forest clearing is even more unexpected – a recreated 1930s railway station, complete with stationmaster's office and bar (partly shared, somewhat bizarrely, with tame farm animals). The cherry on the top is a period train comprising carriages from the legendary Orient Express headed by a large steam locomotive.

The time-warp interior of the Château de La Ferté Saint-Aubin.

Basilique Notre-Dame de Cléry

15 km southwest of Orléans, entrance on rue du Cloître, Cléry-St-André. Information from the tourist office, T02 38 45 94 33, o-tourismedeclery@wanadoo.fr.

From a distance this vast church rises from the surrounding plains like a beached ocean liner. The cathedral-like scale becomes even more impressive as you draw closer, the symphony of 15th-century flamboyant Gothic contrasting with a *clocher* (bell tower) which is clearly much older. The vast building's presence here is due to a single item which survives inside – a beautifully carved wooden statue of the Virgin and Child unearthed by a farm labourer's plough in 1280. Acquiring a reputation for miraculous powers, the statue was installed in a chapel, which soon proved inadequate for the number of pilgrims it attracted. In 1309 Philippe IV sanctioned construction of a much larger Gothic collegiate church, of which all but the tower perished at the time of the siege of Orléans in 1429. The interior of the present church (declared a Basilica by Pope Leon XIII in 1894) soars, the nave piers rising all the way to the 27-m-high rib vaults in a seamless flight, with not a capital in sight – and with nothing between the arcades and the upper windows but smooth, tooled stone. Not surprisingly, you can't help but focus on the precious statue, which sits in a shrine-like setting behind the main altar at the far end of the church. Beside the northern aisle stands the tomb of Louis XI, who ordered the enlargement of the nave shortly before his death in 1483. The French monarchy's attachment to Cléry is expressed elsewhere in the choir windows, given by Charles III, and five doorways bearing the arms of Henri II. Notice also the extravagantly decorated chapels of the south aisle and the huge panels on the western wall recording a quite extraordinary succession of visitors throughout the centuries.

If you're visiting the area in late July look out for *son et lumière* spectacles.

La Collégiale St-Liphard & Château de Meung-sur-Loire

Entrance to La Collégiale and the Château on place Martroi, Meung-sur-Loire (18 km west of Orléans), chateaux-valdeloire.com. Château 1 Mar-31 Oct daily 1000-1900, 1 Nov-28 Feb Sat and Sun 1400-1800. €7, €4 children (over 12).

You could easily miss the charming small town of Meung-sur-Loire altogether, which might explain how it has managed to retain such a palpable sense of the past. In 1429 Meung witnessed a decisive battle during the Hundred Years' War, being freed from English occupation by forces led by Joan of Arc. It retained its defensive ramparts for centuries, and the main gatehouse c.1629 survives at the northern end of rue Porte d'Amont (if you look carefully you'll notice that the tower's ancient clock dial displays 61 minutes). Retrace your steps through the heart of the town to place Martroi, a broad, sunny square with a restaurant terrace popular with lunchtime diners. Ahead is the substantial collegiate church dedicated to St-Liphard, who was buried in the monastery he founded here during the sixth century. Its 11th-13th-century replacement retains the spirit of an earlier style, and the main doorway and rounded transepts are essentially pure Romanesque. Inside it's light and airy, if rather over-restored, and the apse in particular is surprisingly plain. But odd details are interesting: the far left-hand corbel below the organ sprouts three carved heads, while the junction of the choir and the transept from which you entered features the head of an ox with an endearingly comical smile. On the wall of the transept is a large section of a medieval painting. As you leave turn left and you'll find the church tower base still mated to the circular bastion of a chateau built during the early 12th century by Bishop Manasses de Garlande. Just 50 or so years later one of his successors constructed a second chateau, whose stern and satisfyingly crumbly rear façade overlooks the church.

Beaugency

For centuries this historic town on the north bank of the Loire offered the only crossing between Orléans and Blois. Its celebrated 26-arch former toll bridge dates from the 14th century, and once incorporated a chapel for pilgrims on the route to Compostela. Its melancholy cobbled quays tell of long-departed port activity, but Beaugency's real charm lies elsewhere, in the heart of the old town, which has escaped modern development and is a joy to explore on foot. Overlooking it all are the vast Tour de César, part of an 11th-century feudal chateau built to defend the town and its river crossing, and the handsome bell tower of a 16th-century church lost during the Revolution. Three times daily (0800, 1200 and 1900) its fine peal sounds the *Carillon de Vendôme* (see page 97).

Joan of Arc is overlooked by the Clocher Saint-Fermin.

Around the Old Town

The layout of the town – which is almost village-like in look and spirit – takes some working-out, but you'll soon discover that everything is neatly packed into the surprisingly small area defined by its original medieval defences. Almost every street has a story to tell, via a wealth of architectural survivors. One of the earliest is the **Maison des Templiers**, a 12th-century former Knights Templars' hall in rue du Puits de l'Ange, whose sober Romanesque decoration is in total contrast to the exuberantly sculpted Renaissance façade of the Hôtel de Ville (1526-1528) in rue du Change. You'll find medallion busts, bas-relief friezes, the salamander emblem of François I, the arms of Beaugency's own Dunois-Longueville family and more. Things became almost surreal with the addition of a pair of fanciful watch towers when the building was 'restored' during the 19th century. Inside, the first-floor Council Chamber conserves a series of magnificent 17th and 18th century embroidered panels from the Abbaye Notre-Dame, which ended up here (minus their borders) after being seized during the Revolution. Nearby, roughly parallel to the abbey, is the Château de Dunois, originally a fortress occupied by the Lords of Beaugency and much modified for more civilized living during the 15th century. In its heyday it entertained both Louis XI (after his coronation at Reims in 1461) and Francis I (who spent 10 days here in October 1526 after being freed from captivity in Madrid). The guest-list took a dive, though, after the building was confiscated during the Revolution and eventually ended up homing beggars and the insane. In 1928 it finally became a museum for arts and traditions of the Orléans region. It is due to reopen its doors during 2010 after major refurbishment.

Tip...

If you're feeling weary from sightseeing don't miss the upper end of rue du Pont, where restaurant terraces are tucked away among an explosion of flowers in tubs and window-boxes.

Essentials

➲ **Getting there** Beaugency is served by train from Paris, via Orléans or Blois and Tours from the west. The Ulys bus services numbers 8 and 9 operate between Orléans Gare Routière and Beaugency.

➔ **Getting around** The historic centre of Beaugency is so compact that you'll have no problem exploring the town on foot.

⊖ **Bus station** Buses to Beaugency stop at various locations; the stop on rue Nationale is just above the old town.

◑ **Train station** Rue de la Gare, T02 38 44 50 28.

⊗ **ATMs** Place du Martroi.

⊕ **Hospital** Hôpital La Source, 14 avenue de l'Hôpital, Orléans, T02 38 51 44 44, chr-orleans.fr.

✚ **Pharmacy** Pharmacie Tardif Hervé, 17 place du Martroi, T02 38 44 50 22.

➐ **Post office** 15 rue des Chevaliers, T02 38 45 00 45.

❶ **Tourist information offices** 3 place du Dr Hyvernaud, Beaugency, T02 38 44 54 42, beaugency.fr; 47-49 rue Poterie, Vendôme, T02 54 77 05 07, vendome.eu.

Around the region

L'Abbatiale Notre-Dame

Rue de l'Abbaye.
You are free to visit any time except during prayer.

Chance upon it from rue du Pont and you'll be startled by the smoothly curving apse of a giant abbey looming over the former convent (now a hotel) huddled against it. Round in the more peaceful place St-Firmin, though, things look very different. The western façade looks pretty dull apart from two Romanesque doorways, a line of corbels and a single *clocher* barely taller than the gable of the nave. But don't be put off, for inside it's huge, and has a real sense of medieval mystery. The rich (modern) stained glass windows make it quite dark, but as your eyes acclimatise you'll notice signs of the serenity of Romanesque giving way to the dawning of the Gothic spirit; the nave arcade arches sit on simple drum piers but are pointed, not rounded, and the side aisles have *Angevin*-style rib vaults. Less immediately obvious is the fact that the nave ceiling is a dazzling piece of all-timber construction created in 1663-1665 to replace the original stone vaults lost during the Wars of Religion. The entire southern aisle was also painstakingly rebuilt after being destroyed by aerial bombardments in 1940. It's nevertheless still possible to picture the scene in 1103 when the Council of Beaugency heard Philippe I's plea to reconsider his excommunication for leaving his wife Berthe de Hollande in favour of Bertrade, Comtesse d'Anjou – or when in 1152 it forbade the marriage of Louis VII and Eleanor of Aquitaine (who were considered too closely related). In the square outside is a stirring bronze statue of Joan of Arc, erected in 1896, before the 50-m-high Clocher St-Firmin of 1530. This handsome bell tower is all that remains of a Romanesque church dating from the 11th century and lost during the Revolution.

Château de Talcy

About 16 km east of Beaugency off the D15, T02 54 81 03 01, talcy.monuments-nationaux.fr. 2 May-4 Sep daily 0930-1200 and 1400-1800, 5 Sep-30 Apr daily 1000-1230 and 1400-1700. Closed Tue 1 Oct-31 Mar, 25 Dec, 1 Jan and 1 May. €5, under 18s free.

While other gracious chateaux have their origins in feudal military strongholds, Talcy was originally the manor house of a nobleman. Its subtle reverse transformation began in 1517 when the estate was acquired by Florentine banker Bernard Salviati, a financial supporter of Francis I during the Italian wars and cousin of Catherine de' Medici. Around 1520 he added defensive features to the chateau (stopping short of the drawbridge which would have made things more secure) in an austere form of French Gothic, rather than the Italianate style which was proving fashionable elsewhere. The mood had obviously relaxed by the time his wife Isabelle enlarged the domestic accommodation between 1533 and 1543. On 21 April 1545 Talcy entered literary history when 21-year-old Pierre de Ronsard attended a party given by the Salviatis and fell in love with their daughter, who at the time was just 14. The result was the epic series of love poems entitled *'Les Amours de Cassandre'*.

In 1704 the estate passed to the Burgeats family, who added further refinements and created Renaissance gardens, which are today bounded by productive fruit orchards. Nearby are a 16th-century dovecote and a 17th-century barn, complete with a huge and venerable wine-press. For the majority of visitors, though, Talcy's greatest attraction is undoubtedly the château itself, whose interior layout and furniture have survived intact from the 18th century.

The Angevin-influenced side-aisle vaults.

Vendôme is a fascinating town of towers and spires.

Vendôme

31 km northwest of Blois.

This attractive and atmospheric town sits below its ruined feudal chateau in a fork of the Loir, whose waterways then subdivide to create the sensation that you are moving among a series of islands. If your time is limited simply follow one of two discovery trails marked by brass studs in the town centre paving. This way you won't miss the 15th-century **Porte St-Georges**, sole survivor of the four gates which once controlled access to the town, or a handsome iron-framed covered market

Tip...

When you feel like a coffee break in an atmospheric setting, place St-Martin provides a café/bar in the 15th-century Maison St-Martin, which is decorated with carved figures of the Saint and his colleagues Jacques, Louis and Jean-Baptiste.

opened in 1896. The adjoining **place du Marché** was formerly the place du Pilori and, until the 16th century, witnessed public executions. More conventionally elegant is the **Hôtel de Ville**, built in French Classical style between 1639 and 1777 as the Collège des Oratoriens (among whose pupils was Honoré de Balzac) and which also later served as a royal military academy. Further echoes of the town's long military associations survive (but only just) in the former Benedictine abbey buildings which became the **Rochambeau Barracks**, home to an illustrious mounted cavalry regiment which was decimated by the horrors of 1914.

Perhaps most surprising of all, however, is the genuine charm which persists in the town centre, despite TGV rail services having placed Vendôme firmly in Parisian commuter territory. Rue du Change, for example, successfully blends modern prosperity with medieval-style half-timbering. Not all of the façades are as old as they appear, though, since this cost-effective construction style survived locally until the 18th and even 19th century.

Eglise de la Trinité

Rue de l'Abbaye.
Daily. Free.

The greatest of Vendôme's many historic assets is a cathedral-like abbey founded around 1032 which later blossomed into one of the very finest examples of flamboyant Gothic in all France. Seen from the nearby place St-Martin, the vibrant western façade smoulders coyly and invitingly behind an early 12th-century *clocher* (bell tower) soaring skywards. Between them lie the Benedictine abbey cloisters, which are worth visiting to appreciate part of an 11th- and 12th-century fresco lost for 600 years before being rediscovered in 1972. You'll find the characters in the *Miraculous Catch of Fishes* gazing with a conspiratorial glow from the wall of the *salle capitulaire* (Chapter House) in the far left-hand corner of the square.

Enter the church by the western door to get the full impact of the medieval Gothic *tour de force* which lies within – the side aisles alone rise higher than many lesser churches. Notice too the slender piers of the nave launching straight up to lightweight rib vaults suspended above tall windows and a skeletal glazed triforium stage. At the far end of the choir is a rounded apse (or *déambulatoire*) with five radiating chapels. In the centre, and most beautiful of all, is the Chapelle du St-Sacrément, where you'll find the stained glass panel of Notre-Dame, a miraculous survivor created for the previous Romanesque abbey in 1125. And don't miss the choir stalls, whose 16th-century carved misericord panels depict characters including wine producers at their daily labours.

Le carillon de Vendôme

During the Hundred Years' War, the legacy of the Dauphin, the 11th of 12 children of Isabeau of Bavaria, and later King Charles VII, was limited to Bourges – where he installed his little court – and the small towns of Beaugency, Cléry-St-André and Vendôme. A 15th-century rhyme tells the tale of his much-reduced circumstances:

Mes amis que reste-t-il
à ce Dauphin si gentil?
Orléans, Beaugency,
Notre-Dame de Cléry,
Vendôme, Vendôme.

Les ennemis ont tout pris
Ne lui laissant par mépris
Qu'Orléans, Beaugency,
Notre-Dame de Cléry,
Vendôme, Vendôme!

The accompanying chimes sound hourly in Vendôme, and three times each day in Beaugency and Cléry-St-André. If you try singing along with these words, remember that the French usually extend the last syllable, as in: *Frère Jacques* (*Frèr-e Jacq-ues*).

Rochambeau was Commander-in-Chief of the French Army in 18th-century Yorktown (USA).

Sleeping

Château de la Verrerie €€€€-€€€

Oizon (32 km southwest of Gien), T02 48 81 51 60, chateaudelaverrerie.com.
Choose from 12 guest rooms, all cosy, charming and romantic, in this restored 15th-century chateau in the heart of the Sologne. Its early 16th-century Renaissance gallery overlooks a large lake surrounded by woodland. The Maison d'Hélène restaurant, created in the former farm, offers intimate dining and, for those to whom the idea appeals, the chateau can arrange a day's hunting or stalking.

Le Domaine des Roches €€€

2 rue de la Plaine, Briare, T02-38 05 09 00, domainedesroches.fr.
A 19th-century manor house set in its own park in the heart of Briare-le-Canal, with beautifully appointed rooms opening out onto gardens. There are also cottages to rent within the grounds, and a restaurant with a terrace.

Hôtel du Rivage €€€

1 quai de Nice, Gien, T02 38 37 79 00, hoteldurivage@orange.fr.
The hotel enjoys a superb location overlooking the Loire and Gien's Vieux Pont, or the gardens to the rear. The rooms have private bathrooms, free Wi-Fi and are simply but adequately furnished, although the hotel's best feature is undoubtedly its setting. The town and the riverside restaurants are just a few minutes' walk away.

Hôtel Le Panoramic €€€

Rempart des Augustins, Sancerre, T02 48 54 22 44, panoramicotel.com.
An aptly named hotel with sweeping views across the vineyards. Many rooms share the same panorama and are fully equipped to a high standard. The luxury suites are sumptuous, with separate lounge areas furnished in classic French style.

Rustic country chambre d'hôte.

Standard rooms are less charming with plainer decor and contemporary furniture. Rooms on the town side are significantly cheaper. Free Wi-Fi.

Les Logis du Grillon €€
3-5 rue du Chantre, Sancerre, T02 48 78 09 45, chambres-hotes-sancerre.com.
Offering bed and breakfast or gîtes full of period charm, with stone fireplaces and exposed beams. The guest rooms are individually styled and decorated in fresh colours and traditional French fabrics. Guests can expect high levels of comfort, a gourmet breakfast with regional produce and home-made jams, calm surroundings, a/c and free Wi-Fi.

Hostellerie du Grand Sully €€
10 bd du Champ de Foire, Sully-sur-Loire, T02 38 36 27 56, grandsully.com.
A comfortable, quiet hotel with a range of accommodation. The cheapest rooms are comfortably furnished and have their own bathroom. Pay a little more for elegantly furnished bedrooms with antique furniture and lovely fabrics adorning the beds and windows. The hotel serves a really rather nice breakfast with plentiful fresh bread and pastries, delicious coffee and home-made jams in china pots. Private parking, free Wi-Fi and a/c.

The hotel restaurant, offering a range of excellent regional menus from €28-52, is one for special occasions (open Tue-Fri).

Hôtel du Parc €€
5 place Aristide Briand, Châteauneuf-sur-Loire, T02 38 56 13 13, hotel-du-parc-45110-chateauneuf-sur-loire.com.
Situated opposite the park and entrance to the Musée de la Marine de Loire, the hotel offers reliable and clean accommodation at an affordable price. The rooms are light and bright although very plain, but there is a/c and secure parking. Expect a basic buffet breakfast. Some rooms have wheelchair access. Free Wi-Fi.

Hôtel-Restaurant Le Laurier €€
29 rue du Commerce, St-Satur (a few km north of Sancerre), T02 48 54 17 20, bossley18@orange.fr. **Closed Sun evening and Mon.**
Entering this ivy-clad former post house is like stepping back in time, with many original features, low beams and a classic French dining room with crisp white table linen. The rooms are traditional, too, but brightly decorated and comfortable (don't be surprised to find a rather old-fashioned bathroom). Sancerre is just a few minutes' drive away.

Château de Champvallins €€€
1079 rue de Champvallins, Sandillon (about 10 km southeast of Orléans), T02 38 41 16 53, chateaudechampvallins.com.
This 18th-century chateau hotel in the heart of the Sologne near Orléans is set in 10 ha of woodland and has an outdoor swimming pool. Five spacious rooms all overlook the park and are luxuriously decorated with silk and antique furnishings in the purest French tradition.

Hôtel d'Arc €€€
37 rue de la République, T02 38 53 10 94, hoteldarc.fr. Map: Orléans, p86.
A fully modernized hotel, centrally located behind a striking art nouveau-style façade. The rooms are light and spacious with neutral decor punctuated by additional, more individual splashes of colour, giving an overall sense of elegance and simplicity. All rooms have high levels of comfort and services, including free Wi-Fi, international TV channels and a mini-bar. The location is just 10 mins' walk from the heart of Orléans, tram services stop almost at the front door and the rail station is within a few minutes' walk.

L'Orée des Chênes €€€

Route de Marcilly-en-Vilette,
La Ferté-St-Aubin, T02 38
64 84 00, loreedeschenes.fr.
A charming hotel-restaurant
surrounded by superb grounds
in the heart of the Sologne.
Decorated in neutral shades with
classic French-style furniture, the
bedrooms are restful and
elegant. If possible, compare
Standard and Superior room
choices before you commit, and
note that rooms are quieter on
the first floor. The excellent
restaurant is highly
recommended – but not for
those on a tight budget.

Relais Louis XI €€€

2 rue St Pierre, Meung-sur-Loire,
T02 38 44 27 71,
lerelaislouisxi.com.
Strategically located by the river,
this collection of ancient
buildings around a courtyard
was fortified by the British during
the 100 Years' War. In 1429 Joan
of Arc and her troops surrounded
the place and destroyed the
bridge between here and the
road to Beaugency. Opened as a
'completely environmental' hotel
in late 2008 it employs
geothermal energy, organic
cotton bed linen and, of course,
only organic wines and produce
are served in the gourmet
restaurant. The rooms are light
and airy, with simple
contemporary furnishings in
varying styles, and all have views
to the Loire River.

Hôtel de l'Abeille €€

64 rue Alsace Lorraine, T02 38
53 54 87, hoteldelabeille.com.
Map: Orléans, p86.
A traditional French hotel with a
certain charm – there's a small
café-bar at the entrance, plus
balconies decorated with
greenery and flowers. Rooms are
individually decorated with
patterned wallpaper and draped
fabric in typical French country
style but have modern
bathrooms and free Wi-Fi, plus
24-hr room service. The roof
terrace affords good views of
the cathedral.

Hôtel Escale Océania €€

16 quai St-Laurent, T02 38
54 47 65, oceaniahotels.com/
escale-oceania-orleans.php.
Map: Orléans, p86.
On the quays, just a few minutes'
walk from the medieval quarter
and the centre of Orléans, this
quiet hotel has functional, bright
and modern rooms with free
Wi-Fi. Private parking is a big
bonus in this part of the city.

Hôtel Villa Marjane €€

121 route de Sandillon, St-Jean-
le-Blanc (2.5 km south of
Orléans), T02 38 66 35 13,
villamarjane.com.
The villa sits in its own wooded
grounds on a main road
southeast of the centre of
Orléans (about 5 mins drive
from the centre) and offers a
restful ambiance with a warm
and personal welcome. The

rooms are slightly old-fashioned
classic French style but have
modern bathrooms and
represent good value for money.
Free Wi-Fi available.

La Ferme des Foucault €€

Ménestreau-en-Villette
(6 km east of La Ferté-St-Aubin),
T02 38 76 94 41,
ferme-des-foucault.com.
This typical red-brick late
19th-century farmhouse in the
heart of the Sologne has been
fully restored by its French-
American owners. The result is a
beautiful haven with charming
rooms, plenty of light and views
to the surrounding forest. Guests
enjoy a hearty breakfast and
modern comforts including free
Wi-Fi and a swimming pool.

Campsites

Parc des Alicourts

Pierrefitte-sur-Sauldre
(30 km southeast of La Ferté-
St-Aubin), T02 99 73 53 57,
top-tree-houses.co.uk.
Nature lovers might like to try
living in their very own tree
house, hidden away in a holiday
resort in the heart of the
Sologne. Choose between the
6-m-high cabin with its own
staircase and bridge, or ladder
tree houses – not quite so
vertigo-inducing.

Beaugency

Hostellerie de l'Ecu de Bretagne €€€
Place du Martroi, T02 38 44 67 60, ecudebretagne.fr.
A stone-built former coaching inn, the hotel encompasses the main building (which overlooks the square) and completely restored annexes. Rooms are beautifully and luxuriously furnished. Parking, heated swimming pool and free Wi-Fi available. The fine hotel restaurant serves traditional regional dishes.

Le Saint George €€€
14 rue Poterie, Vendôme, T02 54 67 42 10, hotel-saint-georges-vendome.com.
Situated in a prominent position in the heart of the town, the hotel has modern, comfortable rooms, each with a useful kitchenette and some with a spa bath. The restaurant is decorated with South American artefacts and the menu features dishes from around the world accompanied by an equally international wine list. Hotel parking available and free Wi-Fi throughout.

Hôtel de la Sologne €€
6 place St-Firmin, T02 38 44 50 27, hoteldelasologne.net.
A charming hotel on the prettiest square in town. Individually styled traditional rooms face onto the square or the inner courtyard, and are incredibly quiet, apart for the thrice-daily *Carillon de Vendôme* from the nearby clock tower. Other attractions are a warm welcome and delicious breakfasts served in a cosy dining room or sunny terrace. Free Wi-Fi and secure area for bicycles.

Hôtel le Relais des Templiers €€
68 rue du Pont, T02 38 44 53 78, hotelrelaistempliers.com.
Situated at the end of this pretty street, the hotel provides a warm welcome for tourists and offers good value accommodation in basic but adequately furnished rooms. The public lounge downstairs offers a cosy corner, and there's free Wi-Fi and a computer available for guests. Secure area provided for bicycles.

Campsites
Val de Flux
T02 38 44 50 39, camping@ville-beaugency.fr.
Apr-end Aug.
A large, well managed municipal site in a calm and shady position on the banks of the Loire, with views across the river to the town.

Hotel de la Sologne, Beaugency.

Eating & drinking

Côtes et Jardin €€€
8 rue Grand Sully, Sully-sur-Loire,
T02 38 36 35 89, cotes-jardins.fr.
1200-1430 and 1900-2130.
Closed Tue evening and Wed.
Situated in Sully's main street,
the restaurant is in a fine
Renaissance building with a large
and airy dining room. Choose
from a sumptuous menu of
classic French dishes and several
seasonal daily specials.

La Poularde €€€
13 quai de Nice, Gien,
T02 38 67 36 05, lapoularde.fr.
Closed Sun evening and Mon.
A super restaurant situated on
the banks of the Loire a short
distance from the town centre.
Menus are both traditional and
inventive, and served in the
charming dining room of La
Poularde hotel.

Auberge l'Écurie €€
31 Nouvelle Place, Sancerre,
T02 48 54, 16 50,
auberge-ecurie.fr.
Relaxed dining in what comes
close to a British pub in style and
ambiance. Varied menu
including grills, salads and Italian
dishes served in generous
portions. There's also a tempting
display of gateaux and flans.

Le Petit Saint Trop €€
5 rue Tissier, Briare,
T02 38 37 00 31, le-petit-saint-
trop@wanadoo.fr.
Closed Sun evening and Mon.

Next to the bridge on the
Port de Plaisance, this brasserie
restaurant has built up a faithful
local clientele with its
refreshing menus and friendly
service. Apart from standard
brasserie fare, look out for
more refined fish courses with
fresh vegetables.

Le Trevi €€
5 rue Faubourg St-Germain,
Sully-sur-Loire, T02 38 36 26 92.
A friendly Italian restaurant and
grill a short walk from the
château where you'll receive a
warm welcome and efficient
service. Arrive promptly, before
the dining room fills up with
locals enjoying a convivial
evening with friends.

L'Epicerie de la Borne €
La Borne d'en Bas, Henrichemont
(23 km west of Sancerre near
Henrichement), T02 48 26 90 80.
Restaurant mid-Jul to end Aug
daily 1230-1430 and 1930-2200,
rest of the year Tue-Sun
1230-1430 and 1930-2100
(closed Sun evening and Mon).
Salon de Thés 1500-1900.
Tucked away in this working
potters' haven, enjoy a
wholesome lunch or
scrumptious cake in the leafy
garden or rustic salon. Local fresh
produce makes up the daily
menu surprise or *plats du jour,*
which includes a vegetarian
option. Reservations preferred.

Tip...
Opening times have been
provided where they are
available. Note that many places
prefer to be 'flexible' in their
hours. If in doubt, phone ahead.

Terrace dining high above the vineyards in Sancerre.

A popular meeting-place in Vieux Orléans.

Orléans

Chez Jules €€€
136 rue de Bourgogne,
T02 38 54 30 80.
Closed Mon lunch, Sat lunch
and Sun, annual holidays
mid-Jul.
Map: Orléans, p86.
Chez Jules looks rustic and rather
small but provides a warm
welcome and generous servings
of traditional dishes with a
modern approach.

Restaurant de la Marine €€€
12 l'Embouchure, Combleux
(8 km east of Orléans), T02 38 55
12 69, restaurant-la-marine.com.
Daily.
Situated in a picturesque village
on the banks of the Loire, La
Marine is delightful for dining
outside under the lime trees in
summer. The delicious menu is
based upon classic French
dishes, using regional produce.

Eugène €€€
24 rue Ste Anne, T02 38 53 82 64,
restauranteugene.fr.
Mon evening, Tue-Fri and
Sat evening, 1200-1400
and 1915-2115.
Map: Orléans, p86.
Chef Alain Gérard is Breton by
origin but draws inspiration from
the south of France – which
clearly makes his diners very
happy indeed, since this is one of
the most popular restaurants in
the Loiret. Booking essential.

Le Girouet €€€
14 quai du Châtelet,
T02 38 81 07 14, legirouet.com.
Tue-Fri, Sat evening only.
Map: Orléans, p86.
The interior of the Girouet is
distinctly nautical, as befits its
position on the river bank – the
terrace has views directly over
the Loire. The enticing menu
changes twice weekly and
reflects what is in season, much
of it organic and river-fresh.

Restaurant Le Lift €€€
Place de la Loire, T02 38 53 63 48,
restaurant-le-lift.com.
Daily.
Map: Orléans, p86.
With its contemporary interior
design and elevated terrace
overlooking the Loire, Le Lift is
one of the more chic addresses
in Orléans. The menu has
unmistakable regional and
seasonal origins but chef
Philippe Bardau brings his own
refreshing personality to the
dishes. Booking advised.

Les Toqués €€€
71 chemin du Halage, St-Jean-
de-Braye, T02 38 86 50 20.
Closed Sun and Mon.
A fashionable address with a
stylish terrace on the towpath
just a short distance from the city
centre. It brings a contemporary
twist to traditional dishes using
seasonal produce and has a
divine choice of desserts.

A summer evening in the heart of Orléans.

Au Bon Marché €€
12 place du Châtelet,
T02 38 53 03 35,
aubonmarche-orleans.com.
Daily 1200-1430 and 1900-2200.
Map: Orléans, p86.

In the bustling heart of old
Orléans, this is a restaurant, a
cave à vins and an *épicerie*. Expect
regional dishes using fresh
produce plus a good selection of
local wines, with an excellent
plat du jour at around €8.

Le Brin de Zinc €€
62 rue Ste-Catherine,
T02 38 53 38 77.
Map: Orléans, p86.

Tucked away in a side street off
place du Martroi, this is a lively
brasserie restaurant – the terrace
is always packed with diners on
summer evenings – with an
extensive menu.

La Parenthèse €€
26 place du Châtelet,
T02 38 62 07 50.
Tue-Sat 1200-1345 and
1930-2145. Annual holidays
late Aug.
Map: Orléans, p86.

An elegant restaurant in the
heart of the old city with a
lovely little terrace in summer
and a simply decorated dining
room. Excellent service from
friendly staff and a refined
traditional menu.

Cafés & bars

Head for rue de Bourgogne, in
the heart of the pedestrian area,
for a seemingly endless selection
of bars and restaurants. Look
out for Le Paxton's Head or
L'Atelier for a drink, or Le bÔ bar
(see below) for an aperitif.
Otherwise, make for the busy
place du Martroi, where Le
Martroi is worth a look for its
art deco interior.

La Chancellerie
27 place du Martroi, T02 38
53 57 54, lachancellerie.fr.
Map: Orléans, p86.

Once a favoured rendezvous for
Chopin and his lover, novelist
George Sand, this splendid
building houses a gastronomic
brasserie. Its large new terrace
is a great place to watch the
world go by.

Le Bô bar
193 rue de Bourgogne, T02 38 53
83 18, baravins-lebobar.com.
Tue-Sun 1800-0100
(May-Oct 1800-0200).
Map: Orléans, p86.

A wine bar and cocktail lounge
with a warm and welcoming
atmosphere. Occasional music
throughout the year, and a
permanent exhibition of
paintings and photographs.

Le Petit Bateau €€€
54-56 rue du Pont, T02 38 44 56
38, lepetitbateau@wanadoo.fr.
Closed all day Mon and
Tue lunch.

Traditional French menu served
in a character dining room with
exposed beams and fireplace.
Evening menus between €28
and €45.

Le Patio €€
5 place du Petit Marché,
T02 38 44 02 43,
berrier.yves@wanadoo.fr.
Closed Mon and Tue lunch
in summer, Sun and Mon
in winter.

An Italian restaurant whose
friendly chefs also serve at your
table. Good value pizzas, along
with some original pasta dishes
such as: 'Spaghetti à la
Mauricienne' – featuring an
improbable-sounding, but tasty,
creamy sauce with curry spices.

Cafes & bars
Bar le Saint Martin
Place St-Martin, Vendôme,
T02 54 77 23 63.
Daily (closed Mon low season).
This half-timbered building is a
popular meeting place, and ideal
for a light lunch on the large
terrace. There's a good selection
of bottled and draught beers,
and you might catch one of the
regular music nights.

Entertainment

Orléans

Cinema

Les Carmes
7 rue des Carmes, T02 38 62 94 79, cinemalescarmes.com.
Map: Orléans, p86.
Showing international films in original language and art house French films. €7.50.

Festivals & events

International Music Festival, Sully-sur-Loire
T02 38 24 05 05 (tourist office), festival-sully.com.
End May to mid-Jun.
Classical music festival with concerts staged at various venues throughout Le Loiret, such as the cathedral in Orléans or the Collégiale at Meung-sur-Loire.

Orléans Jazz Festival
T02 38 24 05 05 (tourist office), orleansjazz.fr.
Mid- to late Jun.
Two weeks of music centred around the Place au Jazz Bourgogne, le Jardin de l'Evêché and the Campo Santo in the heart of Orléans. Internationally renowned names (which included Jamie Cullum in 2009), jazz musicians of tomorrow and local jazz performers produce a packed programme of entertainment.

The annual Festival de Loire, Orléans.

La Caravane de Loire
caravanedeloire.com
Beginning of Sep, every even year.
This bi-annual festival of music and fun starts off at Montargis, moves to Briare along the canal, then down the Loire to Gien, Orléans, and finally Meung-sur-Loire – 26 towns and 200 km in all. The Caravane brings together performers, music, food, traditional boats and crafts, plus festivities including firework displays and jazz nights.

Festival de Loire, Orléans
T02 38 24 05 05 (tourist office), festivaldeloire.com.
Late Sep.
The riverside quays come alive with the sound of sea shanties and a visual feast of traditional and unusual river craft. Visitors can take short river trips and see all manner of crafts and regional produce on the stalls lining the quays. The weekend can get very crowded, but it's well worth joining the throng for the atmosphere and to see the fabulous fireworks reflected in the river.

Fêtes de Jeanne d'Arc, Orléans
T02 38 24 05 05 (tourist office), fetesjeannedarc.com.
End Apr to early May.
There's plenty to see and do, including a medieval festival and market, concerts, exhibitions, *son et lumière* around the cathedral plus parades. The city becomes crowded, so book your accommodation well in advance.

Shopping

Sancerre to Orléans

Emaux de Briare Museum Boutique
1 bd Loreau, Briare,
T02 38 31 20 51.
After visiting the museum (see page 78), call in at the ceramic company's factory shop – it stocks everything you need to create your own mosaics, plus a good selection of ideas for the home.

La Ferme des Chapotons
Le Bourg, Mentou-Râtel (near Sancerre), T02 48 79 36 38, lafermedeschapotons.com.
Producers of Crottin de Chavignol goat's cheese and other regional products and wines. You're invited to visit the farm (where children will love meeting the animals), see the goats being milked (Mon-Sat at 1700) and then observe the cheese-making. You can also taste local products and buy them direct from the farm.

Chavignol's inquisitive goats.

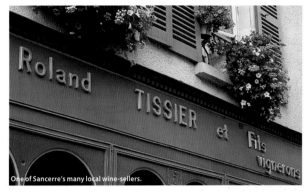
One of Sancerre's many local wine-sellers.

Gien Factory Shop
78 place de la Victoire, Gien,
T02 38 05 21 05, gien.com.
Mon-Sat and also Sun in Jul and Aug (closed lunch).
Full range of Gien tableware and gifts at ex-works prices.

Orléans

Halles Châtelet
Place du Châtelet.
Tue-Sat 0730-1900,
Sun 0730-1230.
The large market hall where locals head to buy fresh produce and where you will find local specialities and wines.

Hédiard
310 rue de Bourgogne,
T02 38 68 13 77, hediard.fr.
Tue-Sat 1000-1300 and 1400-1900, Mon 1400-1900.
Luxury fine foods and gift hampers from the famous delicatessen first established in Paris by Ferdinand Hédiard 150 years ago.

Les Musardises
38 rue République,
T02 38 53 30 98.
Mon-Sat 0900-1800.
Chocolatier confiseur and salon de thé, Les Musardises make the extraordinary *Cotignac d'Orléans.* Cotignac is a jelly made from quince, harvested in the region in October. The colourful syrup is poured into spruce bark boxes called *friponnes* while still hot. The appealing packages bear the stamp of Joan of Arc on the cover.

Beaugency

Rodolphe
9 place St Martin, Vendôme,
T02 54 77 32 58.
Artisan *chocolatier* and *confiseur* making local specialities such as the *Pralinés du Vendômois* and the *Carrés Ronsard* – all beautifully presented and gift wrapped if required. There is a cosy *salon de thé* at the rear of the shop.

Activities & tours

Canal boat hire
Charmes Nautiques
Port de Plaisance, Briare,
T02 38 31 28 73,
charmes-nautiques.com.
Boat hire company based in
Briare offering a choice of
vessels with plenty of helpful
advice before you set off on
your canal adventure.

Cycle hire & routes
vélo+
Information and subscription
T08-00 00 83 56,
agglo-veloplus.fr.
See page 69.

Detours de Loire
(locationdevelos.com), has the
following partners where you
can hire or leave your bikes:
Auberge de la Maille d'Or, 3 av
de Blois, Beaugency, T02-38 46
43 43, mailledor.com. 0900-1200
and 1400-1900.
Hôtel Le Cerf, 22 bd Buyser,
Briare, T02-38 37 00 80,
hotelducerf.com, 0800-2100.

Kit Loisirs, 7 av Dauphin, Orléans,
T02 38 66 57 81, kitloisirs.com,
Tue-Sat, 0930-1230 and
1330-1900 (also Sun and Mon
by appointment).

Loire à Vélo
Cyclists following the *Loire à Vélo*
route can begin in Sancerre or
enjoy a brief glimpse of the Loire
at St-Thibault before following
the route of the Canal Latéral. At
the time of writing there is still a
large gap between Briare and
the outskirts of Orléans but a
provisional route is planned from
Châteauneuf-sur-Loire. Continue
along the Loire through the
centre of Orléans, a city where
cyclists enjoy over 350 km of
signed routes and instant access
to bicycles at 32 vélo+ stations
(see page 89). Route descriptions
are available in English from a
tourist office or can be
downloaded (French only) from
the website (loire-a-velo.fr).
See full details page 69.

Gardens
Château de la Bussière
La Bussière (between Gien and
Briare), T02 38 35 93 35,
chateau-labussiere.com.
Apr to mid-Nov Wed-Mon
1000-1200 and 1400-1800,
Jul-Aug open daily all day.
€7.50, €4 children.
Originally a medieval fortress,
this impressive residence in
red brick typical of the region
is noted for its fishpond and
its remarkable vegetable and
fruit gardens.

Le Jardin de Roquelin
Meung-sur-Loire (cross the
bridge to the left bank and
turn left), T06 70 95 37 70,
lesjardinsderoquelin.com.
1 May-14 Jul and 29 Aug-18 Oct,
Wed-Mon. €5, under 18s free.
Beautiful rose gardens in a
superb setting, just metres from
the Loire river. The nursery is
open all year.

Parc Floral de la Source
About 7 km south of Orléans,
T02 38 49 30 00,
parc-floral-la-source.com.
Access via the tramway Ligne A
(about 20 min journey time),
alighting at Université - Parc
Floral. It's then just a short,
level walk through the campus.
Open all year except 25 Dec
and 1 Jan; times vary according
to season. €6, €4 children (6-16).
See the source of the River Loiret
and wander around this peaceful
parkland setting enjoying the

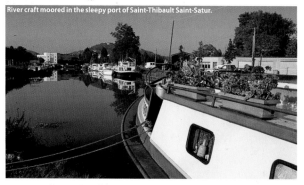
River craft moored in the sleepy port of Saint-Thibault Saint-Satur.

various collections including a rose garden, *potager* (kitchen garden), butterfly house, flamingos and, in autumn, a glorious display of dahlias.

Golf
This part of the Loire Valley is famous for its magnificent golf courses. They range from 18 to 27 holes, where amateurs and experienced players can test their skills in exceptional natural settings. For a list of courses in the area visit golf.tourismloiret.com.

Brittany Ferries Golf Breaks
T+44(0)871-244 0808 (Golf Line), brittany-ferries.co.uk/golf.
Book your ferry, hotel accommodation and pay your green fees with Brittany Ferries – choose from seven golf courses in the Loire Valley, including the renowned Les Bordes.

Boats & cruises
Les Bateaux Touristiques de Briare
Port de Plaisance or Port de Commerce, Briare, T02 38 37 12 75.
Enjoy a slower pace of life on the canal. Cruises on the Pont-Canal and the Canal de Briare run from late Mar to 31 Aug.

Les Passeurs de Loire
45 rue de Gabereau, Châteauneuf-sur-Loire, T06 74 54 36 61, passeursdeloire.fr.

Memorable trips on the Loire between St-Benoît and Sigloy in traditional river boats. Introduction to the natural history of the river, opportunities for picnics and special dawn or dusk itineraries.

Raod trips/scenic routes
Sancerre to Romorantin-Lanthenay
This scenic drive on the D22, via Crézancy-en-Sancerre, meanders through the vines and ancient oak woodland towards Henrichement. Along the way you can stop in the pottery village of La Borne. Continue through Neuvy-sur-Barangeon towards Romorantin-Lanthenay on quiet roads amid forests and lakes. Visit the Musée de Sologne (see page 131) in Romorantin for an excellent introduction to this beautiful and mysterious region.

Wine
Maison des Sancerre
3 rue du Méridien (next to the church), Sancerre, T02 48 54 11 35, maison-des-sancerre.com.
1 Apr-11 Nov, daily.
Modern exhibitions helping visitors understand the complexity of the soils and the surprising world of viticulture. The visit ends in a superb perfumed garden designed to highlight the aromas and flavours of the Sancerre wines. (See also page 77.)

Transport

Bus
The bus operator **SEMTAO** has a useful website (semtao.fr) which shows clearly all bus and tramway routes around Orléans. The operator **Ulys** (ulys-loiret. com) serves towns throughout the Loiret.

Train
Orléans is currently only served by **TER** (ter-sncf.com) regional trains, which include regular services from Paris (just over 1 hr) and stations along the western Loire Valley.

Tram, Orléans.

The Gare SNCF rail station in Orléans.

Contents

Blois & the Sologne

The early 17th-century Château de Selles-sur-Cher.

Introduction

B eyond Orléans the Loire flows towards the town of Blois, where giant golden salamanders burst from the innocent-looking Maison de la Magie, and whose sumptuous Château Royal was once the favoured seat of the French monarchy. South of the river lies la Sologne, among whose vast hardwood forests, countless man-made lakes and open, undeveloped landscapes lie noble hunting estates such as Cheverny and the greatest of all the Loire Valley chateaux: Chambord. It's the perfect place to get away from it all, particularly for walkers, cyclists and lovers of wildlife. Dramatically less visited are the cheerful villages of local red-brick, smaller chateaux such as le Moulin and the courses of rivers including the Seaudre and Beuvron which help drain this former marshland. You can learn how it was reclaimed and much more about this fascinating and little-known area at the Musée de la Sologne in Romorantin-Lanthenay, whose other museum (the Espace Matra) recounts the town's long involvement with motoring and motor sport. On the southern edge of the Sologne the River Cher is joined by the Canal du Berry at Selles-sur-Cher, where you can discover renowned locally produced goat's cheeses and visit the huge, and now beautifully restored, 900-year-old Romanesque abbey church of Notre-Dame-la-Blanche.

What to see in...

...one day
Visit the incomparable **Château de Chambord** before the crowds arrive, then hire a boat on the canals or take a horse-drawn coach ride around the estate. Enjoy a picnic lunch or dine on the terrace of the **Hotel Grand Saint-Michel** – either way, you'll still be in sight of the chateau. After lunch explore Blois, see the **Château Royal** façade and the golden salamanders of the **Maison du Magie**, then descend the stone steps for a cool drink or a meal on the square.

...a weekend or more
Begin your second day at **Chaumont** to tour the Festival gardens in the cool of the morning, then visit the chateau and stables. After a relaxed lunch in one of the excellent estate restaurants, return to Blois to see the **Cathédrale St-Louis**, the **Eglise St-Nicolas** and the dazzling interiors of the **Château Royal**. Dine in the atmospheric heart of the old town then round things off in unforgettable style with a magical *son et lumière* performance at the chateau.

Gargoyles displayed in the Château Royal de Blois.

Blois

The sumptuous Château Royal de Blois provides a timely reminder of the period when this expanding town on the north bank of the Loire enjoyed political influence second only to that of Paris. Much may have since changed, but you can still cross one of the broader stretches of the Loire via the graceful 18th-century Pont Jacques Gabriel and discover a medieval network of narrow streets hidden away behind the town's vibrant but less instantly lovable commercial heart. Among the ancient alleys and *degrés* (stone steps) things are much calmer, to the point where you almost feel as if you've stepped straight into an archive photograph. Powerful echoes of an even earlier spirit haunt both the Cathédrale St-Louis and the former abbey of St-Nicolas, each of which offers cool solace on a hot summer day. On the other hand, for instant immersion into modern-day Blois, grab a table beneath the plane trees and parasols of the elegant café terraces in place Louis XII, just below the Château Royal. On balmy summer evenings, or when the area resonates with the buzz and bustle of a Saturday street market, there's nowhere better to tap into the spirit of this atmospheric town.

The Château de Chaumont-sur-Loire.

Château Royal de Blois

Place du Château, T02 54 90 33 33,
chateaudeblois.fr.
Daily (except 25 Dec and 1 Jan) from 0900,
closing times vary. €8, €6 concessions,
€4 children (6-17). Ask at the desk or tourist office
(near Château entrance) about money-saving
combined tickets. Daily guided tours are
available at no extra charge, with tours in
English every day at 1030, 1300, 1730, or on
request. The 'Visite Insolite' (available on
request) allows visitors to discover parts of the
chateau normally closed to the public. *Son et
lumière* shows in summer: for details see the
events listing page 142.

For all its obvious (and less obvious) restored
features, the chateau still resonates with the proud
spirit of the Kings of France at the height of their
power and influence, and presides over the town
with a magisterial air. The northern façade of the
François I wing looks vast, detached and Italianate,
with long rows of ornate, *loggia*-like galleries
beneath a covered walkway. Climb to the Place du
Château, though, and you come face to face with a
more accessible, mostly Flamboyant Gothic façade,
whose sizzling stonework embellishes decorative
red and black brickwork laid in a diamond pattern.
Above the main entrance is an imposing niche
figure (a 19th-century replica replacing the original
destroyed during the French Revolution) of Louis
XII mounted on horseback along with the royal
porcupine emblem and the letters L (for Louis XII)
and A (for Anne de Bretagne).

Self-guided visits begin with a climb to the
Salle des Etats Généraux built in 1214 and
beautifully restored during the 19th century. The
vast hall is divided by a slender central arcade while
neo-Gothic decoration covers virtually every
surface, including the rich blue roof vaults adorned
with almost 7000 golden *fleurs-de-lys*. Descend a
flight of stairs at the end of the hall and you'll enter
the **Musée Lapidaire**, a series of rooms filled with
gargoyles, pinnacles, capitals and many other
chunks of ornamental stonework (some of them

Essentials

❶ **Getting around** Blois is relatively small and has
multi-storey car parks within easy walking distance of
the main sights. Radio Taxis, place de la Gare (in front
of the train station), T02 54 78 07 65 also offer 'Circuits
Châteaux', liaisons with TGV stations and airports.
Outside Blois roads are generally quiet, apart from peak
periods around big attractions such as Chambord and
Cheverny. Cyclists have miles of dedicated tracks in the
Domaine de Chambord, and the *Loire à Vélo* routes are
well signed.

❷ **Bus station** 2 place Victor Hugo, T02 54 78 15 66,
tub-blois.fr.

❸ **Train station** Boulevard Daniel Dupuis north of
the town.

❹ **ATMs** Place de la Résistance, rue Denis Papin and
on place Louis XII in Blois.

❺ **Hospital** Centre Hospitalier de Blois, Mail Pierre
Charlot, T02 54 55 66 33, ch-blois.fr.

❻ **Pharmacies** Pharmacie de Trois Clefs, 30 rue
Denis Papin, Blois, T02 54 74 01 35; **Pharmacie
Cassagnol**, 5 place Louis XII, Blois, T02 54 78 00 29.

❼ **Post office** Rue Gallois in Blois.

❽ **Tourist information offices** Loir-et-Cher Tourism,
5 rue de la Voûte du Château, Blois, T02 54 57 00 41,
chambordcountry.com; 23 place du Château, Blois,
T02 54 90 41 41, bloispaysdechambord.com;
Bracieux, 10 Les Jardins du Moulin, T02 54 46 09 15;
Chambord, place St Louis, T02 54 33 39 16;
Chaumont-sur-Loire, 24 rue du Maréchal Leclerc, T02
54 20 91 73; Cheverny-Cour-Cheverny, 12 rue du Chêne
aux Dames, T02 54 79 95 63; Montrichard, 1 rue du Pont,
T02 54 32 05 10; Romorantin-Lanthenay, place de la
Paix, T02 54 76 43 89.

Royal apartment, Château Royal de Blois.

plaster casts) replaced during restoration works. Climb a stairway from here and you reach the François I wing via the **Grande Salle**. Among the vibrant decoration, notice the two huge fireplaces decorated with gilded salamander emblems. Adjoining this room is a **guard room** displaying armour, swords, pikes and other weaponry. Also present is the porcupine emblem, along with another salamander over an ornate doorway leading to a **music room**. There's a welcome lightness here, more sumptuous floor-to-ceiling decoration and an interesting selection of objects including an early clavichord, *faïence* (glazed earthenware) violin and mandolin ornaments, plus a series of busts of French monarchs. Beyond is **Catherine de' Medici's study**, whose 237 intricate restored, original 16th-century panels conceal the secret compartments described by Alexandre Dumas in *La Reine Margot*.

On the second floor, accessed by the famous lavishly decorated *grand escalier* (spiral staircase), are the sumptuous **Royal Apartments**. In 1588 the King's Chamber was the scene of the assassination of the Duc de Guise on the orders of Henri III (who watched events unfold while concealed behind a large wall-hanging).

When you finally descend to the large central courtyard you'll see clearly how changing fashions inspired the various portions of the chateau, starting with the early 13th-century Salle d'Etats Généraux and Flamboyant Gothic Louis XII wing of 1498-1501. Just 12 years or so later the radically different François I wing was begun, drawing inspiration from the Italian Renaissance. Last came the much more sober Gaston d'Orléans or Classical Wing, begun in 1634 and designed by François Mansart. A casualty of Mansart's work was the Chapelle St-Calais, whose nave was among the sections demolished to make way for the new wing. Only the holiest part of the King's private chapel (in which Henri III attended a thanksgiving mass immediately after dispatching the Duc de Guise) has survived. The tall, richly coloured 1950s windows are by master glass-maker Max Ingrand and substituted previous (19th century)

replacements lost during Second World War bombardments. Outside, the neo-Gothic western façade and portal, created by Félix Duban and Jules de la Morandière in 1870, restore some dignity to this wounded but still beautiful survivor.

Maison de la Magie

1 place du Château, T02 54 90 33 33, maisondelamagie.fr.
4 Apr-31 Aug daily 1000-1230 and 1400-1830, 1 Sep-20 Sep Mon-Fri 1400-1830, weekends 1000-1230 and 1400-1830, 24 Oct-4 Nov (school holidays) 1000-1230 and 1400-1830. Last entry 30 mins before closing. €8, €6.50 concessions, €5 children (6-17). 30-min shows 3-4 times daily.

The golden salamanders of La Maison de la Magie, Blois.

Around the region

It takes something pretty spectacular to instantly grab your full attention after the chateau visit, but an innocent-looking townhouse across the place du Château will do just that. Every hour the peace is shattered by dark, horror-movie sounds, shutters open of their own accord and six golden salamander heads emerge amid clouds of smoke, followed by claws and a forked tail. As the dragon-like creatures peer around at the startled onlookers in the square below, they begin to open and snap their jaws menacingly. A few minutes later, having made their point, they retreat, the shutters close and peace returns. It's quite a show, and provides a foretaste of the remarkable museum dedicated to magic and in particular to local illusionist Jean-Eugène Robert-Houdin (who inspired young Erich Weiss to change his name to Harry Houdini). Inside you can expect a live magic show, automatons, memorabilia from both Houdin and Houdini, plus a gallery of optical illusions, the most spectacular of which is the Hallucinascope, a virtual reality experience in which visitors wear special inverting glasses. The result is a sensation of walking on air through other worlds, across oceans, etc (the scenery responsible being in fact mounted high above them). Pure magic.

The Saint-Louis window, Cathédrale Saint-Louis, Blois.

Cathédrale St-Louis

Place St-Louis, T02-54 78 17 90.
Daily 0900-1800.

Relatively few visitors climb the old stone steps which wind from the heart of the historic quarter behind quai St-Jean to Place St-Louis. Take this time-worn approach, though, and the cathedral suddenly towering above you looks a lot less underwhelming than from most other viewpoints. Blame the present jarring lack of unity on a troubled history stretching back to the 10th century, when a crypt was created to house relics of St-Solenne, an early Bishop of Chartres. Two successive, and much larger, structures followed, the second (built by order of François I) being virtually destroyed by a hurricane in 1678 and

rebuilt in Gothic style. Bizarrely, though, the single tower was later topped off in French baroque.

Against all expectation, the interior is beautiful and a picture of Gothic harmony, despite a lack of transepts and the fact that only three of the huge stone slabs above the nave arcades ever received their planned bas-relief decoration. Second World War bombardments claimed the original stained glass but their worthy contemporary replacements by Dutch conceptual artist Jan Dibbets tint the entering sunlight, warming the pale stone interior. Real enough are the mystical qualities of the Carolingian crypt, which survives (complete with the bones of the Saint) below the floor of the nave. A world apart, it's in the eerie silence of early sacred places like this that you'll still tap into the spirit of the dawn of Christianity which transformed ordinary sites into important centres of pilgrimage – which in turn would inspire the creation of vast medieval abbeys and cathedrals.

Eglise St-Nicolas

Rue St Laumer, T02 54 90 41 41.
Daily 0900-1830.

The three handsome slated spires rising assertively between the Château Royal and the Loire belong to the 12th- and 13th-century Eglise St-Nicolas, originally the centrepiece of a Benedictine abbey destroyed by Huguenots and partly rebuilt during the 17th century. The startling effect of the tall, Chartres-influenced western façade is sustained by the soaring height of the interior, whose modest window areas make things much darker and more mysterious than the Cathédrale St-Louis. The narrow span of the vaults has the effect of making the nave look even taller, with things being taken a stage further by suspending a lantern tower above the mighty piers of the transept crossing. Above its

The handsome Gothic spires of the Eglise Saint-Nicolas, Blois.

low windows is a stone cupola symbolizing the waiting Heaven, a sensational effect which must have seemed even more so when this eastern portion was completed between 1138 and 1186. Smaller, less obvious details around the choir are also worth a closer look, particularly the outer chapels and the pier capitals, whose surprisingly irreverent imagery hints at a much earlier Romanesque spirit. The large axial or central chapel, on the other hand, is a 14th-century addition. Before leaving you'll find it well worth walking slowly around the exterior for an object lesson in how an early medieval Gothic building is constructed, and to see the whole thing still comfortably upstaging the surrounding rooftops.

Muséum d'Histoire Naturelle de Blois

Les Jacobins, 6 rue des Jacobins, T02 54 90 21 00.
Jul-Aug Tue-Sun 1400-1800 and Tue and Fri mornings 1000-1200. €2.80, €1.40 concessions and 12-18 years, free under 12s.

The museum's permanent displays concentrate on the natural history, landscapes and geology of the Loire Valley including the plains of the Beauce, the lakes heathland and forests of the Sologne, plus the river itself. Interactive and audiovisual displays bring it all to life in the setting of a former convent founded in 1273. The museum also hosts a programme of temporary exhibitions.

Château & Parc de Beauregard

Allée de Beauregard, Cellettes, 7 km south of Blois off the D956, T02 54 70 36 74, beauregard-loire.com.
Apr-Sep daily, Oct-Feb closed Wed, closed for lunch outside Jul-Aug and closed for much of Dec-Jan. €7 for chateau and park, €5 park only. Guided visits available for a small supplement.

The chateau exudes Franco-Italian grace and beauty from every pore, with a setting to match in landscaped parkland bounded by the dense Forêt de Russy, on the northern fringes of the Sologne. Beauregard has been occupied since the 15th century, serving as a hunting lodge for both Louis XII and François I before being acquired by Henri II's Secretary of State Jean du Thier in 1545. A man of culture (and patron of poet Pierre de Ronsard), his workplace, the exquisitely decorated Cabinet des Grelots, survives on the first floor of the building for which he was largely responsible. The outer wings, though, were added after the estate passed, in 1617, to 72-year-old Paul Ardier, who also began the celebrated Gallerie des Illustres, whose walls would eventually display 327 portraits of key figures from European history. The work took three generations to complete and the floor has around 5500 Delft tiles emblazoned with military horsemen. The room remains the centrepiece of visits to the chateau, whose decor represents the creative input of a succession of aristocratic owners. Other surprises include a Dutch long-case clock dated 1711, the complete jawbone of a whale (also dating from the 18th century) and the original chateau kitchens, used until 1968. In the park are the ruins of a 15th-century chapel inscribed with the shell emblem of St-Jacques de Compostelle and the cross of the Knights Templar.

View across the Loire to the Château de Ménars.

Château de Ménars

Closed to visitors – riverside viewpoint signed from lay-by on D951 about 10 km east of Blois.

If you intend driving between Blois and Orléans it's worth taking the slower, less-travelled road which hugs the *rive gauche*, or southern bank, of the Loire – not least to get the definitive view of an important, privately owned chateau rarely accessible to visitors. The Château de Ménars was begun around 1645 by Royal Councillor Guillaume Charron and purchased in 1670 by the newly ennobled Madame de Pompadour. With the help of Court architect Ange-Jacques Gabriel (who conceived the Petite Trianon at Versailles and the Place de la Concorde in Paris) she enlarged the original building by adding symmetrical wings, updated the interior in a lighter, more fashionable style and laid out the parkland and formal parterre gardens. Disliking the smell of cooking, she had the

kitchens removed from the house and installed in a separate new building linked to the dining room by an underground passage. On her death in 1764 the estate passed to her brother, Abel-François Poisson de Vandières, who was by then Director General of Buildings to the King. On his instructions, his architect Jacques-Germain Soufflot effectively doubled the size of the main building and covered the wings added by Gabriel with pitched slate roofs *à la Française*. So sensitive was the work that the chateau became one of the most perfect examples of surviving 18th-century French architecture. Add to this a perfect setting, amid substantial landscaped gardens with elevated, uninterrupted views across the river, and you'll have every reason to hope that one day the chateau will once again reveal some of its secrets to visitors. As it is, if you visit the village of Ménars hoping for a closer view of the chateau you'll be disappointed. There's the pleasant village bar-restaurant Café de la Pompadour, however, and if you follow the small sign to the Loire you'll find ample parking and space for a picnic overlooking the river with access onto the cycle route along the bank.

Chambord

In 1519 the young King François I resolved to create a definitive statement of absolute power. Almost five centuries later, from the moment its unmistakable outline rears up on a horizon bounded by dense forest you already know that the largest and most celebrated of all the Loire chateaux is not going to disappoint. When you eventually finish exploring the wonders which lie within, climb the celebrated double-helix staircase to the rooftop terraces, from whose privileged viewpoints you can admire the surrounding landscapes of ancient forest. So is this the ultimate hunting lodge or a decadent pleasure palace? You decide.

François I's unashamedly romantic Château de Chambord.

Some of the Château de Cambord's Hunting memorabilia.

Domaine & Château de Chambord

T02 54 50 40 00, chambord.org.
Daily except 1 Jan, 1 May and 25 Dec from 0900, closing times vary (last entry 30 mins before closing). €8.50 low season, €9.50 high season, €7/8 concessions, under 18s free with family. Purchase tickets at the central office or walk direct to the chateau entrance and pay there. The audio handset (€4, available in 10 languages, deposit of a passport required) provides an excellent commentary when and where you want it. Parking €2 per day for a car. Access to the chateau grounds and estate free. There's also a variety of restaurants and shops, an ATM, tourist information and toilets (payable) on site as well as cycle and boat hire facilities and carriage rides. For details of evening *son et lumière* shows see the event listing page 142.

The sheer scale of Chambord defies belief: 156 m long and 56 m high, with 426 rooms (containing 282 fireplaces) served by no fewer than 77 staircases. From a distance it appears almost weightless in the landscape, but draw closer and you can see how the construction consumed 220,000 tonnes of pale *tuffeau* limestone from Bourré which was worked on site by around 1800 masons and labourers. Surprisingly, however, the identity of the architect is a mystery, although it's tempting to ascribe at least some of its features to Leonardo da Vinci, who spent his last years nearby in Amboise as the King's guest. Despite its apparent complexity, Chambord was planned around a square donjon (keep) with four massive corner towers. However, being essentially symbolic, it had no need for outer defences, so the courtyard walls are little more than wings for the central building.

Today's visitors enter lofty doors on the far side, feeling suddenly dwarfed by the towering scale of the surroundings. Inside you're free to explore three floors whose layout is broadly similar, with rooms served by four central hallways converging upon an ingenious double-helix staircase. Notice the exquisitely carved decoration including the salamander of François I. The ground floor reception rooms display hunting paintings and computer-generated presentations outlining the chateau's layout and construction.

The first-floor rooms have been furnished to replicate their appearance during key periods in the chateau's varied history. The **Royal wing** houses the apartments of François I, a council chamber and a small oratory. Alongside is the **Queen's Apartment** occupied by the two wives of Louis XIV: Maria-Theresa of Spain and Françoise d'Aubigny. In the opposite wing is the chateau's largest room, a serene vaulted **chapel** completed by Jules Hardouin Mansart, architect of Versailles, while the central body of the building presents **state rooms** in their last-known decorative style. On this floor you can also visit the apartments of two of the chateau's 18th-century governors, exiled King of Poland Stanislaus Leszynski and Maréchal Maurice de Saxe, who had been handed Chambord for life by Louis XV in 1748 (and who died here just two years later). Further rooms are dedicated to Henri V, Comte de Chambord from 1821-1883, who spent just three days here. Perhaps the most remarkable of the related exhibits is a huge glass case containing the intended future French king's childhood toy collection – beautifully engineered large-scale models of contemporary weapons of warfare.

The second-floor rooms display huge tapestries and other historic hunting imagery, although at least as interesting are the vast shallow-arched Italianate stone vaults of the hallways, with 400 sculpted salamander emblems, plus the Royal 'F' and rope-work monogram. Above lie the roof terraces created to survey the estate and the point where the architecture finally lets rip. Gaze in awe at a forest of 365 chimneys, assorted towers and spires reaching skywards, then peer over the balustrades to the courtyard spread far below.

The surrounding 5440-ha hunting domain is enclosed by 32 km of impenetrable stone walls (enough to encircle the city of Paris) whose construction took 100 years. Around 1000 ha of the estate are freely accessible to walkers, riders, cyclists and wildlife watchers.

Château de Villesavin

8 km south of Chambord via Bracieux off the D52, T02 54 46 42 88, chateau-de-villesavin.com. Mar-May 1000-1200 and 1400-1900 (closed Thu in Mar), Jun-Sep daily 1000-1900, Oct-15 Nov daily 1000-1200 and 1400-1800. Closed 15 Nov-1 Mar. €6 unaccompanied, €7.50 guided.

After the unbridled magnificence of Chambord, Villesavin (whose name derives from the Roman Villa Savini which once stood nearby) looks calmer and much more human. However, the two estates are much more closely linked than you'd imagine, since this chateau was built (between 1527 and 1537) by François I's Financial Secretary (and Seigneur de Villandry) Jean le Breton, who had been appointed to project-manage the King's great adventure. It's hardly surprising, then, that with both construction sites running concurrently, Chambord's teams of masons also worked here, or that the many shared visual references include the Royal emblems adorning Villesavin's stone gables. Otherwise it's essentially a single-story country manor house, with dormer windows permitting attic space accommodation, and it remains privately owned. Guided tours visit a selection of 16th- and 18th-century interiors, and you can also include in this tour the Musée du Mariage, whose 1500 or so display items retrace traditions of marriage since 1840. Marginally more mainstream is a display of *hippomobiles* (horse-drawn carriages) and *voitures d'enfants* – early forerunners of prams and pushchairs. Transcending it all is Villesavin's serene chapel, which was visited by Catherine de' Medici in 1611. Its walls and vaults are adorned with late 16th-century frescoes (currently undergoing patient restoration) by the influential Modenese artist Nicolò dell' Abate, who also worked at the Château Royal de Fontainebleau. Don't miss seeing the estate's huge 16th-century dovecote – and look out for some of the big, furry Baudet du Poitou donkeys which are bred on site.

Cheverny

Here on the borders of Touraine and the Sologne you sense that you're in the very heart of chateau country. The undoubted star attraction is Cheverny, the definitive French country hunting estate, which is still occupied by descendants of the family which built it almost four centuries ago. As a result, the chateau's opulent apartments offer a rare glimpse of aristocratic French country living that you'll long remember. And there's insight into more down-to-earth country life nearby in a museum at the Château de Troussay, a 15th-century gentleman's residence, and one of the Loire Valley's smallest chateaux. Almost as close, and altogether more feudal looking, is the Château de Fougères-sur-Bièvre, whose assertive towers dominate the heart of an otherwise unassuming country village. Dramatically less visible, but well worth discovering, is the Château de Gué-Péan, tucked away in a clearing among gently undulating forests above the River Cher. Its owner, a talented architect responsible for styling the famous Futuroscope theme park further south near Poitiers, dedicates his spare time to patiently restoring this ancient family chateau.

The spirit of Tintin lives on at the Château de Cheverny.

Château de Cheverny

T02 54 79 96 29, chateau-cheverny.fr.
Jan-Mar daily 0945-1700, Apr-Jun daily
0915-1815, Jul-Aug daily 0915-1845, Sep daily
0915-1815, Oct daily 0945-1730, Nov-Dec daily
0945-1700. Min €7.40, max €16.70, concessions
under 7s, students, families, disabled visitors
and groups.

The efficiency of Cheverny's visitor management
gives some idea of the numbers who since 1914
have been converging on this small village to see
one of the largest privately owned chateaux in
France. Beyond the gift shop and ticket sales point
the vast and immaculately groomed lawns of this
historic hunting estate unfold against a backdrop
of dense forest. The chateau remains largely
hidden by trees to your right, but walk on and it's
slowly revealed, looking surprisingly youthful
despite the passage of almost four centuries. The
unmistakable Louis XIII-style exterior in pale *tuffeau*
stone quarried in Bourré was designed by Jacques
Bougier, who also worked at Blois and Chambord.
Classical details include dentil cornices, arched
window lintels plus medallions sculpted with
heads of Roman Emperors. Perfect symmetry and
deeply incised horizontal banding holds
everything together visually.

Tip...

In peak season arrive early, beat ticket queues and
enjoy a cool, leisurely visit before tour operator
coach parties arrive.

As you enter the interior you'll receive an
informative brochure describing the main rooms
to be visited at your own pace. To your right is a
large dining room sizzling with decorative panels
of scenes from Don Quixote plus a huge gilded
neo-Renaissance fireplace surmounted by a bust of
Henri IV. Above is an appropriately intricately
decorated beamed ceiling.

Climb the Louis XIII main staircase, clearly dated
1634, whose sculpted decoration includes several
Green Man fertility symbol references – something
of a recurring theme at Cheverny. On the first floor
you'll discover beautifully preserved private
apartments, beginning with a salon reserved for
the presentation of newborn babies. Next come a
nursery with a Napoléon III rocking horse, a ladies'
drawing room and a bridal chamber, complete
with early ensuite facilities. The family dining room
is set with a specially commissioned *Autumn in
Cheverny* dinner service and tablecloth, while in the
small salon is a life-sized statue of Anne-Victor

Formal gardens link the chateau with the 18th-century orangerie.

The orangerie's interior houses an upmarket boutique.

Hurault de Vibraye, whose descendants still own the estate.

A very different aspect of this elegant family home is revealed in the huge **Arms Room**, whose collection of polished armour includes a complete suit made for the four-year-old Duc de Bordeaux (who became Comte de Chambord). There's also 15th- to 17th-century weaponry, Henri IV's travelling chest and a still-vibrant 17th-century Gobelins tapestry. This room also preserves the meticulous decorative work of Jean Monier, who created the next room, the **King's Chamber**, designed to welcome the monarch and other distinguished guests. Its walls are hung with huge Paris-made tapestries, beneath a ceiling emblazoned with gilded panels decorated with romantic themes from Greek mythology. Their dazzling effect was no doubt appreciated by Henri IV, who occupied the Royal bed (covered in 16th-century Persian embroidery) during a visit to the estate.

The visit continues on the ground floor among hunting trophies, portraits, a large family tree plus a 17th-century Flemish tapestry in the vestibule.

The **Grand Salon**, whose intricate pastel-toned panelling adorns even the ceiling, displays fine portraits of great historical significance (one is attributed to Titian) and a Louis XVI table is signed 'Stockel', cabinetmaker to Marie Antoinette. Beyond lies the **Galerie**, with canvases by François Clouet, portrait artist to François I, a coronation portrait of Louis XVI and a document signed by George Washington. Completing the visit are a **library** with 2000 leather-bound works and a **salon** hung with giant 17th-century Flanders tapestries. Its Louis XV longcase clock remains in perfect working order.

Leave by the rear doors, crossing the stone bridge spanning a dry moat. Ahead, beyond the Apprentices' Garden created in 1996, lies a large 18th-century orangery. During the Second World War it housed many of France's greatest art treasures, including the *Mona Lisa*, but now contains an upmarket gift boutique.

Cheverny (minus its outer towers) will be familiar to Tintin aficionados as Moulinsart – Marlinspike Hall in English texts – a fact celebrated in a colourful museum created between the exit

Around the region

gates and the estate's walled *potager* (vegetable garden). A spectacle in itself, the garden's aromatic qualities also help offset those wafting, not always pleasantly, from the nearby kennels of around 100 handsome hunting dogs. Late afternoon feeding times are frenzied affairs that you might decide to miss.

Château de Troussay

Route de Troussay, Cheverny, a short distance southwest of Cheverny, T02 54 44 29 07.
Apr-Jun and Sep daily 1030-1230 and 1400-1800, Jul-Aug daily 1030-1830, Oct-Nov Sat-Sun 1030-1230 and 1400-1730.
€5.50, €3.50 exterior only.

One of the smallest of the Loire chateaux, Troussay is nevertheless a delight, with a nobility and grace out of all proportion to its physical dimensions. The central body, constructed around 1450 for Robert de Bugy, *écuyer* (equerry) to François I, clearly took its design cues from great structures like Blois, Chambord and Cheverny, as you'll discover during a guided visit of six rooms of the privately owned chateau.

The original brick-and-stone Renaissance façade was extended two centuries or so later with wings framed by handsome circular towers topped with decorative *clochers*. Completing the effect is a broad courtyard with a 500-year-old holly tree sheltered on either side by long, low *dépendences* (farm-style outbuildings) which are now occupied by a museum giving worthwhile insight into bygone rural life in the surrounding Sologne region. The rear of the chateau bears Louis XII's porcupine emblem, the salamander of François I plus an *escalier* (staircase) tower added during the 19th century and decorated with playful corbel figures. Little remains of the original formal gardens apart from the tell-tale depression of a former lake, venerable cedars and sequoias, plus a still-productive *potager*. But the spirit survives, and the beautiful, secluded location completes this perfect antidote to the occasional sensory overload of its big-league neighbours.

Château de Fougères-sur-Bièvre

11 km southwest of Cheverny on the D52, T02 54 20 27 18, fougeres-sur-bievre.monuments-nationaux.fr.
8 May-10 Sep daily 0930-1230 and 1400-1830, 11 Sep-7 May Wed-Mon 1000-1230 and 1400-1700. Closed 1 Jan, 1 May, 1 Nov, 25 Dec. €5, €3.50 18-25 years, under 18s free.
Guided visit by arrangement, otherwise self-guided visit with literature in 9 languages.

The chateau has more of a dual personality than most. Its upper parts look the very epitome of the French country castle, with its massive towers, cannon, arrow-slits and sentry walk. However, instead of being isolated within a protective moat (which was filled in around the 17th century) it's now bounded on one side by a meadow and on the other by the grassy roadside verges of the slightly laid-back village. But the building can trace its history back to 1030, and was occupied during the Hundred Years' War by the English who, after their defeat in 1429, left it in ruins. In 1470 Louis XI's Chancellor Pierre de Refuge rebuilt the structure, adding the square donjon and most of the other defensive features we see today. The purely decorative Renaissance-inspired embellishments of 1510-1520 were the work of his grandson Jean de Villebresme, who also removed the upper crenelated battlements and added the present steeply pitched slate roofs. Sadly, the interiors were stripped when the site was acquired by Réné Lambot, who already owned the nearby Château de Boissay and who used Fougères from 1812 until 1901 for a milling enterprise. Happily the chateau and its dignity have now been fully restored, and the self-guided visit offers a worthwhile insight into medieval military construction techniques. Undoubted highlights are the sentry walk and the forest of massive roof timbers.

Château du Gué-Péan

13 km east of Monthou-sur-Cher, about 23 km south of Cheverny, T02 54 71 37 10, guepean.com. May-Sep 1030-1230 and 1400-1830. €6.50, €5 child, groups 20+, students, under 8s free.

In contrast to the long-celebrated sites of the Loire Valley, Gué (pronounced 'gae')-Péan is that rarest of things: a romantic chateau in a peaceful clearing amid ancient hunting forests, so far largely undiscovered by the outside world. To visit you must cross the remains of a medieval drawbridge and tug a modest bell-pull beside a stone gateway. Soon the gate will open, welcoming you to an unimagined haven in largely Renaissance style. The self-guided visit begins in a vaulted family chapel and continues with a winding climb to the sentry walk of the highest of the medieval towers, whose walls wear the inscriptions of visitors from centuries past. Take a seat beneath the complex supporting timbers of the Imperial bell-shaped roof and you can watch a well-produced video outlining the history and restoration of the estate, formerly the site of a Roman camp. From up here there's also a bird's-eye view of the courtyard and surrounding countryside.

From the 16th century onwards the chateau gradually evolved into a gracious country home, as you'll now discover during a tour (guided only) of several of the more historically important rooms. Highlights include a hunting trophy room, a ladies' salon, the King's bedroom (lest he should decide to drop in unexpectedly) and a music room used by Chopin, a rather more frequent visitor. Further history unfolds in the library housed in another tower, with letters signed by personalities including Napoléon, General de Gaulle and Marie Antoinette. There's also an early map-style illustration of the estate, whose stables are once again occupied, as part of a large equestrian centre.

Gué-Péan's feudal origins are thinly disguised.

Romorantin-Lanthenay

The capital of the Sologne is inexorably linked to French history as the setting in which François d'Angoulême – who would later become King François I – spent his childhood, and also as the birthplace of his future wife, Claude de France. Her father Louis XII so loved the town that he commissioned Leonardo da Vinci to design a chateau here. Although the innovative building never materialized, the old town, beside the River Sauldre, is worth visiting, not least to see the excellent Musée de la Sologne, housed in three ancient water mill buildings. Nearby is the Espace Matra, a very different museum dedicated to the town's former motor manufacturing industry. Meanwhile, tucked away in a romantic forest clearing not far from the town is the fairy-tale castle you've been secretly searching for – the 16th-century Château du Moulin. A little further to the southwest lies Selles-sur-Cher, where you can picnic on the riverbanks before visiting the huge Romanesque abbey-church of Notre-Dame-la-Blanche, close to the spot on which Joan of Arc's 6000-strong army awaited the command of Charles VII in 1429.

Musée de Sologne

Moulin du Chapitre, T02 54 95 33 66, museedesologne.com.
2 Jan-31 Dec Wed-Mon 1000-1200 and 1400-1800. Closed 1 Jan, 1 May, 25 Dec. €5, €3.50 concessions. Ask for an English translation of the exhibition at the desk. Combined tickets available for this and the Matra museum €8.

Simply defining the Sologne region is far from straightforward, but this well-conceived museum gives a firm grounding in so many facets of its landscapes, history, culture, architecture and wildlife that you'll immediately begin to see things differently and start piecing together something of the puzzle. The displays are housed in three former watermills, one of which (the Tour Jacquemart) dates from the 12th century. Contrasts between simple peasant farming and the privileged life in the great chateaux are particularly revealing, and everything is documented in a well translated printed guide to accompany your visit.

Espace Automobiles Matra

17 rue des Capucins, T02 54 94 55 58, museematra.com (French only).
2 Jan-31 Dec Wed-Mon 0900 (1000 Sat-Sun) -1200 and 1400-1800. Closed 1 Jan, 1 May, 25 Dec. €5, €3.50 concessions. Combined tickets for this and the Musée de Sologne €8. Exhibit information provided in English.

The Matra company's motor racing pedigree is celebrated in this extravagant collection of historic vehicles displayed in an appropriately high-tech setting (in which *Beaulieu* cine cameras were once assembled). Each year there's an additional themed display, 2010 being devoted to the ingenious mechanical designs of Leonardo da Vinci. The lower floor, on the other hand, displays some of the concept vehicles developed by the company's styling and engineering studios. Pride of place goes to variations (including a roadster) on the Espace, rejected by Peugeot before Renault turned it into a world-beater and took all the credit, and which for many years the company assembled in Romarantin.

Traditional hand-tools.

Petrolhead heaven.

Château du Moulin

Lassay-sur-Croisne (10 km west of Romorantin-Lanthenay), T02 54 83 83 51, chateau-moulin-fraise.com.
1 Apr-30 Sep daily 1000-1230 and 1400-1830. Guided tours of chateau, museum and garden at 30 mins past the hour from 1030. €8, €6 12-18 years, €4 under 12s; €6 museum and gardens only.

The 'pearl of the Sologne' sits in a romantic and secretive location deep within silent, broadleaf forest, where reflections of its tall, pale pink brick towers shimmer in the dark waters of a satisfyingly wide moat. The chateau was constructed between around 1492 by court architect Jacques de Persigny for nobleman Phillippe du Moulin, who, it is said, saved the life of Charles VIII at the Battle of Fornoue (Italy) in 1495. The initial visual effect today, though, is much more fairy tale castle than feudal fortress, with only one of the four outer bastions retaining its full height, and virtually all the brickwork incorporating the same diamond-pattern decoration found at Blois. That said, the towers feature *meurtrier* openings for archers, outermost faces are curved to maximize their strength and those of the drawbridge gatehouse rise to an impressive height. Renaissance influences are obvious in the main residential building or *châtelet*, whose steeply pitched roof has dormer windows, alongside more typically Gothic touches such as crocketed gables and a small but sturdy chapel. The private chateau remains inhabited, but guided visits include a selection of rooms with period furnishings, looking much as they did after major but sensitive renovation works in 1901-1914. The estate is today home to the Conservatoire de la Fraise, the former chateau stables now housing a museum celebrating the history and culture of the far-from-humble strawberry, 40 or so varieties of which are grown in the adjoining gardens.

The Château du Moulin is the definitive romantic country hideaway.

The tomb of Saint Eusice, founder of the gracious Romanesque abbey-church.

Eglise Abbatiale Notre-Dame-la-Blanche

Selles-sur-Cher (18 km southwest of Romorantin-Lanthenay), mairie-selles-sur-cher.fr.

The pleasant town of Selles-sur-Cher takes its name from the *cella* (Latin for 'refuge') of Eusice, an early Christian hermit who arrived to set up home on a known flood plain, which thereafter remained miraculously dry whatever the state of the river. When he died around 540 he was buried in a simple vaulted chamber beneath the nave of the monastery which by then he'd established. Around 1200-1215 the monastery, an important place of pilgrimage, was replaced by the huge abbey church of Notre-Dame-la-Blanche. Despite the hostile actions of the Revolution, which saw the abbey's prized possessions sold off, the tomb survives. You'll find it by descending a small flight of stone steps from the south aisle (a rather primitive wall-mounted timer activates fittingly

atmospheric lighting). Surprisingly, the Romanesque church above has a timber (slated) roof with Gothic rib vaults in the side aisles, whose interesting carved capitals include vine leaf decoration. The exterior of the apse has a primitive early frieze thought to depict events in the life of the Saint.

In 1429 Selles witnessed a key event in French history unfolding after the liberation of Orléans, when Joan of Arc and the Duke of Alençon assembled an army of 6000 to await the command of Charles VII. At the time, the abbey and the village were protected by a feudal donjon sited on the riverbanks. It was replaced during the early 17th century by an elegant private chateau. There's talk of it becoming a hotel, but for now it remains a tantalising enigma gazing coyly across the river. The town has also given its name to a high quality local goat's cheese, which was awarded AOC (*Appellation d'Origine Contrôlé*) status in 1975.

Domaine de Chaumont-sur-Loire

The Château de Chaumont sits imperiously on a broad plateau high above the Loire. In 1560 Henri II's widow Catherine de' Medici acquired it in order to oust the king's mistress Diane de Poitiers (whom she had long despised) from Chenonceau and instead take up residence here. Today it's hard to see why she never did so, for the estate and its setting seem near faultless, particularly during the annual Festival des Jardins which have made Chaumont world-famous. When you've completed your tour of the chateau and the display gardens created for the festival by some of the best contemporary garden designers, head down to the banks of the River Cher to dine under the stars in Montrichard, or climb to the town's ruined fortress to enjoy an historic re-enactment performance recalling events in the town's history. In the nearby village of Bourré is another unmissable attraction – a traditional village sculpted deep underground in the same pale *tuffeau* stone that was quarried here for centuries to build the great chateaux of the Loire.

Château de Chaumont

T02 54 20 99 22, domaine-chaumont.fr.
Daily from 1000, closing times vary (last entry 45 mins before closing). Closed 25 Dec-1 Jan. Festival des Jardins runs from end Apr to mid-Oct. All-inclusive Domaine ticket including Festival des Jardins €15, €11 12-18 years, €5.50 children (6-11), under 6s free. Festival des Jardins and park €9.50, €7.50, €4.50, free. Chateau only €9, €6, €3.50, free.
The village entrance involves a 10-min gentle uphill walk. Visitors with reduced mobility are advised to enter via the Plateau entrance, which offers adjacent level parking.

At first glance the Château de Chaumont looks like a French castle should, with mighty towers and a commanding strategic placement high above the banks of the Loire. Make the gentle climb from the village for a closer look, though, and its tourelles, Italianate detailing and private chapel tell a very different story. Unlike its predecessor built in 990 to defend nearby Blois, this is less a military fortress and more a showpiece country residence. Look inside and you'll discover a succession of rooms in neo-Gothic and Renaissance styles, replicating as closely as possible the fashionably romantic effect visualised by 19th-century architectural stylist Paul-Ernest Sanson for the estate's last private owners. In 1875 16-year-old Marie Say visited the chateau with her father and instantly fell in love with it. Naturally, the wealthy sugar company magnate purchased it for her. Marie subsequently married Amédée de Broglie and the couple began pouring a vast fortune into the radical transformation of both the chateau and its estate, along the way producing fantastic creations including a guardroom complete with polished arms and armour and a council chamber hung with 16th-century tapestries and floored with 17th-century majolica tiles shipped from a palazzo in Palermo. Then for good measure they restored the bedchambers of Catherine de' Medici and her personal astrologer Cosimo Ruggieri.

After these visual fireworks, the beautiful Flamboyant Gothic *grand escalier* spiraling back down to the ground floor provides a welcome interlude of serenity, and a curtain-raiser for the long, Pugin-esque ground floor salon, whose monumental fireplace is emblazoned with a large painted porcupine. Louis XII's curious emblem reappears outside as a stone bas-relief overlooking what must have been a rather dark, enclosed central courtyard up until 1739, when the north

Expect the unexpected at Chaumont's summer-long garden festivals.

Festival des Jardins

Chaumont is today renowned the world over for its summer-long International Garden Festival which has been hosted here since 1992 and which showcases the art of contemporary garden design. Landscape designers, horticulturalists and artists are invited to submit designs expressing imagination and resourcefulness for gardens of 210 sq m (average for a typical home garden) and within a set maximum budget. A jury selects the best designs, whose creators then bring them to life in 26 plots at Chaumont. Each season there's a new theme to be interpreted and the results vary from subtle to spectacular, attracting widespread press coverage. Visitors, too, keep returning in search of fresh inspiration for their own gardens.

See listings page 144 for details of the Festival des Jardins opening times and nocturnal visits.

wall was demolished. The result is a vast terrace bathed in sunlight and affording panoramic views across the river.

Don't leave without visiting the palatial *écuries* (stables) created by the Broglies for their beloved horses, and whose fully stocked tack room is curiously atmospheric. Dominating the buildings is an immense bastion-like tower looking like a classic piece of English Arts and Crafts architecture. In fact it began life as the kiln of a pottery and glass works which stood on the site, and was spared demolition to serve as an indoor pony training school. Perhaps unsurprisingly, the family fortunes eventually declined, and in 1938 the estate passed into state ownership (now the Region Centre).

Chaumont offers something for just about everyone (including wheelchair-users) and its two restaurants are outstanding, offering inspired, wholesome menus in a choice of settings; dine in style in an elegant marquee or less formally beneath tall, mature lime trees. There's also a sandwich bar for smaller budgets. In its additional role as Centre d'Arts et de Nature the Domaine is adding an experimental farm-style *potager* (vegetable garden), hosts open-air film festivals inspired by nature (Jardin d'Images) and will be welcoming and encouraging fresh artistic talents. But the underlying spirit remains undiluted, as you'll discover during Les Nocturnes – evenings when the chateau is entirely candlelit, or when the festival display gardens are transformed by thousands of coloured LED lights.

Montrichard

Museum and Donjon entrance on Grand Degré Ste Croix, T02 54 32 05 10, officetourisme-montrichard.com. Apr-Sep daily times vary. €5, €3 7-12 years.

Seen from across the river Cher on a sunny day, the town of Montrichard (whose 't' is pronounced) looks perky and contented, as if refusing to be dominated by the blockhouse-like donjon of its forlorn, ruined chateau. Cross the ancient multi-arched bridge, continue past a time-warp saddler's workshop and you'll enter a square shaded by a huddle of billowing lime trees. A seat beneath one of the pastel parasols of of the various bar-restaurants is the perfect spot in which to relax with a cool drink and contemplate the medieval half-timbered façades just across the square. You can thank the sturdy *clocher* (church tower) rising behind the most colourful pair for having protected them when part of the chateau walls collapsed in 1753. The Eglise Ste-Croix itself (in which Jeanne de Valois married the future King Louis in 1476) fared less well, only its Romanesque

Tip...

No chocolate lover should leave Montrichard without having visited *Aux Délices*, run by master *pâtissier/chocolatier* Serge Granger in rue National. The local specialities are *les Malices du Loup* ('mischief' or 'cunning' of the wolf), which combine almonds, hazelnuts and honey with a tang of orange and anise.

La Cave des Roches.

façade being spared. Consequently, it's today less visited than the nearby museum of local archeological finds and the chateau ruins, from whose elevated site you can enjoy sweeping views of the river and surrounding landscapes. Each summer the site hosts ambitious medieval re-enactments, whose spectacle value is heightened at nightfall. Stop at the tourist office, in the 16th-century Maison de l'Ave Maria, for a town map with walking tour.

La Cave des Roches

Bourré (4 km east of Montrichard).
See page 144 for opening times and other details.

On the surface, Bourré (whose name means 'drunken' in French) looks like a typical riverside village, but for centuries it provided the beautiful, pale limestone known as *tuffeau*, which was used in the construction of many of the great chateaux. In fact, everybody wanted it and the quarries, pushing deep underground, happily obliged, calling a halt only when hundreds of kilometres of

galleries were beginning to cause real concerns for the safety of the village they had undermined. The site found a new lease of life, though, when dark conditions and consistently low temperatures of around 12°C proved ideal for large-scale mushroom production. You can see for yourself by taking a guided tour, although arguably more compelling is the chance to visit silent, long-abandoned galleries. Here, with upwards of 50 m of stone poised unnervingly above your head, you'll learn about the techniques and tough working conditions of the quarrymen, before moving on to La Ville Souterraine – billed as an underground town in stone. This unlikely creation is being systematically sculpted *in situ* by a dedicated young stonemason in his spare time, for the benefit of future generations. Tours are conducted in both French and English, which slows things down considerably, but your patience will be rewarded with the kind of insight that enables you to see things on the surface very differently. Less surprisingly, while you're here you can purchase mushrooms direct from the producer.

Listings
Sleeping

Blois

Hotel Mercure €€€
28 quai St Jean, T02 54 56 66 66, mercure.com.
Modern and spacious rooms in a riverside location a few steps from the town centre. Parking (payable), Wi-Fi, swimming pool and hotel restaurant make this hotel comfortable and convenient, if slightly lacking in charm.

Le Médicis €€€
2 allée François 1er, T02 54 43 94 04, le-medicis.com.
Closed Jan.
Well-known for its gastronomic restaurant, the hotel, about 1 km from the centre of town, has fully modernized sound-proof and air-conditioned bedrooms. Decorated in warm colours with cushions and throws, the accommodation, which includes family rooms and suites, has a welcoming, cosy feel throughout. Free parking and Wi-Fi.

Anne de Bretagne €€
31 av Jean Laigret, T02 54 78 05 38, annedebretagne.free.fr.
Closed Dec-Feb.
Situated on a tree-lined square close to the chateau and a 5-min walk from Blois centre. The rooms are rather basically furnished, but refreshed with colourful wallpapers and fabrics. Some underground parking and a secure area for bicycles,

free Wi-Fi. The rail station is within 150 m.

Côté Loire €€
2 place de la Grève, T02 54 78 07 86, coteloire.com.
Closed Jan.
A small 16th-century former coaching inn in a quiet spot on the right bank of the Loire. The bedrooms are attractive, bright and airy. Those at the front have river views, while at the rear is a charming courtyard. There's also a secure place for bikes. Its popular restaurant (open Tue-Sat) serves different dishes every day, with ingredients fresh from the market.

Hotel Le Monarque €€
61 rue Porte Chartraine, T02 54 78 02 35, annedebretagne.free.fr.
Closed end Dec-Jan.
A welcoming hotel with cheerfully decorated rooms and a restaurant flooded with light. Situated at the top of the town, there's a pleasant walk down through pedestrianized shopping streets to the centre. Free Wi-Fi, limited car parking plus a secure area for bicycles.

Campsite
Camping Francois 1er
Base de Loisirs Rive Gauche, Vineuil (4 km from Blois centre, direction Chambord on D951), T02 54 78 82 05, camping-francois-1er.com.
Jun-Oct.

Spread around 40 ha of riverbank, this exceptional campsite has plenty of shady pitches and easy access to Blois and Chambord. A good base for cyclists.

Chambord

Hôtel de la Bonnheure €€
9 rue René Masson, Bracieux (between Cheverny and Chambord), T02 54 46 41 57, hoteldelabonnheur.com.
You'll receive a warm welcome at this rural hotel with typical decorative brick features and cosy dining room with exposed beams. Situated in the heart of the village of Bracieux, it's set in its own charming gardens and has quiet rooms overlooking the grounds. Breakfast includes a speciality egg served in a small pot. Secure bike park and enclosed private parking.

Hotel and Restaurant Grand Saint-Michel €€
Place St-Louis, T02 54 20 31 31, saintmichel-chambord.com.
The only hotel in Chambord, and where you'll virtually have the chateau and the grounds to yourself after the visitors have gone. Some rooms overlook the chateau. Ground-floor room available for disabled guests. Breakfast on the terrace with that fabulous view, weather permitting.

La Maison d'à Côte €€
25 route de Chambord,
Montlivault, T02 54 20 62 30,
lamaisondacote.fr.
Closed 15-30 Nov and
28 Dec-15 Jan.
Conveniently situated between
Blois and Chambord, this hotel
and restaurant extends a warm
and friendly welcome to guests.
The stylish and comfortable
contemporary-chic rooms are
for one or two people and all
have a/c and free Wi-Fi.

Le Saint Florent €
14 rue de la Chabardière,
Mont-Près-Chambord,
T02 54 70 81 00,
hotel-saint-florent.com.
A friendly hotel a 10-minute
drive from the heart of Blois and
close to the chateaux of
Chambord and Cheverny. The
rooms are comfortable and
homely with good bathrooms,
though they are now a little
dated. Rear bedrooms are
quieter. Free Wi-Fi on request.
Evening meals can be taken in
the restaurant (closed Mon) to
the rear of the hotel.

Cheverny

Domaine Le Clos Bigot €€
Le Clos Dussons, Chitenay
(12 km south of Blois), T02 54
44 21 28, gites-cheverny.com.
Peaceful accommodation in
Sologne-style buildings set
around a courtyard. There's a

selection of lovely rooms
including a suite on two floors
in a former *pigeonnier*. Breakfast
includes home-made jams and
cakes – a good start for a day
exploring all the remarkable
sites nearby.

Les Chambres Vertes €€
Le Clos de la Chartrie, Cormeray
(13 km south of Blois), T02 54 20
24 95, chambresvertes.net.
An eco-friendly bed and
breakfast with spacious and
simply furnished rooms, with
one twin room specially adapted
for disabled visitors. There is a
bright and welcoming common
room (with internet access)
which leads onto the terrace
and garden. Evening meals
are served five days a week
(€24 including wine, reservations
required) and are made with
organic, locally sourced
ingredients. Vegetarian meals
are available on request.

Domaine de la Rabouillère €€
Chemin de Marçon, Contres
(21 km south of Blois), T02 54 79
05 14, larabouillere.com.
Closed Nov-Easter.
Set within a wooded estate with
its own lake, this Sologne-style
farmhouse offers delightful
rooms in the main house or a
pretty cottage for families. All
rooms are immaculately
furnished, some have fine views
over the parkland and there is a
ground-floor suite with easy
access. Free Wi-Fi.

Chaumont

Le Clot du Verêt €
9 Route des Vallée,
Bourré, T02 54 32 07 58,
lestabourelles-leveret.com.
In the troglodyte village of
Bourré on the northern banks of
the River Cher, the Domaine des
Tabourelles wine estate offers
very pleasant rooms in an
18th-century home which is full
of character. Guests have their
own entrance into a common
area which includes a handy
small kitchen. There is a family
suite and two doubles, one with
a small terrace and another with
views over the Cher valley.

Château de Chissay €€€
1-3 place Paul Boncour,
Chissay-en-Touraine, T02 54 32
32 01, chateaudechissay.com.
Closed Nov-Apr.
A beautiful chateau hotel in pale
tuffeau stone not far from
Montrichard and convenient for
many magnificent sites. Some of
the rooms are very grand, others
not so – but whatever the
budget, everyone can enjoy the
extensive grounds, outdoor pool
and dine in style.

Eating & drinking

Au Rendez-vous des Pêcheurs €€€
27 rue du Foix, T02 54 74 67 48, rendezvousdespecheurs.com.
Daily except Sun and Mon lunch.
Chef Christophe Cosme established this bistro-style dining room in 1999 and has become a star of local cuisine. He expresses the Loire in his menus using seasonal vegetables and locally caught river fish such as *sandre* (pike-perch). Menus are from €30, although the menu *découverte* at €69 (per table only) best illustrates what modern Loire cuisine has to offer.

Les Banquettes Rouges €€€
16 rue des Trois Marchands, T02 54 78 74 92.
Daily lunch and evenings. Closed for 10 days in Jun and in Aug.
A mouth-watering culinary journey through French tradition, with portions to satisfy the biggest appetites. Bistro-style dining room with welcoming staff.

Le Bouchon Lyonnais €€€
25 rue des Violettes (just off place Louis XII towards rue St Lubin), T02-54 74 12 87, aubouchonlyonnais.com.
Mon-Sat.
Immerse yourself in a huge and very traditional Lyonnais menu – not for the fainthearted. There's a set menu for €20, although many dishes have supplements (and the wine is expensive).

Le Castelet €€
40 rue St Lubin, T02 54 74 66 09, le-castelet.eu.
Closed Wed and Sun, otherwise open 1200-1345 and 1900-2145.
Traditional menus served in a cosy, characterful dining room. Expect to find fresh and seasonal produce, with the opportunity to savour particular local *charcuterie* or river fish with an appropriate wine for around €16. There's also a vegetarian option.

Character dining in the backstreets of Blois.

Le Duc de Guise €€

13-15 place Louis XII,
T02 54 78 22 39.
Apr-Aug daily, Sep-Mar
closed Sun and Mon evenings.
A popular Italian restaurant
serving a good range of pizza
and pasta dishes. Efficient and
friendly service from the staff,
regardless of how busy they are.
The upper terrace and dining
room are quieter than those on
the square.

Cafés & bars
Ben's Blues Bar

L'Orangerie, 41 rue St Lubin,
bensbluesbar.com.
Thu-Tue 1830-0200.
Live blues and occasional gypsy,
manouche-style jazz at this small,
atmospheric venue in the old
quarter of Blois.

Le Clipper

13-15 place Louis XII,
T02 54 78 22 39.
Daily 0900-0100, closed public
holidays, 24-26 Dec and
31 Dec-2 Jan.
Le Clipper bar has comfortable
covered seating in the shade
of the trees in the square. At
night it's a popular meeting
place and serves as the
street-level dining area for the
Duc de Guise Italian restaurant.

Velvet Jazz Lounge

15 bis rue Haute, T02 54 78 36 32,
velvet-jazz-lounge.com.
Tue-Sat 1700-0200.

Relaxed country style in leafy La Borne.

Situated at the foot of the Denis
Papin steps; relax in the velvety
interior and enjoy some smooth
jazz sounds.

Romorantin-Lanthenay

Grand Hôtel du Lion d'Or €€€

69 rue Georges Clemenceau,
T02 54 94 15 15, hotel-liondor.fr.
Daily except Tue lunch, closed
mid-Feb to end Mar.

A Michelin-starred restaurant
within a beautiful 16th-century
Renaissance building which is
now an unashamedly luxurious
hotel in the centre of town.
Chef Didier Clement is
celebrated for his creation of
harmonious flavours in dishes
which are a feast for both the
eye and the palate.

Entertainment

Festivals & events

Tous sur le Pont
T02 54 58 84 56,
toussurlepont.com.
Mid-Jul.

An established summer festival of lively French *chanson*-style music held over five days. Major pop/rock concerts are staged in the courtyard of the Château Royal supported by free live events in Blois centre, plus dancing and fireworks.

Château Royal de Blois
Son-et-Lumière
T02 54 90 33 33,
chateaudeblois.fr.
Presentations every evening from 11 Apr-30 Sep except 21 Jun. English version every Wed. €7, €5.50 concessions, €4 6-17 years; combined ticket with chateau €13. Audience arrives 30 mins before the show, which starts at 2200 (2230 Jun-Jul).

This 45-minute performance set to an original text and musical score tells the story of the loves, tragedies and mysteries of the chateau.

Chambord *Son et Lumière*
T02 54 50 40 00, chambord.org.
Every evening at nightfall from Jun-Sep. €12, €10 concessions, combined ticket with chateau €17. Bookings at the central ticket office.

A nocturnal sound and light show (about 50 mins duration) projected onto the façade of the chateau.

Festival spirit, Domaine de Chaumont-sur-Loire.

Festival des Jardins, Domaine de Chaumont-sur-Loire
T02 54 20 99 22,
domaine-chaumont.fr.
Daily end Apr-end Aug 1000-2030, Sep 1000-2000, 1 Oct to mid-Oct 1000-1930 (last entry 90 mins before closing). Illuminated visits 2200-2400 Fri-Sat evenings in Jun, every evening (except Fri) Jul-Aug. €9.50, €7 concessions, €4 children (6-11), free under 6s and for disabled visitors and their helper companion.

Donjon de Montrichard
T02 54 32 05 10, officetourisme-montrichard.com.
Jul-Aug.

A company of professional actors, experts in medieval sword fighting and local amateurs stage daily entertainment ('Amaury, Son of the Dragon' in 2009) from 25 Jul to mid-Aug at 1600. €8, €5 children (6-12). At night during the same period (but not every day) a different show ('1249 – Fairies and Knights' in 2009) is performed in a magical setting. €15, €8 children (6-12). Details and bookings from the tourist office in Montrichard.

Journées Gastronomiques de Sologne
Romorantin-Lanthenay, information from the tourist office T02 54 76 43 89, romorantin.fr/jgs/.
€7 1 day, €9 2 days.

This massive food and wine fair takes place on the last weekend in October. There's a different theme each year, featuring a region or country, but pride of place goes to the enormous range and quality of Sologne and Loire Valley regional produce.

Shopping

Blois

Food & drink
La Caf Thé
*14 rue du Commerce,
T02 54 74 50 65, lacafthe.fr.*
Tue–Sat 0830-1300 and
1400-1900.
The smell of freshly roasted
coffee and shelves full of
colourful tea caddies draws you
into this fascinating emporium
packed with everything you
could desire for a small moment
of caffeinated pleasure.

Comtesse du Barry
*5 rue St-Martin (opposite
the steps just off Place St Louis
XII), T02 54 78 80 00,
comtessedubarry.com.*
Mon 1430-1900, Tue-Sat
0930-1230 and 1430-1930.
One of a chain of stores, but a
good place to buy a little
souvenir from a wide choice of
fine foods and regional produce.

Max Vauché
*51 rue du Commerce,
T02 54 78 23 55,
maxvauche-chocolatier.com.*
Tue-Fri 0930-1200 and
1400-1900, Sat 0900-1230
and 1400-1900.

The beautiful window display
will stop you in your tracks. You
can also go on a guided tour of
the Max Vauché chocolaterie in
Bracieux (see page 146), but if
all you want to do is buy and
enjoy it, come here.

Le Théâtre du Pain
*26 rue Trois Marchands,
T02 54 78 05 91.*
Fresh bread baked in the shop,
all flavours of macaroons and
fantastic selection of sandwiches
and tarts to take away. Ideal for a
picnic lunch or sandwich.

Spoilt for choice in La Caf Thé, Blois.

Activities & tours

Balloon flights
France Montgolfières
T02 54 32 20 48,
franceballoons.com.
Hot-air balloon flights from eight locations and offering various different packages.

Cycle routes & hire
Cyclists following the *Loire à Vélo* cycle path (for full details, see page 69) have the option of two routes between Candé-sur-Beuvron and St-Dyé-sur-Loire passing through the forests around Chambord, or through Blois and along the Loire river (loire-a-velo.fr). If based in the Blois and Sologne area take advantage of 300 km of possible bike rides and 11 themed circuits on the *Châteaux à Vélo* routes around Chambord, Blois and Cheverny (chateauxavelo.com). Below are two bike hire places in

Blois but there are other hire shops in Bracieux, Chambord and Cour-Cheverny.

Rando Vélo
29 rue du Puits Neuf, Blois,
T02 54 78 62 52, randovelo.fr.
Apr-Oct Mon-Fri (open weekends on request).
Hire and repair of bikes, plus wide choice of self-guided itineraries or ready-made packages. Prices start from €57 per adult per week.

Bike in Blois
3 av Jean Laigret, Blois,
T02 54 56 07 73.
Daily Apr-1 Oct.
Hire of road or mountain bikes and accessories, plus a large selection of itineraries. Large number of pick-up and drop-off sites along the Loire.

Food & drink
Chocolaterie Max Vauché
22 les Jardins du Moulin,
Bracieux, T02 54 46 07 96,
maxvauche-chocolatier.com.
1 Jul-31 Aug Mon-Sat 1000-1230 and 1400-1900 (guided tours 1030, 1530 and 1630, 1430 in English), 1 Sep-30 Jun Tue-Sat 1000-1230 and 1400-1900 (guided tour 1430), all year round Sun 1500-1830 (guided tours 1530 and 1630). €5. Disabled access.
On entering the factory you will be given a sample to taste before moving on to discover the world of chocolate-making from the

raw cocoa to the final product. There's also a boutique.

La Cave des Roches
40 route des Roches, Bourré,
about 3 km from Montrichard
signed left off the D176, T02 54 32
95 33, le-champignon.com.
Cave Champignonnière or Carrière and the Ville Souterraine open daily mid-Mar to Sep with hourly guided tours Jul-Aug (website gives details of visiting times throughout the year).
€6.50 or €11 duo visit, €4.50 children (7-14) or €6 duo visit.
Visit a former *tuffeau* quarry and incredible underground town or the mushroom cellars where rare varieties of fungi are grown in the clean, subterranean atmosphere. Either of the guided tours takes about an hour and it's possible to do both on a combined ticket. There's a shop selling varieties of mushrooms and related speciality products and a restaurant with terrace open at lunchtimes (May-Sep) to savour simple mushroom-based dishes.

Guided tours
Boat Rides
Departures from Port de la
Creusille, rive gauche (left
bank), Blois, T02 54 90 41 41
(tourist office).
May, Jun and Sep Tue-Sat 1500 and 1615, Jul-Aug Mon-Sat 1100, 1500 and 1615.
€9, €7 under 12s.

Test of willpower, Blois.

Non-polluting transport, Blois.

Transport

Horse-Drawn Carriage Rides
Place du Château, Blois,
T02 54 90 41 41 (tourist office).
Tours run Apr-Jun and
Sep 1400-1800, Jul-Aug
1100-1900. €6, €4 children
(2-12). Disabled access.
Departing from the chateau
entrance, for a 25-min circuit of
the town (with commentary) in a
covered horse-drawn carriage.

Wellbeing
Spa du Domaine des
Thomeaux
12 rue des Thomeaux, Mosnes
(between Chaumont-sur-Loire
and Amboise), T02 47 30 40 14,
domainedesthomeaux.fr.
The calm and relaxing Thomeaux
spa, health and beauty centre

offers hammam, sauna, indoor
swimming pool, hydro-massage
bath, body and facial treatments
and body sculpting massages
from around the world.
See website for details of
wellbeing packages.

Wildlife
Zooparc de Beauval
St-Aignan, T02 54 75 74 26,
zoobeauval.com.
Open all year.
€20, €14 children (3-10).
The largest collection of its
kind in France with over 4000
animals in 22 ha. See lions and
tigers, primates, koala bears,
a large tropical aquarium
and vast tropical glasshouses
and botanical trail.

Blois

Bus
A bus journey costs €1.10 for up
to an hour. Pay the driver as you
board the bus (try to have the
correct change) or purchase *un
carnet de dix voyages* (a book of
10 tickets, €8.90) from POINT BUS
on place Victor Hugo, or from
newsagents around the town.
You can see all the routes on the
website, with bus stops,
timetables and where to buy
your ticket books.

TLC buses, T02 54 58 55 55,
transports-du-loir-et-cher.com,
offer a 'Circuit Châteaux' with
three services departing daily
from Blois Gare SNCF (train
station) from 11 Apr to 30 Sep.
There is a single tariff for any
journey (€12.10, €9.70 under 12s,
students and over 60s). You'll also
receive a discounted entry to the
chateaux on production of your
ticket. Purchase tickets at the
tourist office or on the bus.

Train
You can travel east by train from
Blois to Beaugency (20 mins),
Meung-sur-Loire (30 mins) and
Orléans (45 mins), or west to
Tours (30 mins), Saumur (60 mins)
or on to Angers and Nantes.
Most services will carry bikes
free of charge.

Contents

The Touraine

Rennaissance style, Château de Chenonceau.

Introduction

The medieval world looked on in startled awe as the French taste for elegant country living found its ultimate expression here, in the heart of the Valley of Kings, in a string of Renaissance chateaux, each seemingly more extravagant than its predecessor. If anything, the passage of time has only heightened their beauty. But look beyond international celebrities like Amboise, Azay-le-Rideau and Chenonceau and you'll find lesser-known sights like the graceful Chanteloup Pagoda, a section of Gallo-Roman aqueduct near Luynes, a rediscovered trogolodytic farming valley at Les Goupillières, the Musée Maurice Dufresne's fantastic mechanical collection and an entire town constructed by Cardinal Richelieu, not to mention the perfect country village of Montrésor. Along the way lie renowned AOC wine producers, fruit and mushroom farmers, market gardeners, river fishermen and countless talented chefs who between them will give you a real taste for Touraine. There's atmosphere, too, in historic chateau towns like Chinon, Langeais and Loches – and real big-city buzz when you need it in Tours, which also has its own historic heart for you to explore. And when you eventually need to stop and smell the roses you'll have Villandry's world-famous Renaissance gardens, and La Chatonnière's more eclectic Jardins Remarquables.

Summer idyll, Parc du Domaine de Richelieu.

What to see in...

...one day

Start in Tours at the **Cathédral St-Gatien** as the morning sun enters the interior, then stroll through the heart of Vieux Tours to visit the market in **Les Halles,** reaching **place Plumereau** in time to find a café table for lunch. Continue exploring with some antiques browsing in **rue de la Scellerie,** or perhaps visiting one of the huge flower markets beneath the ancient plane trees of **boulevard Béranger.** Head just out of town to visit the **Prieuré de St-Cosme.** In the evening stroll down **rue Colbert** for an aperitif and dinner.

...a weekend

Next morning drive past **Vouvray,** stopping for a *dégustation* at a wine producer, en route for **Amboise.** Visit Leonardo da Vinci's last home in **Clos Lucé** then dine al fresco in the terrace crêperie. After lunch, visit the nearby **Château Royal,** then explore the narrow streets of the old town. Visit the **Bigot Chocolaterie** for beautiful handmade chocolates then head a few kilometres out of town to climb to the summit of the **Pagode de Chanteloup** for fabulous sunset views.

Amboise

Amboise gets its fair share of road traffic but its buzz and sheer charisma are irresistible; having long been a halt for pilgrims on the route to Santiago de Compostela, the place knows how to make visitors feel welcome. The chateau rises above the old town like a slumbering giant from the rocky promontory which in earliest times made it an obvious place for settlement. During the 11th century Comte d'Anjou Foulques Nerra (see page 27) built the first stone fortress here, but the effect today is more gracious than threatening, thanks to the chateau's transformation into a Renaissance-style royal pleasure palace during the reigns of Louis XII and François I. For maximum effect, see it from across the river at sunset, or simply take a seat at your preferred bar on place Michel Debre and admire the closer view – an option which adds a sense of drama, courtesy of the vast stone walls which rise almost sheer from the square to the chateau terraces. Projecting from them on a tall pillar of stone is an exquisite Gothic chapel in which Leonardo da Vinci lies buried. A few minutes' walk will bring you to his last home at Clos Lucé.

Château Royal d'Amboise.

Essentials

❷ **Getting around** Amboise itself is small enough to visit on foot and it's a pleasure to wander through its narrow streets and stroll along the embankment. If using public transport, the rail station is a short distance from the town on the north bank. Cyclists will find plenty of secure places to leave their bikes while visiting the town.

❷ **Bus station** Buses to Amboise run from Tours (about 45 mins) on a regular service (except on Sun).

❷ **Train station** Gare SNCF, boulevard Gambetta (on north bank). There is a good service to stations throughout the Loire Valley and you can travel direct to Paris in just over two hours.

❷ **ATMs** Near the bridge on quai du Général de Gaulle and on rue Nationale.

⊕ **Hospital** Centre Hospitalier Intercommunal, Amboise–Château-Renault, rue des Ursulines, T02 423 33 33.

✚ **Pharmacy** Pharmacie Centrale, 30 rue Nationale, T02 47 57 09 04.

➔ **Post office** 20 quai du Général de Gaulle, T02 47 30 65 00.

❶ **Tourist information office** Quai du Général de Gaulle, T02 47 57 09 28, amboise-valdeloire.com.

Château Royal d'Amboise

Access on rue Victor Hugo, T08 20 20 50 50 (€0.09/min), chateau-amboise.com. Daily from 0900 all year (except 25 Dec and 1 Jan), closing times vary, closed lunchtimes in winter. €9.50 (night visit €6.50), €6 children (7-14) and disabled. Additional €4.50 per person to access underground passageways and towers. When leaving the chateau, take the route via the Heurtault Tower if possible. Starlit Stroll *son et lumière* shows every Friday Jul (2200) and Aug (2230). €6.50, €5 students and children.

Shallow steps set against the western ramparts take you through a dark archway to the visitor ticketing area. You'll emerge beside the inevitable gift shop, and climb to a grassy plateau around which lie the remains of the original chateau buildings. The visit begins in the Gothic **Chapelle St-Hubert**, dedicated to the patron saint of hunting (hence the vivid scene carved above the doorway and copper antlers incorporated into the spire). The royal chapel sits, like its predecessor created by Louis XI, on a vast pillar of stone clinging dramatically to the ramparts, and is breathtakingly beautiful inside; note the delicate snowflake-like

The Château Royal d'Amboise offers elevated views of the town and the Loire.

central bosses adorning the complex vaulting. In the tiny south transept is the simple tomb of Leonardo da Vinci (see page 156).

Continue along the ramparts to the **Tour des Garçonnets** for panoramic views of the town and river. The large building nearby was begun by Charles VIII in French Gothic style and enlarged by Louis XII and François I, who added a new Italianate Renaissance wing. Inside is a primary guardroom displaying 16th-century armour and weaponry, followed by the **Promenoir des Gardes**, a vaulted open gallery overlooking the Loire, whose stonework bears traces of much later conflicts. Next comes the **Salle des Gardes Nobles**, protecting the royal apartments on the floor above. The room displays 16th-century armour plus an early mariner's chest. Creature comforts improve in the **Salle des Tambourineurs** (Drummers' Room), which contains a Renaissance table, a Charles VIII chest plus the throne of Cardinal Georges d'Amboise, who conducted the marriage of Charles VIII and Anne de Bretagne. Floor tiles feature *fleurs-de-lys*, and a 16th-century Flemish tapestry depicts Alexander the Great. The architectural showpiece, though, is the **Salle du Conseille** (council chamber), whose pink brickwork complements stone features including ornate Renaissance fireplaces and lightweight rib vaulting. The capitals of the slender piers depict hunting scenes plus grape-laden vines being filched by animals and birds.

Renaissance rooms begin with the **Salle de l'Echanson** (Cupbearer's Room) used for court banquets conducted around large Italian-style tables. Notice the large 17th-century Aubusson tapestries. Next is Henri II's bedchamber with a suitably regal four-poster bed, a false-bottomed jewel chest and 16th and 17th-century Belgian tapestries. The following **Antichambre de la Cordelière** has a Renaissance fireplace bearing a royal crest above decorative ropework of the Ordre de St-Michel, founded at Amboise in 1469 by Louis XI. The mood changes in the apartments of King Philippe I, displaying fine family portraits amid the vibrant colours of the mid-19th century.

After leaving the apartments you can stand on the roof of the mighty **Tour des Minimes**, 40 m or so above the river. The tower's dark secret is revealed when you peer through the central iron grille or descend a staircase to discover a huge spiral ramp conceived by Charles VII's military engineers to permit cavalry and carriages to reach the chateau terraces. Another tower just like it was created on the opposite side of the plateau, providing a (relatively) safe descent. Between the two lie the Loire Valley's very first Renaissance garden (the Terrasse de Naples) and a contemporary Tuscan-style garden planted with cypresses, muscat vines and countless clipped box spheres. Above is the **Porte des Lions** and a raised terrace overlooking defensive ditches created by the Romans.

Make your exit via the ticket area, or (for a more climactic experience) the spiral ramp of the dimly lit **Tour Heurtault**, accessible from the gift shop.

The Italianate gardens.

Tip...

A *Pass Châteaux* gives reductions on entry to a variety of attractions, eg a four-chateaux pass including Amboise, Clos Lucé, Chenonceau and Chambord for €38 (a saving of only €3 but it's valid for a year and you won't have to queue to get into the attractions). You can buy them from tourist offices or in advance online at amboise-valdeloire.com.

Château du Clos Lucé & Parc Leonardo da Vinci

2 rue du Clos Lucé, T02 47 57 55 78, vinci-closluce.com.
Daily (except 25 Dec and 1 Jan) Jan 1000-1800, Feb-Jun 0900-1900, Jul-Aug 0900-2000, Sep-Oct 0900-1900, Nov-Dec 0900-1800. Chateau and park (1 Mar to mid-Nov) €12.50, €9.50 concessions, €7 6-15 years, €32 family ticket (2 adults and up to 2 children). Château only (mid-Nov to 28 Feb) €9.50, €7 concession, €6 children, family ticket from €25, under 6s and disabled visitors free.

A short walk from the heart of Amboise lies Clos Lucé, the 15th-century brick and limestone *manoir* (mansion) in which Leonardo da Vinci spent his final years as a guest of François I. The visit begins with a steep ascent up a narrow spiral staircase to his **bedroom**, whose richly carved dark oak furnishings include a grand four-poster bed. Next are the **kitchen** in which his vegetarian meals were prepared, the **study** where he worked on refining his inventions, plus several Renaissance-style rooms hung with vast Aubusson tapestries. Numerous framed quotes from his writings give valuable insight into this remarkable man, who no doubt enjoyed gazing from the Italianate loggia connecting the upper rooms.

From here descend to the Gothic **chapel**, whose vaults feature frescoes by his companion and pupil Francesco di Melzi, then to the large **cellar rooms**. A museum in themselves, they contain scale models of his most important inventions, bilingual information panels plus the entrance to a mysterious tunnel believed to have once been connected to the Château d'Amboise.

Leonardo also apparently loved observing nature during walks around the beautiful private **parkland**, a pleasure which you can share. You can also see giant canvasses of his works and full-size replicas of his inventions. A terrace overlooking the park has an exquisite formal Renaissance garden with shaded tables for relaxed *crêperie* dining.

A visit to Clos Lucé is an education.

The restored pagoda and its park give a tantalizing glimpse of how things were.

La Pagode de Chanteloup

3 km south of Amboise direction D31 Bléré/Loches,
T02 47 57 20 97, pagode-chanteloup.com.
Apr-Jun and Sep daily from 1000 (closing times
vary), Jul-Aug daily 0930-1930, Oct to mid-Nov
weekends and bank holidays 1000-1200 and
1400-1700. €8, €7 students, €6 children (7-15)
and disabled, €25 family ticket (2 adults and up
to 6 children), under 7s free. Last entry 1 hr
before closing, guided visits by arrangement.

Glimpsed from the far end of a broad, tree-lined
avenue, the pagoda's romantic coyness is
irresistible. Give in to temptation and, a few
minutes later, you'll discover that it sits beside a
huge, semi-circular lake bounded by the slightly
melancholy remains of once-grandiose
landscaped parkland laid out in 1762. The pagoda
was constructed in 1775, and while there are
arguably more elegant structures, it's not short on

period charm and rises (with a hint of a Pisa-esque
lean) through seven storeys to an impressive 44 m,
giving it real presence in the landscape. It also
simply begs to be climbed, which you can do if you
have a cool head for heights – you'll need it when
you reach the topmost slender ironwork parapet.
The views, though, are sensational, taking in the
lake and 4000 ha of surrounding forest. On the way
down you can compare what you've seen with a
display of archive material, including the
photographs of the heroic restoration work carried
out in 1909-1910 which saved the pagoda from
certain collapse.

If you'd like to know more, you'll find a small
museum dedicated to the estate in a nearby
gatehouse well worth visiting. Set beside the lake
are a Chinese garden and a collection of traditional
games, a good quality gift shop and a café with
parasol-shaded tables.

Château de Chenonceau

However many pictures you've seen, nothing comes close to seeing for yourself this exquisite chateau reflected in the waters of the River Cher. Adding to the effect are not one but two extravagant Renaissance gardens conceived on the banks of the River Cher by two powerful women. To the left, lawned *parterres* and swirling filigree plantings of Santolina radiate from a central fountain in the immense garden of Henri II's mistress Diane de Poitiers. In 1533 the King married Catherine de' Medici who, upon his sudden death in 1559, forced her rival to leave Chenonceau for Chaumont (see page 135). Her own garden, on your right, is more intimate but just as elegant with its box topiary, standard roses and well over a thousand lavender plants laid out around a large fountain. The estate also preserves its 18th-century farm and the *potager* (kitchen garden) which supplied fresh vegetables for the chateau.

A picture of serenity, mirrored in the waters of the Cher.

Chenonceaux

34 km southeast of Tours, T02 47 23 90 07, chenonceau.com.
You can travel from Tours to Chenonceaux by train (25 mins). The rail station is just 50 m from the entrance. Daily though opening times vary. €10, €8 children and students. Audio guide €4. Arrive early during peak periods to avoid overcrowding inside the chateau. However, if you're keen to see the gardens at their best, visit them in late afternoon, when the light softens. Romantic evening walks in the gardens accompanied by music, early evenings Jul and Aug. €5, under 7s free.

The chateau is reached via the two footbridges of a small island, where the lone **Tour des Marques** survives from the feudal chateau acquired by Thomas Bohier in 1513. Pressure of his duties as François I's Financial Receiver led him to leave

project managing of its Renaissance replacement to his wife Catherine Briçonnet, who oversaw the creation of the beautiful turreted main building and its chapel (built on the site of a former mill). The costs eventually proved ruinous, however, and when Bohier died in 1535 his son was forced by accumulated debts to relinquish the chateau to the Crown. Eight years later Henri II gave Chenonceau to Diane de Poitiers, who carried out a series of embellishments, including the multi-arched bridge across the river, which her successor Catherine de' Medici transformed by adding the celebrated Italianate gallery visible today.

Self-guided visits are unaffected by prolonged restoration works on the exterior of the chateau, and begin in the vaulted vestibule, whose curiously offset rib vaults date from 1515. On your left is the **Salle des Gardes**, whose pale stone walls are hung with large tapestries beneath an intricately decorated beamed ceiling. A magnificent doorway

> ## Tip...
> If you take a river cruise from Chisseaux, you'll pass beneath the arches of the chateau.

Chenonceau in reflective mood.

Detail of the monumental fireplace in Diane de Poitiers' bed-chamber.

leads to the Renaissance-Gothic chapel – notice the shell emblems where the peers meet the vault ribs, and the niches below them which doubtless once contained sculpted figures. Beyond the guardroom lies the **bedchamber of Diane de Poitiers**, complete with a huge, pure white fireplace now hung with a somewhat sinister-looking portrait of Catherine de' Medici. The imagery adorning her adjoining study is more uplifting, and includes a vast wall-hanging featuring exotic birds in a sea of verdure. Now comes the 60-m-long gallery, cunningly designed with window openings positioned above the load-bearing arches of Diane de Poitiers' bridge, alternating with deep niches set above its sturdy piers. A small wall plaque records the many casualties treated here during the First World War, when the gallery served as a hospital.

After the palatially decorated **bedroom occupied by François I**, climb the visibly Italian-influenced stone staircase to a light hallway extending the full width of the building and dedicated to Catherine Briçonnet. The **Chambre des Cinq Reines**, on the other hand, honours Catherine de' Medici's two daughters and three daughters-in-law, and is followed by her own equally sumptuous bedroom. Beyond it the **Cabinet d'Estampes** displays interesting early engravings of Chenonceau beneath a richly painted Florentine ceiling. After the capacious bedchambers of **César de Vendôme** and **Gabrielle d'Estrées** (son and daughter-in-law of King Henry IV) who acquired Chenonceau in 1624, the visit continues on the second floor, where another beautifully decorated hallway (this time in 19th-century taste) contrasts with the movingly funereal bedchamber of **Louise de Lorraine**, to which she retreated after her husband Henri III's assassination in 1589. Descend to the ground floor to see a room occupied by **Louis XIV**. Note the stirring portraits and a huge fireplace emblazoned with gilded salamander and ermine emblems before you plunge into the very different world of Chenonceau's vast kitchens.

After the visit you can recover on the café terrace of the nearby former stables, or dine in the elegant Orangerie Restaurant, tucked away beside the Jardin Vert behind them. Don't miss visiting the *potager* (kitchen gardens) and the preserved 18th-century estate farm.

Loches

Loches is a small town on the banks of the River Indre divided into two distinct parts by the ancient fortifications protecting its upper town, one the most important surviving examples of defensive medieval architecture in Europe. Much of the lower town also has a considerable air of antiquity, with weathered façades of pale stone beneath steeply pitched roofs of slates or terracotta tiles. Rearing 52 m skyward from amongst them is Touraine's only Renaissance belfry, the 16th-century Tour St-Antoine. A century older, but well-preserved and much less aloof, is the nearby Porte des Cordeliers, a fortified drawbridge gatehouse from the outermost of the three walls which once defended the town. Just across the River Indre lie attractive public gardens, where you can picnic on a shady bench while admiring unrivalled views of the chateau. Meanwhile, it's a very different world up on the plateau, where you'll discover the Logis Royal in which Joan of Arc met Charles VII in 1429 and convinced him to go to Reims to fulfil his destiny as King of France. At the opposite end of the plateau the monolithic Donjon de Loches provides a powerful reminder of a military complex founded during the 11th century by Comte d'Anjou Foulques Nerra.

Cité Royale de Loches & Collégiale St-Ours

Enter the old town through the mighty **Porte Picois**, a 15th-century gatehouse which you'll find off place du Blé. Beyond this medieval time-tunnel lies a cobbled square overlooked by the Renaissance **Hôtel de Ville** clinging to the Porte and bearing the salamander emblem of King François I. The gentle climb here continues as you turn right into rue du Château, where you'll pass the **Maison du Centaure** and **La Chancellerie**, whose 16th-century decoration includes Italianate friezes, humorous capitals and a large bas-relief of Hercules confronting the Centaur Nessus. Their delicacy only heightens the effect of the nearby 13th-century **Porte Royale**, whose immense scale injects real drama to the final entry into the *citadelle* or upper town.

Turning left brings you first to a charming small museum dedicated to the local 19th-century landscape artist Maurice-Etienne Lansyer. A little further on lies the **Eglise St-Ours**, a former collegiate church, whose – mercifully unique – feature is a pair of octagonal pyramids set between its main towers. The real interest lies within, however, starting in the porch with a section of a Gallo-Roman pillar whose carvings include fighting gladiators. Beside it a huge, richly sculpted Romanesque-meets-Gothic doorway retains some of its original rich colouring, while just inside in a side aisle you'll find the beautiful recumbent tomb figure of Charles VII's mistress Agnès Sorel.

Logis Royal

Entrance on rue Fossés St-Ours, T02 47 59 01 32, monuments-touraine.fr.
Daily (except Dec 25 and Jan 1) Apr-Sep 0900-1900, Nov-Mar 0930-1700.
The Logis Royal and Donjon are on a combined entry ticket. €7, €4.50 concessions, under 12s free. Free guided visits, advance booking recommended for groups or English language tours. Disabled access to the Logis Royal only.

Essentials

➊ Getting around You can stroll around Loches on foot and explore the medieval city. It's quite a steep climb up but cars can get as far as the entrance if necessary.

➋ Bus and train stations Gare SNCF and Gare Routière, place de la Gare. Public transport from Tours is mostly geared around getting young students in and out of the city and some daytime services only run during term time. Most TER services are actually buses, which stop outside the train station, not far from the town centre.

➌ ATM Rue Picois, in the centre of Loches.

⊕ Hospital Centre Hospitalier de Loches, off rue du Dr Martinais, T02 47 91 33 33, ch-loches.fr.

⊕ Pharmacy Pharmacie Bourget, 1 rue de Tours, T02 47 59 02 35 (near tourist office).

➎ Post office 7 rue Descartes, T02 47 91 87 20.

➊ Tourist information office Place de la Marne, T02 47 91 82 82, loches-tourainecotesud.com.

The 15th-century Porte des Cordeliers.

Son et lumière shows

❶ **Night of 1000 Fireworks** Over 2000 candles and a huge firework display light up the gardens at Château de Villandry. On two consecutive nights in early July.

❷ **Royal Nights** A magical fire dance and dramatized street tours around the historic royal city of Loches. Every Tuesday night during July and the first half of August.

❸ **Starlit Stroll** A contemporary and highly original sound and light creation at the Château Royal d'Amboise. Every Friday for most of July and August.

❹ **Evening Strolls** Romantic lighting and beautiful music create lots of atmosphere in the gardens at Chenonceau. Early evenings during July and August.

❺ **Midsummer Dreams and Lights** Visitors can wander freely and marvel at the beautiful light effects on both the chateau and gardens at Azay-le-Rideau. Every evening during July and August.

Not far beyond the Collégiale is the Logis Royal, or Royal Lodge. The original *Vieux Logis* dates from the 14th century, although its severe military Gothic aspect was softened a century or so later by the addition of larger windows similar to those of the Renaissance-flavoured remainder of the building. Inside the rooms are hung with Flemish tapestries and paintings, including a vibrant triptych of The Passion (c1485) attributed to Jean Fouquet of Tours. There's also a transcript of the trial of Joan of Arc, who met Charles VII in the Grande Salle in 1429 and convinced him to go to Reims to fulfil his destiny as King of France.

Le Donjon

The Donjon shares the admission ticket with the Logis-Royal (see details above).

For raw, no-frills military might, simply walk to the opposite end of the plateau, where the monolithic Donjon de Loches rises defiantly 36 m from the site of a once-powerful military complex founded during the 11th century by Comte d'Anjou

Foulques Nerra. The fact that it's now merely a hollow shell has an upside, in the form of steel mesh interior walkways which allow you to climb all the way to the summit for a free vertigo test. If this doesn't appeal, you can admire the venerable edifice while cooling off in the welcome shade of mature trees in the park-style area between the donjon and the ramparts.

Chartreuse & Corroirie du Liget

On the D760 between Loches and Montrésor, there is a small car park in front of the imposing gateway of the Chartreuse. The Corroirie is a little further on, to the left of a bend in a shallow valley. T06 80 43 38 75, corroirie.com.

The Chartreuse (charterhouse) sits in the heart of the Forêt de Loches and was founded as a Carthusian monastery in 1178 by Henry II, Plantagenet-in-penance for his part in the murder of Thomas Beckett. Although much damaged during the Revolution, what remains is impressive enough to give some idea of the former importance of the site. By 1360 its lands included 880 ha of pastures, vines and garden, plus a further 526 ha of forest and 43 ha of lakes. In 1361 during the Hundred Years' War the occupants were forced to flee via a previously dug underground passage to the nearby *corroirie* (leather tannerie), their secure place of refuge. Here they survived the siege and later added the fortifications visible today, including a classic feudal donjon-style gatehouse and drawbridge. The complex also includes a 10th-century mill.

In 1790 the post-Revolutionary National Assembly decreed that the Chartreuse estate should become public property and its possessions dispersed. The monks and fathers departed the following year. In 1837 the Chartreuse was purchased by a former Mayor of Loches, and remains in private hands, having undergone various campaigns of conservation. The exterior is visitable, although the process is somewhat informal – pass beneath the swallows nesting in the grandiose 18th-century gateway and look for a

The Tour Saint-Antoine fails to impress 19th-century poet Alfred de Vigny.

small sign beside the next gate inviting you to knock on a door and await the arrival of someone to greet you. It's worth persevering, as the setting is beautiful, and the charterhouse itself has all the grace and elegance of a good-size chateau.

Château & village of Montrésor

Rue Potocki, Montrésor (17 km east of Loches), T02 47 92 60 04, loches-tourainecotesud.com. Apr to mid-Nov 1000-1800 (1900 Jun-Sep), mid-Nov to Mar weekends and school holidays only. €7, concessions €4 chateau and park, disabled access to the park and ground floor only. Guided visits of the interior.

The archetypal French village of your dreams is presided over by a fairy-tale chateau originally constructed in the 11th century. It was substantially enlarged and rebuilt, however, by generations of French nobles who have either lived here or taken an interest in its strategic value. The present owners are descendants of Polish Count Xavier Branicki, whose extensive mid-19th-century restoration works added the present interior refinements, including both Italian and Polish works of art. Slumbering contentedly at its feet is officially one of the 'Most Beautiful Villages in France' – to see why follow an idyllic riverside walk

Vouvray AOC vineyards

Wine has been produced here since the fourth century AD, when the first vines were planted at the Monastery of Marmoutier. The Vouvray AOC (*Appellation d'Origine Contrôlé*) was defined in 1936 and today covers around 2000 ha, divided between 300 or so wine producers and eight villages. The only grape variety authorized is Chenin Blanc – also known locally as Pineau d'Anjou, Pineau de la Loire or simply 'Chenin'. The name is thought to derive from Mont-Chenin (now Monchenain), which lies below the rivers Loire and Cher.

known as *Les Balcons de l'Indrois* between lush meadows and the gently flowing Indrois river. It passes a restored early hydraulic ram installed by Count Branicki in 1856 to supply water to the chateau, and a traditional *lavoir* (communal washhouse) before crossing the river on an iron footbridge created by Eiffel and offering the definitive view of the chateau. Follow the route up to the plateau, where you'll discover the Collégiale St-Jean-Baptiste, a vision of pale limestone loveliness and founded around 1520 by Imbert de Batarnay, who lies with his wife and son in the nave of his largely Flamboyant Gothic creation.

You can learn more about Montrésor and key figures in its long history by climbing the massive

Leave the world behind on Montrésor's Balcons de l'Indrois riverside walk.

staircase to the *grenier* (upper storey) of the village centre's restored 17th-century timber-framed market hall known as La Halle des Cardeux. The old wool-carders' hall now contains a well-presented museum of local life (free admission).

Eglise Notre-Dame-et-St-Jean-Baptiste

Rue du Commerce, Vouvray (10 km downstream from Tours).

The cupola-topped *clocher* (bell-tower) rises high enough from its 11th-century base to be clearly visible from the celebrated vineyards of the adjacent plateau. Otherwise, though, the exterior of this modest parish church was probably far more arresting prior to the drastic 19th-century restoration and enlargement works which included walling-up the original entry portal. Beside the present doorway is a charming sculpted monument depicting two choirboys. The monument celebrates Charles Bordes (1863-1909), a prolific composer born in Vouvray who founded *La Schola Cantorum* to revive Gregorian and other early sacred choral music. Inside, the church feels dark at first, particularly in the two trogolodytic, slightly creepy chapels created beyond a north wall and constructed tight against the rock face. As your eyes adjust the beauty and complexity of the 13th- and 14th-century Gothic construction of the interior become clear, along with some interesting details. The pier capitals, for example, are sculpted with grapes and vine leaves, celebrating centuries of local wine production, and on the south wall is a large 14th-century memorial tablet to Johanna, wife of Renaut, Seigneur (Lord) of le Manoir du Plessis, beautifully carved in full period costume. There's an appealing irony in the fact that the model for a large early-20th-century painting of the Madonna was one Madame Santenac, a local mother of 11 children.

Organic wines from hand-picked grapes.

Eglise Notre-Dame-et-St-Jean-Baptiste.

Tours

At first sight Tours appears big, brash and in a world of its own, but penetrate the ancient heart and you'll see things very differently. This cultured city is the official home of definitive spoken French, and is a thriving language learning base. Its large student population also injects a vibrant café culture, which even extends to the banks of the Loire, beside the graceful Pont Wilson. And when the streets fill to bursting during one of the regular markets the buzz is irresistible. The historic heart of the city is centred on the famous place Plumereau. At peak times you'll need an eagle eye to grab a vacant café table, but when you do you can enjoy a magical setting ringed with beautifully restored medieval half-timbered townhouses. You'll be transported even further back in time in the glorious Gothic interior of the Cathédrale St-Gatien, whose exquisite cloister was equally touched by the Renaissance. A few steps away is the former Bishop's Palace, which provides an elegant setting for the internationally renowned collections of the city's Fine Arts Museum. Finally, for a note of belle époque elegance, don't miss the fabulous façade of the famous Gare de Tours.

AU BUREAU 7J/7

Daily bustle in the Place Plumereau, Vieux Tours.

Cathédrale St-Gatien

Place de la Cathédrale, T02 47 05 63 87.
Daily summer 0900-2000, winter 0900-1900.
Visitors not permitted during worship (Sun 1100
and 1830). Illuminations 1900 Mon, Wed and
Thu. The Cloître la Psalette opening times vary,
closed Sun morning and lunchtimes, entry €3.
Map: Tours, F2, p170.

Vieux Tours is still dominated by the cathedral's
twin towers rising assertively from the deliciously
ornate western façade. Forty years and two
architects separate their construction, and there
are countless subtle variations in the swirling
surface decoration. Sixteenth-century Italianate
summits and carefully disguised Romanesque
bases aside, the fourth religious structure to have
occupied the sacred site is pure Gothic.

The interior is surprisingly unified, despite the
300-year construction period which began in 1236.
As you enter your attention will be drawn to the
distant wall of stained glass supported on a
miraculously slender stone skeleton, the panels
looking as vibrant now as when they were created
around 1270. Around the choir ironwork are

Tours listings

① Sleeping
1 Hôtel du Manoir *2 rue Traversière* **F3**
2 Hôtel du Théâtre *57 rue de la Scellerie* **D2**
3 Hôtel l'Addresse *12 rue de la Rôtisserie* **B3**
4 Hôtel Ronsard *2 rue Pimbert* **D2**

① Eating & drinking
1 Au Martin Bleu *4-6 place des Aumônes* **E4**
2 Aux Delices de Michel Colombe *1 place François Sicard* **E2**
3 Bar le Tourangeau *36 place Grand Marché* **B3**
4 Café du Vieux Mûrier *11 place Plumereau* **B2**
5 Comme Autrefouée *11 rue de la Monnaie* **B2**
6 La Chope *25 bis avenue de Grammont* **E5**
7 Le Molière *1 rue Corneille* **D2**
8 Le Petit Patrimoine *58 rue Colbert* **D2**
9 Les Frères Berthom *5 rue du Commerce* **C2**
10 Rive Gauche *23 rue du Commerce* **C2**
11 Scarlett *70 rue Colbert* **D2**
12 The Pale Irish Bar *18 place Foire-le-Roi* **E2**

Essentials

❯ Getting around The city is easily explored on foot
and major sites within the Touraine are accessible by
bus, train and by bicycle via the Loire à Vélo network.
Car users will find ample parking in the centre.

❷ Bus station Halte Routière, in front of the railway
station on place du Général Leclerc. The urban service in
Tours is called the **Fil Bleu** (T02 47 66 70 70, filbleu.fr).
Fil Vert buses (T02 47 31 14 00, tourainefilvert.com)
serve outlying villages and towns and key tourist sites
around the Touraine.

❸ Train station Gare SNCF, place du Général Leclerc
in the heart of the city. Travellers arriving by TGV must
change at St-Pierre-des-Corps on the outskirts of
Tours for the short connection to Tours centre.
Taxis (T02 47 20 30 40, taxis-tours.fr) wait outside
the main station entrance.

❺ ATMs Around place Jean Jaurés and on rue
Nationale.

❻ Hospital Hôpital Bretonneau, 2 boulevard Tonnellé,
T02 47 47 47 47, chu-tours.fr. The general hospital
with an accident and emergency department.

❼ Pharmacies Pharmacie Principale, 53 rue
Nationale, T02 47 05 21 29; **Pharmacie Vinci**, 2 place
du Général Leclerc, T02 47 05 52 78.

❼ Post office 1 boulevard Béranger and 153 avenue
Grammont.

❶ Tourist information offices Touraine Tourism,
30 rue de la Préfecture, T02 47 31 47 48, tourism-
touraine.com; 78-82 rue Bernard Palissy, T02 47 70 37 37,
ligeris.com; place du 14 Juillet, Langeais, T02 47 96 58 22.

Medieval Gothic fireworks on the Cathédrale Saint-Gatien de Tours.

Tip...

See the western façade at its very best late in the day, when the sinking sun transforms the pale grey stone of the western façade to dazzling gold.

descriptive panels detailing individual windows, the subjects include St-Martin (whose tomb is in the Basilique St-Martin), several early Bishops of Tours and Canons of Loches. There's more fine glass in the huge 14th-century Rayonnant Gothic rose windows of the transepts and the five chapels radiating from the apse. Beside the south transept is the sad but exquisitely sculpted Carrara marble tomb of Charles VII and Anne de Bretagne's two sons, who died aged three years and just 25 days respectively. Watched over by four angels, the monument is ringed with a delicate Florentine frieze. Rather more distant are the decorative central bosses of the stone rib vaults, poised 29 m above the floor of the nave.

Complete your visit in the Cloître la Psalette, a beautiful 15th-century Gothic/Renaissance cloister preserving the library and writing room of the canons of the cathedral. It's accessible from the north aisle.

Cathedral quarter

Map: Tours, E/F2, p170.

Behind the cathedral lies the cobbled Place Grégoire de Tours, which offers the perfect view of the huge *chevet* (apse) rising above its chapels within a spidery framework of tall piers and slender flying buttresses. A little further on, behind the rear corner of the Bishops' Palace, lies the insignificant-looking rue Général Meunier, whose gentle curve follows the exact trace of a vast circular Gallo-Roman arena said to have diverted water from the Loire for more spectacular events. The street eventually joins up with rue Manceau to return through what was once the central axis of the arena. To see what little now remains, retrace your steps beside the cathedral, turn left and follow rue Lavoisier, then left again into rue des Ursulines. Behind the Centre des Archives Historiques de Touraine building lies a garden area which is bounded by otherwise hidden substantial masonry of huge stones and pink bricks, dating from the settlement's fourth-century defences. To see more continue and turn left into rue du Petit Cupidon and look for a similar garden area.

Musée des Beaux-Arts

18 place François Sicard, T02 47 05 68 73, musees.regioncentre.fr.
All year Wed-Mon 0900-1245 and 1400-1800. Closed Tue, 1 Jan, 1 May, 14 Jul, 1 and 11 Nov, 25 Dec. €4, €2 concessions, under 13s free and free entry 1st Sun every month.
Map: Tours, F2, p170.

Tours' Fine Arts Museum enjoys an impressive setting in the former Palais des Evêques (Bishops' Palace) dating from the 17th and 18th centuries. The Revolution saw the building playing a succession of different roles, including theatre, school and library, before becoming a repository for the countless seized works of art. An inventory was then drawn up, and the collection opened its

The former Bishop's Palace now houses the Musée des Beaux-Arts.

doors on 4 March 1795, being officially established as a museum in 1801. When the building was later returned to the archdiocese, however, the collections were shunted between a series of homes, before finally returning to the Palais after its acquisition by the city in 1910. Today elegant former reception rooms like the Salon Louis XV display treasures 'acquired' from private homes, churches and monasteries, plus the great lost chateaux of Chanteloup and Richelieu. Highlights from the museum's formidable collection of 18th- and 19th-century paintings include works by François Boucher, Eugène Delacroix and Claude Monet. Non-French artists including Rembrandt, Rubens, Degas and Andrea Mantegna are also well represented, as are lesser-known local painters and notable figures of the 20th century. The museum's reputation and influence enable it to attract state funding to host a world-class, year-round programme of temporary exhibitions.

Outside the ornamental gardens are dominated by a magnificent 200-year-old Lebanon cedar. A less immediately obvious curiosity is Fritz, the Indian elephant who arrived in Tours in June, 1904 with the circus of Barnum & Bailey and never left. The 80-year-old pachyderm apparently became dangerous, paid the ultimate price and his body was presented to the town, who promptly had it stuffed and mounted on a substantial plinth. He now lives safely behind glass across the gardens, in a small building to the right of the venerable cedar.

Place Plumereau & Vieux Tours

Map: Tours, B2, p170.

It may not exactly be an acknowledged shrine of regional gastronomy, but for a cool drink, lively conversation and a spot of shameless people-watching you're unlikely to find a more visually pleasing and generally buzzy location than place Plumereau ('*place Plum*' in local student slang). During the 15th century wives and mistresses of privileged courtiers would come to the *carroix aux chapeaux* to purchase flowers to adorn their hats, but today the square is filled with chic bar tables

Restored medieval façades radiate from the Place Plumereau.

and spreading parasols. Providing the perfect backdrop are rows of tall, half-timbered façades dating from the 15th century, all lovingly restored and with the odd 19th-century interloper in pale local stone to inject a more balanced Touraine identity. Dwarfing them all, on the corner of rue du Change and rue de la Monnaie, is a handsome four-storey slate-hung medieval house whose lower timbers are decorated with Biblical carvings including a mercifully time-worn circumcision scene. In the opposite corner is an ancient survivor from the countless *mûriers* (mulberry trees) which once nourished the town's army of silkworms. A nearby archway off the square leads to place St-Pierre-le-Peullier, in and around which you'll discover Gallo-Roman excavations and more character façades. One of them, in Rue Briçonnet, preserves a fine medieval exterior staircase. Most of the narrow streets tucked away around place Plumereau are similarly worth exploring, and rue de la Rôtisserie and rue du Grand Marché also offer a wealth of possibilities for dining out.

Around the region

Nouvelle Basilique St-Martin

Rue Descartes, T02 47 05 63 87,
paroisse-cathedrale-tours@catholique.fr.
Daily 0730-1900, mass held every day at 1100.
Map: Tours, C3, p170.

The 'new' basilica built between 1886 and 1924 replaced a grand 11th- to 13th-century church constructed over the tomb of St-Martin of Tours, itself a replacement for a much smaller, fifth-century structure destroyed by the Normans in 996. In 1562 it was the turn of the Huguenots, whose destructive efforts began a spiral of decay which culminated in the nave being demolished in 1802 to create rue des Halles. The Tour Charlemagne remains (thanks to rebuilding after a partial collapse in 1928) and is emblazoned with a stirring bas-relief of the Saint, whose remains now rest just across the street in the present basilica. Although its heavy neo-Byzantine style is not to everyone's taste, the dimensions are impressive. The interior is a similar story; decoration is restrained, apart from cylindrical tall arcade piers of polished granite topped with foliated pale stone Corinthian capitals. There are no transepts but four huge piers beyond the nave rise assertively to a lantern tower crowned with a cupola. The tomb of the Saint is in a crypt beneath the raised sanctuary, and reached by flights of steps on either side of those which rise to the central altar. The scene below, for all its deep religious significance, lacks the powerful sense of mystery of other medieval holy places, resembling instead a scene uncomfortably close to that of a Turkish Bath. The reliquary containing the Saint's mortal remains sits deep within the base of the shrine, as you'll see by peering through the heavy wrought ironwork grilles. When you return to the nave follow the left-hand side aisle to the far end to see a life-sized glazed bas-relief of the Saint, plus a series of panels recounting (in French) his life, the history of the Basilica and that of its illustrious Gothic predecessor.

Château de Candé

Monts (10 mins south of Tours on the N10),
T02 47 34 03 70, monuments-touraine.fr.
Apr-Jun Fri-Sun 1000-1800, Jul-Aug Wed-Sun 1000-1800. €4.50, €2 12-18 years. Includes free guided visit, though book ahead for tours in English.

This lesser-known French chateau witnessed an important event in 20th-century history when the Duke of Windsor, formerly Edward VIII, married American divorcee Wallis Simpson (for whom he had recently renounced the British throne) on the 3 of June 1937. It was a fittingly romantic setting, which can trace its history back to 1313, when it was a fortress owned by Macée de Larçay. The present chateau was begun much later during the early 16th century as a Renaissance-style retreat by Mayor of Tours François Briconnet. In 1853 Santiago Drake del Castillo, a wealthy Anglo-Cuban plantation owner, purchased the property and tripled its size, employing both Renaissance and neo-Gothic styles designed by architect Jacques-Aimé Meffre of Tours. In 1927 Franco-American millionaire Charles Bedaux acquired the estate and set about installing more refinements including central heating, a solarium, a telephone system, tennis courts and an 18-hole golf course. In 1951 his widow bequeathed Candé to the French Presidency which in turn eventually handed it to the Conseil Général d'Indre-et-Loire. The visit reveals, in a selection of the 50-odd rooms, the refined elegance of the 1930s, via a dining room, music salon, bedrooms, library and one of a series of jaw-dropping art deco bathrooms. The estate, which by 1876 was already equipped with del Castillo's innovative irrigation system, covers over 250 ha and is home to a large herd of roe deer and countless species of birds.

Prieuré de Saint-Cosme

*La Riche (follow signs on D88, 10 min west of Tours),
T02 47 37 32 70, prieure-ronsard.fr.*
Daily except 25 Dec and 1 Jan, entry times vary.
€4.50, €3 concessions, under 12s free. 55-min
guided tours in English, free on request.

Despite a deeply unpromising suburban approach,
this ancient site, for centuries a place of rest and
renewal for those on the route to Compostela, still
inspires peaceful contemplation. Just enough
remains of the priory founded in 1092 to give some
idea of its former importance. By way of
compensation for the ruined state of the
15th-century Romanesque church, a huge early
12th-century monks' refectory is essentially intact.
Passing through the saw-tooth incised doorway
reveals a vast hall complete with colossal roof
timbers and an ornate oratory incorporated into
the far wall. Modern-day pilgrims, though, are
mostly of the literary kind and make first for the
lodging house in which France's greatest romantic
poet of the Renaissance, Pierre de Ronsard, lived
and worked during his time here as Prior from 1656
until his death in 1585. The original one-up,
one-down internal layout was later modified
substantially, but the spirit of the place remains. He
was buried in the chapel, surrounded by the
gardens and orchards he tended lovingly, and
which were visited by Catherine de' Medici and her
sons, Charles XI and Henri III. Following a decline in
the fortunes of the priory during the 18th century,
the site served briefly as the Archbishop's
residence, before being pillaged for its stone and
exploited by vegetable growers. The assorted
barns, houses and cattle sheds have now been
cleared and the gardens are being lovingly
restored to their former glory, as continuing
archeological excavations reveal fresh evidence of
the site's history are completed. The rose gardens
in particular are already beautiful, and destined to
become even more so in years to come.

The home of Romantic poet, Pierre de Ronsard, during his time as Prior.

Around the region

Château de Luynes

Av du Clos Mignot, Luynes (about 12 km from Tours on the northern bank (rive droite) of the Loire), T02 47 55 67 55.
Apr-Sep daily 1000-1230 and 1400-1800.
€9, €4 children. Visit time about 45 mins, guided tours available (60 mins).

Time has been kind to Luynes, mainly by appearing to have largely bypassed the heart of the town, which is thus well worth exploring. At first the settlement was called Maillé, after the powerful family who built the first chateau in the 10th century. By the Renaissance the barons had become dukes, and were transforming their severe chateau into a more comfortable and fashionable residence. In 1619 it was purchased by Charles d'Albert de Luynes, a close friend of Louis XIII, who renamed the town. In time the Ducs de Luynes would control much of northern Touraine while the town prospered as a major silk producer. When the industry declined, so did the town. It's now very much back on its feet, and holds Saturday morning markets in its handsome early 15th-century covered market hall. Close by are several immaculately restored stone and half-timbered former merchants' houses. Overlooking it all is the **chateau**, still occupied by the 14th generation of the Ducs de Luynes and looking stern and aloof from the town. The high walls and seven circular towers, though, are deceptive; around the courtyard things are much more refined, with Blois-style decorative brickwork and even the odd tourelle. The visit takes in the family art collection, fine tapestries and antique furnishings, in addition to secluded landscaped gardens and a Gothic chapel. There's also a picnic area, and of course the chateau's privileged views of the town and surrounding countryside.

Gallo-Roman aqueduct

2 km northeast of Luynes – follow the old enamelled signs from the town centre.

In what appears at first to be a solitary setting you'll find this series of 44 tall stone piers, nine of which are still linked by their original stone-and-brick arches. The still-impressive ruins are all that remain of an aqueduct constructed during the first or second century by the occupying Roman legions. It's believed to have supplied pure water from a nearby spring to *Malliacum*, on which the priory of St-Venant was founded around the 10th century. Another intriguing, but perhaps less plausible, theory is that it ran all the way to *Caesarodunum* ('the hill of Caesar'), which became *Civitas Turonorum*, before eventually blossoming into the city of Tours. Either way, it required a precisely calculated fall throughout its length in order to achieve a gravity-fed flow, and seems to have functioned for at least six centuries, repairs to the system having been documented during the reign of ninth-century Carolingian king Charles le Chauve.

High-rise, Roman-style, near Luynes.

Cinq-Mars-la-Pile

East of Luynes.

The village takes its name from a curious Gallo-Roman brick pillar (or pile) sited high on a hillside. It's signed from the village centre but is easier to spot on your right when arriving from Luynes, before you enter the main village. Getting to it involves following a steep, narrow footpath which climbs beside private houses and up the hillside. Only when you draw closer to the tower does its great size (5.8 sq m and full 30 m high) become apparent. The summit is crowned by four corner piers, adding a further 3.5 m, and the whole thing is estimated to have consumed around 104,000 bricks during its construction. Although its purpose is uncertain, it's thought to have been a burial monument, and its relatively good state of preservation puts it among the Loire Valley's most important Roman remains. On the upper section of the façade facing the Loire you'll notice 12 rather weathered looking mosaic panels, whose decorative style was also employed briefly in Ostia, the ancient port of Rome – a fact which enables archeologists to date the structure to within a 50-year period during the second century AD. Recent excavations revealed a stone bearing a representation of Sabazios, son of Persephone and Zeus. In 1840 the site became one of the very first in France to be listed officially as a *'Monument Historique'*, and is now maintained by the state.

Château de Langeais

24 km west of Tours, T02 47 96 72 60, chateau-de-langeais.com.
Jul-Aug daily 0900-1900, other months times vary. €8.20, €5 children, under 10s free. Last admissions 1 hr before closing. Guided tours in English (50 mins) on reservation, animated tours in costume in Jul and Aug.

Constructed by order of Louis XI, the chateau was designed to send a powerful reminder of the absolute power of the monarchy to local dissident groups. However, once across the drawbridge

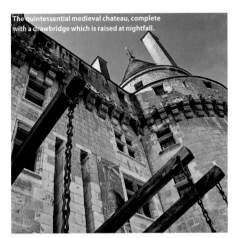

The quintessential medieval chateau, complete with a drawbridge which is raised at nightfall.

(which is still raised at the end of each day) another, gentler side is revealed, as symbolic medieval might is replaced with Renaissance refinement. The chateau was completed around 1469 and in 1491 witnessed the marriage of Charles VIII and Anne de Bretagne, an historic event recreated for today's visitors in atmospheric *son et lumière* presentations starring eerily lifelike waxwork figures in authentic costumes. This attention to detail is complemented by the low light levels which would have accompanied medieval life, and which add to the sense of authenticity throughout the visit. The decoration and furnishings are outstanding examples of 15th- and 16th-century Flamboyant Gothic style, and the decoration and monumental scale of the fireplaces almost defy belief. Completing this extraordinary experience are over 30 large tapestry wall-hangings from the same period. By way of total contrast, a draughty parapet walk surmounts the entire eastern façade, offering vertiginous views of the town and surrounding landscapes.

Behind the chateau the site rises, via formal gardens, to the ruined 10th-century fortress built by Foulques Nerra, Comte d'Anjou. Beyond, in wooded parkland, lie a ruined chapel, a children's tree house and a viewpoint to a neo-Gothic 1930s bridge across the Loire.

Château de Villandry

Completed around 1536, Villandry was the last (and arguably the most French) of all the great Renaissance chateaux of the Loire Valley. There's real history, too, in the form of a huge and much older square tower from the original 12th-century fortress in which the defeated Plantagenet King Henry II signed the Paix de Colombiers treaty before Philippe II of France. Climb to the summit of the tower and you'll be rewarded with the definitive overview of the legendary Renaissance gardens which continue to attract visitors from the four corners of the world.

Renaissance serenity meets medieval might.

Gardens

Villandry is on the D7 18 km west of Tours,
T02 47 50 02 09, chateauvillandry.com.
Gardens daily all year from 0900, chateau closed
mid-Nov to Feb, opening times vary. Chateau
and gardens €9, gardens only €6; €6, €3.50
concessions, under 8s free. €3 audio guide.
Allow 1½ hrs for a self-guided visit. Night of
1000 Fireworks, with entertainment and
gardens illuminated by candlelight, on two
consecutive nights in early Jul.

While much of the chateau itself is visible to
passers by, the greater part of its iconic formal
gardens (19th century recreations of the original
16th century Renaissance layouts) remain
tantalizingly concealed from view. All is revealed by
following the 'Jardins' signs which will lead you
through the ground floor of the chateau to an
elevated walkway overlooking the main garden
areas. In the foreground immaculately clipped box
forms symbolize love and music, along with
fleurs-de-lys and both Maltese and Basque Crosses.
From here continue to the end of the level path (or
follow another into the adjoining woodland via a
second viewpoint 30 m above the gardens) to
planted terraces, greenhouses and the elegant
Pavillon de l'Audience, constructed during the
18th century by the Marquis de Castellane for
meetings with his estate workers. At the far end of
the walkway is a delightful shaded grassy avenue
giving the perfect overview of the **Jardin d'Eau**, a
classically inspired water garden whose
centrepiece is a huge pond shaped to resemble a
Louis XV mirror. Continue and you'll reach the
Jardin du Soleil (created in 2008), whose three
sections depict clouds (with billowing waves of
box and Perovskia, or Russian sage), the sun (raised
beds radiating from a star-like central fountain) and
a children's play area with ornamental apple trees.
Next comes a suitably large clipped hornbeam
labyrinthe (maze), followed by a long, slender
aromatic and medicinal herb garden known as the
Jardin des Simples, laid out in formal *parterres* and

bounded by another elevated walkway. This time
welcome shade is provided by a full-length
pergola supporting highly productive vines, whose
delicious fruit adds a whole new dimension to
late-summer visits.

By now you'll have encircled the world-famous
Renaissance *potager* – nine formal **vegetable
gardens** planted with colourful combinations
evoking the medieval plantings favoured for abbey
gardens. The monks themselves, represented by
standard roses, provide the finishing touches to
this dazzling recreation of Italian and French
influences of the 16th century.

Tip...

The gardens are best seen before mid-morning
and from mid-afternoon onwards, particularly on
wiltingly hot summer days.

Formal gardening, par excellence.

Around the region

Château

For opening times and prices see the Gardens above.

The U-shaped plan is obvious, as is the purity of the architecture – or at least most of it. On the opposite corner overlooking the gardens is a sturdy crenellated donjon, which was somehow spared when Jean le Breton (Finance Minister to François I) demolished the fortress in order to create something a little more in tune with the times. Today around 15 rooms are visitable, beginning with a hall displaying a large-scale model of the chateau and gardens, plus photographs and engravings illustrating the chateau's surprising architectural evolution. In 1754 the Marquis de Castellane acquired the estate and began various modifications, including dividing up internal rooms and almost doubling the number of windows. During the 19th century the gardens were replaced by English-style parkland and the chateau fell into near-ruin. The decline was halted and the lost purity and dignity of the chateau and its gardens restored after Spanish scientist Joachim Carvallo

(whose descendants continue to care for Villandry) purchased the estate in 1906. The visit continues with an 18th-century drawing room, Joachim Carvallo's study and the Louis XV-meets-Provençal dining room created by the Marquis de Castellane. His monumental stone staircase leads to an Empire-style bedroom dedicated to former owner Prince Jérôme, brother of Napoléon. Next is a library offering insights into family life at Villandry, Joachim Carvallo's bedroom and the Vegetable Garden Room, with sweeping views of the gardens. The Moat Bedroom features family portraits by Charles Milcendeau, a friend of Joachim Carvallo and his wife Anne Coleman. A collection of historic Spanish art is displayed in a gallery leading to the Salon Oriental, whose astonishing carved and gilded Moorish ceiling was transported here from the 15th-century Maqueda Palace in Toledo. On the second floor are two children's rooms, after which a spiral staircase finally winds to the donjon roof for the classic overview of the gardens.

The chateau has now been restored to its former purity.

Five of the best

Gardens

❶ Château de Villandry Surely the most sublime kitchen garden in the world.

❷ Château de la Chatonnière A series of delightful gardens including an astounding star-shaped *potager* best viewed from the elevated scented rose walk.

❸ Château de Chaumont Hosts the famous International Garden Festival, where innovative designers are free to experiment on a different theme each year.

❹ Prieuré de St-Cosme Beautiful and romantic gardens are being recreated with roses at the heart of the collection.

❺ Château du Clos Lucé Landscaped grounds display some of the great scientific inventions conceived by Leonardo da Vinci, and there's a beautifully laid-out Renaissance garden.

Azay-le-Rideau

The small town on the *rive droite* of the Indre owed its pre-tourism prosperity to the water mills which divided the flow of the river. Eventually the chateau did likewise, creating the lake-like moat on whose surface the building's elegant form shimmers as if floating weightless – an effect to which a summer evening *son et lumière* performance adds an even more magical dimension. But, as a visit reveals, the chateau was never completed, and we can only gaze in wonder at what Balzac called 'a faceted diamond' and try to imagine what might have been. Nearby, the attractive riverside village of Pont-de-Ruan, with its restored water mill, still corresponds to the writer's impressions of the landscapes he came to love during his stays at the Château de Saché (now a museum dedicated to his life and works). And for centuries daily life has gone on beneath the landscape, too, as you'll discover in the preserved troglodytic valley of les Goupillières.

The chateau now appears to float, as if weightless.

Château d'Azay-le-Rideau

Entrance off rue Balzac or
rue de Pineau, T02 47 45 42 04,
azay-le-rideau.monuments-nationaux.fr.
Oct-Mar daily 1000-1230 and 1400-1730,
Apr-Jun and Sep daily 0930-1800, Jul-Aug daily
0930-1900. Closed 1 Jan, 1 May and 25 Dec.
€8.50, €5.50 concessions, under 18s free.
Audio guides available in 5 languages (€2),
guided visits in French only. *'Songes et Lumières'*
every night Jul-Aug (about 1 hr).

Despite its celebrity status, Azay's chateau remains
hidden until the very last moment. The main
approach, from rue de Pineau, gives a hypnotic
glimpse of its northern façade at the end of a long
avenue of tall, slender oaks. The chateau sits on an
island, and during 1950s restoration works enough
of the river was siphoned off to create a small lake,
purely for the resulting romantic reflections (at
least during periods when the surface has been
cleared of invasive weed). The chateau was begun
by State Treasurer (and Mayor of Tours) Gilles
Berthelot, with stylistic inspiration and project
management from his wife Philippa Lesbahy, who
had inherited the site in 1510. When a close
financial associate was executed after a corruption
scandal in 1528 Berthelot fled France, while his wife
attempted to retain control of the chateau. It was
eventually seized by François I and duly passed to
his military confidant Antoine Raffin, who
apparently had neither the will nor the finances to
complete the project. In 1791 his descendants sold
the estate to Marquis Charles de Biencourt, who
began a long campaign of restoration and
removed the remains of a medieval fortress and
neglected walled gardens to make way for the
present parkland-style landscaping. A century later
the last Marquis, faced with financial ruin, sold the
chateau and the state assumed ownership in 1905.

As one of the earliest of the great Renaissance
chateaux, Azay is also among the most visibly
Italianate in its detailing. The building we see today
has an L-shaped plan, with a single wing extending
from the northern façade. Whatever the original

Essentials

❼ Getting around Azay-le-Rideau is a compact
town midway between Tours and Chinon and makes an
ideal base from which to discover (by car or bike) many
interesting sites and gentle countryside. Cyclists have a
great choice of circuits and trails to follow with guides
available in English from the tourist office. The town is
served by bus (Ligne V) and train services from Tours,
both of which carry bikes on most journeys.

❸ Train station Gare SNCF, Avenue de la Gare, route
de Langeais (2 km from Azay-le-Rideau).

❾ ATM 9 rue Carnot, Azay-le-Rideau.

✚ Pharmacy Pharmacie Picot-Pavy, 22 rue Gambetta,
Azay-le-Rideau, T02 47 45 40 53.

❓ Post office 10 place de la République, Azay-le-
Rideau, T02 47 21 99 59.

❶ Tourist information office 4 rue du Château,
Azay-le-Rideau, T02 47 45 44 40, ot-paysazaylerideau.fr.

intention, entry today is via the almost insignificant
doorway at the base of the four-storey *escalier
d'honneur*, a grand staircase whose loggia-style
upper galleries are the real focus of attention.
Inside, the undersides of the staircase and the
galleries are vaulted and adorned with sculpted
medallion portraits dating from the 16th and 19th
centuries, in the company of Gothic features such
as the royal salamander and ermine symbols.
Among the more notable of the 13 or so rooms
open to visitors are the great bedchamber
occupied during Louis XIII's visit in 1619, and its
antechamber hung with portraits of François I,
Henri III and Louis XIII, along with Jacques-Louis
de Beringheim, equerry to Louis XIV.

Across the landing is the aptly named **Grande
Salle** (great hall), conceived to host balls and
banquets. Superb 16th- and 17th-century tapestry
wall-hangings and an extravagantly sculpted
fireplace are reinforced by skillful mid-20th-century
trompe-l'oeil decoration – a salamander and motto
for the chimney breast and Florentine foliation for
the frieze – suggesting how the room might have
appeared had it been completed. The adjacent
rooms are much more modest, but the **Chambre**

Around the region

du Maître de Maison (Gilles Berthelot's bedchamber) has Renaissance panelling replicated from originals surviving elsewhere in the chateau, plus huge tapestries and furnishings evoking the spirit of the 16th-century Renaissance. The adjoining stone spiral staircase sits within a tower styled after the corner tourelles of the southern façade and was added to improve access during the 19th century.

The visit continues on the ground floor, adapted by the Biencourt dynasty to provide comfortable reception areas. The fireplaces are appropriately grand – neo-Renaissance in the **Bibliothèque** (library), while the **Salle de Billard** (billiard room) has a replica of a 16th-century original in the Château de Montal, in the Lot region. The real show-stopper, however, is in the **Salon Biencourt**. This spectacular full-height Renaissance-meets-Gothic creation is emblazoned with a large fire-breathing salamander surmounted by a royal crown within a scrolled medallion. It holds its own among richly patterned wall decoration, lacquered furnishings and 16th- and 17th-century stained glass.

The remaining, less glamorous areas also have stories to tell: an elegant passageway to the lost Renaissance gardens, and the vaulted kitchen, whose forgotten huge fireplace and indoor well were rediscovered during restoration works.

Eglise St-Symphorien

Place du 11 Novembre, Azay-le-Rideau.

As you leave the chateau you'll notice the handsome outline of this early medieval church. To reach it take the left-hand exit into rue Balzac, turn left again into rue Gambetta and continue until you reach an old market square containing the church. The façade represents something of a power struggle between two churches built side by side. The left-hand façade dates from 1518 and its narrow dimensions are accentuated by a tall, steeply pitched gable set above a large Flamboyant Gothic window and a slate-hung *clocher* (belfry). There's also a low, distinctly un-French looking doorway with an untypical flattened archway. Its wider companion on the right was obviously much lower when constructed during the 11th century – a change of masonry shows where the façade was raised to match the base of the adjoining gable. Notice details such as the sculpted corbel heads dating from an even earlier Carolingian-era structure, plus two rows of niche figures, the lower of which was divided unsympathetically during the 18th century to add a lancet window. A large, rounded-arch doorway is probably another subsequent addition.

Inside, both aisles appear at first to be similar, but note the tall Angevin vaulting (as used in the cathedral of Angers) over the earlier, right-hand aisle. Both aisles have curved eastern apses, the right-hand one being worth a closer look, as it preserves some still-vibrant areas of medieval wall paintings uncovered during restoration works.

La Vallée Troglodytique des Goupillières

3 km from Azay-le-Rideau on the D84 (direction Artannes), T02 47 96 60 84, troglodytedesgoupillieres.fr.
Feb-Mar Sat-Sun 1400-1800, Apr to mid-Nov daily 1000-1900. Last entry 45 mins before closing. Illuminated visits early evenings Jul-Aug. €5.50, €4.50 children (5-12), under 5s free. Car parking is 200 m from the entrance, disabled parking is slightly closer.

Great chateaux like Azay-le-Rideau could not have been created without the back-breaking efforts of countless peasant workers who, armed with little more than a pick-axe and a saw, extracted the celebrated pale *tuffeau* limestone which lay beneath the local landscapes. The caverns they created were then often walled up with slabs of stone to provide a secure family refuge, startling evidence of which survives in this remarkable site. Since its chance discovery in 1962 by 10-year-old Louis-Marie Chardon, he and his family have patiently cleared away the brambles and painstakingly restored a series of three troglodyte farms to reveal just how these tiny communities

Troglodytic caves in the Loire Valley

Along the Loire, in the Touraine and Anjou regions, are two important rocks laid down in huge layers: soft sandstone (*tuffeau*) and limestone (*falun*). It's relatively easy to work *tuffeau*, as prehistoric man discovered when he made dry, warm and relatively safe caves in which to live away from the valley floor. Later many more caves were created during quarrying for building stone. Houses, churches, monuments and chateaux were constructed using stone from these excavations, which often extended far into the hillsides as workers followed a particular seam.

Redundant quarries often became stores, cellars or homes known as *troglodytic* (cave) dwellings. Such homes have several advantages: they were very cheap to create, and both warm in winter and cool in summer. The spaces were also endlessly adaptable, being used not only for human habitation but also for animals, storage and even defence. You can visit the troglodyte village at Les Goupillières near Azay-le-Rideau to understand how a community survived the harsh realities of life, and in the caves at Bourré (see page 137), on the river Cher, you can how the *tuffeau* was cut and removed from the caves – there could not have been a greater contrast in lifestyles between the troglodyte-dwellers and the gentry whom they served.

Over the centuries the troglodyte homes became less popular until by the mid-20th century only a few were still inhabited. Most were abandoned or used only for storage – they were particularly useful as wine cellars because of the constant temperatures maintained underground. In the early 20th century commercial mushroom growing also became established in the caves. Particularly active around Saumur (La Champignonnière du Saut-aux-Loups, for example, see page 215), the mushroom growers produce a large proportion of France's requirements for white button-mushrooms known as *champignons de Paris*, plus more exotic varieties. Today, however, many of the troglodyte houses are being restored as attitudes to cave dwellings have shifted and their potential as eco-friendly homes is realized. Many have been made into charming B&Bs or self-catering accommodation for visitors (see page 36).

Falun was also used as a building stone – you can spot its rich dark yellow tints in buildings around Doué-la-Fontaine and also visit the impressive Les Perrières caves (see page 223), an immense network of characteristically bottle-shaped caverns of cathedral-like proportions. The rock is also suited to Doué's other claim to fame – conditioning the soil of the largest rose-growing area in Europe.

Les Goupillières

functioned. Despite a beautiful and secluded setting, life here was extremely hard for the peasants, and particularly so in times of turmoil; deeper caves were adapted as defensible places of refuge in order to protect the inhabitants from attack. Other deep excavations served as silos for storing precious grain. The homes themselves feel impossibly small, and ambient temperatures remain at a constant 12-14°C throughout the seasons. To minimize the inevitable dampness (a major threat to the occupants' health) they were equipped with large fireplaces incorporating a brick-lined oven for baking bread and drying fruit, connected directly to other caverns occupied by larger farm animals to gain extra warmth. Outside are wells, troglodyte barns plus recreated timber enclosures containing typical farm animals from chickens, ducks, geese and a turkey to rabbits, pigs, goats, donkeys and a pony. A shaded woodland path leads to a small area planted with vines, and a secluded terrace (*Le Trogolodyte Gourmand*) offers refreshments and light meals. Completing the experience are the boundless knowledge and enthusiasm of M. Chardon and his family.

The Lily of the Valley

Honoré de Balzac was born Honoré Balssa in Tours on 20 May 1799 and died in Paris on 18 August 1850. He was a literary critic, journalist, essayist, playwright and printer and is said to have drawn inspiration for his novels from local characters and the local landscape, particularly for his novel *Le Lys dans la Vallée* (The Lily of the Valley). In the book he describes the valley of the Indre between Azay-le-Rideau and Pont Ruan, and the first time he set eyes on the chateau at Saché:

"Then, beyond the bridge, imagine two or three farms, a dovecote, sundry turrets, thirty houses or more, standing apart in gardens divided by hedges of honeysuckle,

jessamine and clematis; heaps of manure in front of every door, and cocks and hens in the road – and you see the village of Pont-du-Ruan, a pretty hamlet crowned with an old church of characteristic style, a church of the time of the Crusades, such as painters love for their pictures. Set it all in the midst of ancient walnut-trees, of young poplars with their pale gold foliage, add some elegant dwellings rising from broad meadows where the eye loses itself under the warm misty sky, and you will have some idea of the thousand beauties of this lovely country."

(Translation by Katharine Prescott Wormley.)

Musée Balzac

Château de Saché, 7 km from Azay-le-Rideau on the D17,
T02 47 26 86 50, musee-balzac.fr.
Apr-Jun and Sep Fri-Wed 1000-1800, Jul-Aug Fri-Wed 1000-1900, Oct-Mar Fri-Wed 1000-1230 and 1400-1700. Closed 1 Jan and 25 Dec.
€4.50, €3 concessions.

If the name of Honoré de Balzac is more familiar than his works, you might decide to remedy this after discovering Saché, the village which the Tours-born writer came to love, and the chateau in which he wrote over 30 novels and short stories. His affectionate description of 'the remains of a castle' is accurate for what appears to be a country manor house that began life as a 12th-century fortress. The 17th and 18th centuries saw the addition of new Renaissance-style wings, and the whole structure acquired its present appearance during the 19th century from Jean de Margonne, who then invited Balzac to live and work in this peaceful setting away from everyday cares in Paris. Since 1951 the chateau has been a museum preserving artefacts from the writer's life and works, including manuscripts and proof pages with corrections handwritten by the author. The beautifully decorated rooms will also inspire lovers of period French Country style, and contain portraits of women who figured in Balzac's life.

The visit concludes on the ground floor, where you can see a 19th-century print workshop, complete with a giant press, and a bronze of the writer sculpted by Rodin. Outside is secluded parkland covering 3 ha.

Balzac is said to have attended mass with his hosts from the chateau in the nearby 12th-16th-century village church. Around the village square are a half-timbered coaching inn said to date from the 12th century and a large 'mobile'-style work created by the highly influential 20th-century American artist Alexander (Sandy) Calder, who for some 20 years lived and worked in and around Saché.

Pont-de-Ruan

La Maison du Meunier, 1 rue de la Vallée du Lys, Pont-de-Ruan (10 km east of Azay-le-Rideau),
T02 47 26 89 17.
Sun 1000-1200 and 1400-1900.

Despite Balzac's atmospheric account, Pont-de-Ruan remains little-known. The beauty of the setting remains, though, and you're unlikely to simply pass it by. The original name of *Rotamagus* indicates that the river crossing was one of a series of halts along the important Gallo-Roman route between Tours and Poitiers. Later, as part of the original pilgrimage route to Compostela, the name evolved into *Pons Rotomagi* and many would visit a small oratory on the riverbank below the **Eglise Ste-Trinité** to seek solace from Ste-Apolline, who is said to have healed those suffering from tooth problems. The church itself was founded in 444 by St Brice, a disciple of St-Martin. The present structure dates from the 11th-13th centuries, and greets visitors with a line of humorous carved corbels above a double-arched entry portal. Inside a timber roof is supported by slender post-and-beam braces which retain a little of their painted decoration. The walls, however, now show no sign of the *ex-voto* messages of the countless pilgrims who once filled the church to join the pre-dawn early morning prayers.

To your right, as you enter the village from Tours, you'll see beside the bridge a small 19th-century mill, one of the many which were a familiar sight along the local waterways. Its water wheels have recently been restored to working order and the **Maison du Meunier** contains a small exhibition showing how a traditional flour-mill functions, and historical insight into the working lives of the millers.

Coopérative Vannerie de Villaines

1 rue de la Cheneillère, Villaines-les-Rochers (6 km south of Azay-le-Rideau on the D57), T02 47 45 43 03, vannerie.com.
Mon-Sat 0900-1230 and 1400-1700 (Jul-Aug, 0900-1700), Sun 16 Oct and 31 Mar 1400-1900. Free.

The village of Villaines-les-Rochers straggles for a considerable distance as the road winds lazily through a broad valley. Along the way you'll pass troglodytic dwellings and numerous signs proclaiming a traditional skill for which the area has long been famous. 'Vannerie' is the art of basket making using willow and rushes, which are cut during winter and left to soften in water until they are ready for 'stripping' (having their bark removed) the following May. The whole process is described in great detail at the Coopérative Vannerie de Villaines, whose origins lie in a society formed in 1849 by local priest (and farm labourer) Jean-

Laurent Chicoisne with financial support from the aristocratic Comte de Villarmois. The workers' cooperative was established in 1937 and since 1971 has opened its doors to talented young craft workers from elsewhere in France. On arrival you'll have an opportunity to watch a brief but interesting video presentation, before seeing the basket makers patiently creating individual items in a large, airy communal workshop. The hypnotic process can produce a surprising range of products, as you'll discover in the boutique displays which fill the remainder of the building. Other products include baskets for bakers, market traders and supermarkets, since around a third of the total French wicker production originates from here in the village.

An age-old craft once again flourishes.

Around the region

Musée de la Vannerie

22 rue des Caves-Fortes, Villaines-les-Rochers,
T02 47 45 23 19.
Afternoons only May-Sep, closed Mon.
€3, €2 12-18 years.

For a detailed history of this local cottage industry, along with other facets of local country life, visit this charming and distinctly eclectic museum. Having outgrown the confines of its small rooms in part of the old village school, it's due to reopen (precisely when was uncertain at the time of going to press) in a newly refurbished hall beside the Mairie, which you'll find in rue de l'Eglise, behind the village centre car park.

Musée Maurice Dufresne

Marnay, 4 km from Azay-le-Rideau
(direction Langeais) on the D120, T02 47 45 36 18,
musee-dufresne.com.
Mar to mid-Nov 1000-1800 (0930-1900 in summer). €10, €7 disabled, €5 children (6-15) and students.

Whatever you were expecting, this is something else. Beyond the imposing wrought-iron gates lies not another exquisite Renaissance chateau but the results of a lifetime's obsessive collecting by an inspired former scrap dealer. The museum fills the 10,000 sq m of a former paper factory buildings in an idyllic location on the banks of the Indre. After steam rollers, traction engines and related early vehicles things become progressively weirder. Highlights include a Second World War tank, a curious tractor used (until requisitioned by enemy forces) to haul shellfish in the Bay of Arcachon, a steam ironing machine for naval uniforms c 1850, a German E-boat awaiting restoration, a wagon-mounted Revolution-era *guillotine* discovered in a cellar in Tours, a 1909 Bleriot monoplane just like the one which made the first Channel flight, a 1911 road-sweeping truck which operated in Boulogne, and an immaculate 1927 Renault which spent the Second World War concealed beneath hay in a

barn. And this barely scratches the surface of this perfect antidote to Chateau Overload.

Les Jardins Remarquables du Château de la Chatonnière

Route de Langeais, about 3 km from Azay-le-
Rideau on the D751 (direction Langeais),
T02 47 45 40 29, lachatonniere.com.
Mar to mid-Nov daily 1000-1900
(closing times vary). €7, €3 children (7-12).

Tucked away in a secluded leafy valley close to Azay-le-Rideau is a Renaissance country manor house whose romantic-looking round towers are reminders of less peaceful times, and whose estate lands once extended from Azay to the banks of the Loire. Over the centuries the chateau flourished

La Chatonnière is a remarkable chateau, too.

while the estate became neglected. Productive vineyards were abandoned along with apple and cherry orchards, plus vegetable and flower gardens. During the mid-1950s a family with a passion for gardens chanced upon the overgrown, unmanaged tangle and purchased it with a dream of completely restoring both the chateau and its remaining estate. Today no fewer than 13 gardens reveal just what Béatrice de Andia and her gardener Ahmed Azéroual (for 20 years head gardener at Villandry) have achieved. Individual themes are expressed in both classic forms and innovative planting plans, sometimes both. The *potager* (vegetable garden), for example, becomes 'The Garden of Abundance', its beds planted in a giant leaf plan. The best view of it is from the Crescent of Fragrances, a 300 m-long elevated arc of rose-clad pergolas above a sea of Californian poppies and 1000 rose bushes. Naturally, the vibrant colour palette varies throughout the seasons, annual highlights being vast waves of poppies and cornflowers in the 7-ha Garden of France, 400 English double roses in the Garden of Luxuriances and – most fleeting of all – the Garden of Danse, an explosion of 40,000 narcissi on a formal Renaissance *parterre*-style plan. This true secret garden appears in March, fading from view without a trace just two months later. For further seasonal discoveries take the woodland path which descends from above the chateau courtyard to the open spaces of the Italianate Garden of Elegance.

Château d'Ussé

Rigny-Ussé (14 km west of Azay-le-Rideau), T02 47 95 54 05, chateaudusse.fr.
Mid-Feb to mid-Nov daily 1000-1800 (-1900 Apr-Aug). €13, €4 8-16 years. Self-guided visit available in English.

It's said that 17th-century author Charles Perrault had Ussé in mind when he wrote both *Le Maître Chat, ou le Chat Botté* (Puss in Boots) and *La Belle au Bois Dormant* (Sleeping Beauty) so naturally the chateau just couldn't resist billing itself as 'Sleeping

Every garden deserves a maze.

Beauty's Castle'. However, even without the association you'd struggle to come up with a more classic vision of a fairy-tale chateau. Ussé takes its name from the fourth-century settlement of *Uceram*, in which the first fortress was built around 1040. The foundations of the present chateau were laid in 1424 by Olivier d'Ussé, whose son Antoine de Bueil married Jeanne de Valois, daughter of Charles VII and Agnès Sorel. Despite her substantial dowry, by 1485 de Bueil was forced to sell the estate to Jacques d'Espinay, who began building the chapel and transforming Ussé into essentially what you see today. All that remained was to demolish the northern portion of the main building (just as at Chaumont, see page 135), opening the courtyard to elevated views of the river. Formal *parterre* gardens attributed to Louis XIV's landscape architect André le Nôtre were then planted on terraces created by military engineer Vauban, a frequent guest after his daughter married Ussé's owner Louis II Bernin de Valentinay.

Today's visitors can tour a series of rooms decorated in the taste of various periods in the chateau's history (complete with slightly creepy costumed mannequins), a guardroom filled with Oriental weaponry arms and painted ivory miniatures, a long gallery hung with magnificent Flemish tapestries and much more. Younger children, on the other hand, will target the gloriously kitsch Sleeping Beauty tableaux and a display of traditional toys and games.

In & around Chinon

Chinon overlooks a broad stretch of the Vienne on the borders of Anjou, Poitou and Touraine, in the heart of some of the Loire Valley's finest wine territory. The town also occupies a key place in history, for it was here in 1429 that Joan of Arc identified the disguised Dauphin and persuaded him to allow her to command an army to rout the English from France. Today the vast chateau is near the end of an equally vast rebuilding programme, while the town's restored medieval quarter is infused with a powerful sense of the past. Nearby are ancient oak forests which still spread as far as Azay-le-Rideau, and, to the north, just above the Loire, you'll find some of the Loire Valley's oldest vineyards established around Bourguiel over a thousand years ago. In its own way no less remarkable is Richelieu, a visionary town created around 1630 on the southern fringes of the area by the powerful Cardinal de Richelieu, Prime Minister to Louis XIII. Its sumptuous chateau may have been lost, but its elegant landscaped parkland survives.

Chinon's continuing restoration is on an heroic scale.

Forteresse Royale de Chinon

*Av François Mitterand (D751), T02 47 93 13 45,
forteresse-chinon.fr.*
Daily (closed 25 Dec and 1 Jan). At the time of
writing, the rebuilding work was expected to
continue until June 2010. Up until this time,
the chateau remains open for a reduced tariff
(€3) and visitors can see the restoration work
in progress.

There's no mistaking the defensive message of
Chinon's vast Forteresse Royale, which smoulders
menacingly from a plateau above the town. The
site was probably occupied in Gallo-Roman times,
although the first significant fortifications were
undertaken around 954 by order of Comte de Blois
Thibaut I. During the 12th century Chinon became
the preferred residence of Plantagenêt king Henri
II, effectively becoming the seat of the English
monarchy after his coronation as King of England
in 1154. By the time he died here in 1189 Henri had
accomplished the enlargement and fortification
works underpinning the fortress whose remnants
we see today. What you won't see is the Fort
St-Georges, which originally defended the eastern
entry from the plateau (the most logical place from
which to attack) and which was named after
England's patron saint. Sure enough, in 1204 the
fort was taken when Philippe-Auguste of France
put the chateau under seige, the remaining
defences falling the following year. The French king
then employed his knowledge of its weaknesses to
rebuild and strengthen the chateau, adding the
25-m-high circular Donjon du Coudray where
captured Knights Templar were imprisoned and
which later accommodated Joan of Arc. The Maid
of Orléans was received in the great hall of the
Logis Royaux, currently nearing the end of a heroic
campaign of reconstruction which will restore as
much of the chateau as possible to its appearance
prior to being dismantled by Cardinal Richelieu,
who used it as a convenient source of construction
materials for his nearby new town (see page 195).

Essentials

❷ **Getting around** It's possible to explore Chinon on
foot but the chateau sits above the town, so for the less
fit it would probably be better to park near the entrance
than walk up. There's a handy pedestrian lift (with
adjacent parking) to the plateau from the town centre,
but at the top there's still a climb. You'll need your own
transport to explore the area and to visit Richelieu to the
south, or to discover Bourgueil.

❿ **Train station** Gare SNCF, avenue Gambetta, Chinon.

❺ **ATMs** You'll find several banks in Chinon.

⊕ **Hospital** Centre Hospitalier du Chinonais, Chinon,
T02 47 93 75 15, ch-chinon.fr.

✚ **Pharmacies** There are two pharmacies on place
du Général de Gaulle and another on quai Jeanne d'Arc,
Chinon.

⌁ **Post office** 80 quai Jeanne d'Arc, Chinon,
T02 47 81 20 41.

❶ **Tourist information offices** 16 place de l'Eglise,
Bourgueil, T02 47 97 91 39, ot-bourgueil.fr; 1 place
d'Hofheim, Chinon, T02 47 93 17 85, chinon-valdeloire.
com; 7 place Louis XIII, Richelieu, T02 47 58 13 62,
tourisme-richelieu.com.

Statue Rabelais & Statue Equestre de Jeanne d'Arc

At the point where the mostly 18th-century Pont
de Chinon meets the Quai Jeanne d'Arc you'll find
Pierre-Eugène-Emile Hébert's slightly aloof bronze
statue of Renaissance writer François Rabelais, who
grew up in Chinon and who has been steadfastly
ignoring the arresting river views behind him since
1880. Quite what he's missing will become obvious
during the course of an unhurried stroll beneath
lines of giant *platanes* (plane trees) with the gently
flowing Vienne on your right for company. Along
the way you'll chance upon benches, should you
feel like pausing to picnic or simply take in the
view. If you continue you'll eventually reach a large
open square on the opposite side of the road to
your left. In the midst of Place Jeanne d'Arc's large
expanse stands a fearsome statue of the Maid of
Orléans charging into battle on horseback with her
sword held straight as an arrow before her.

Around the region

Sculptor Jules Roulleau used some 7 tonnes of bronze in his massive casting, which he exhibited in Paris on Bastille Day then generously donated to Chinon. However, getting it here proved challenging, to say the least. After all attempts to transport it from the capital by rail ended in failure, the load was eventually mounted on a sturdily constructed carriage and hauled here on public main roads by a team of Percheron heavy horses. It was unveiled on 13th August 1893 by Admiral Henri Rieunier.

Medieval Quarter

Vieux Chinon sits between the river banks and the plateau in a compact area long ago bounded by heavy fortifications. The walls have long gone but the streets retain their medieval plan and a high proportion of attractive *maisons à colombages* (half-timbered houses), making this a very pleasant place in which to spend some time. A good starting point is between place Général de Gaulle and place de la Fontaine – follow rue Voltaire to see some of the finest 14th, 15th and 16th century half-timbered façades, interspersed with their pale *tuffeau* stone Gothic and Renaissance counterparts. Just beyond the four-storey, 14th-century **Maison Rouge** is the **Musée d'Art et**

d'Histoire de Chinon occupying the former Hôtel des Etats-Généraux, in which the French Parliament convened in 1428 to debate the continued funding of Charles VII's war with the English. Inside you can discover the history of the town, transport on the Vienne and Loire, see pottery from Langeais and much more besides. Behind it the slender clocktower of the chateau rises from the plateau, while below is **rue du Grand Carroi**. Believe it or not, this innocent looking spot was once the town's most important *carroi* or crossroads, sited at the very heart of the town. There are more medieval façades on the other side of Place de la Fontaine in **rue J.J. Rousseau**, including a beautiful Renaissance creation in *tuffeau* decorated with *fleurs-de-lys*, foliated cornicework and assorted animals. A little further on, near the junction with rue Marceau, are two adjoining façades whose massive oak facia beams have been restored in the style of their original functions (a *sabotier*, or clog-maker, and a linen merchant). After your exploration, return to **place de la Fontaine**, whose café tables provide a pleasant setting for relaxed contemplation over a cool drink. At the top of the square an archway leads to a parking area with a modern elevator up to the plateau.

Restored medieval half-timbered façades in Chinon's historic heart.

Les Caves Painctes

Impasse des Caves Painctes, T02 47 93 30 44.
Closed Mon. There are four guided visits
per day at 1100, 1500, 1630, and 1800.
€3 (Chinon wine-tasting free).

Close to the heart of the old town is a huge
network of caves and tunnels, which until the 15th
century were quarried to provide limestone for the
Chateau Royal and the town itself. The workings
were driven deep into the plateau occupied by the
chateau. When they were abandoned they served
as a wine store, and are now the seat of a local wine
guild or brotherhood – the *Confrérie des Entonneurs
Rabelaisiens*. There's no trace of the paintings
described in the writings of Rabelais, apparently a
frequent visitor, but the scene looks otherwise
little-changed since the 16th century (they are,
after all, caves) and provide an atmospheric setting
in which to enjoy a wine-tasting.

La Chapelle Sainte-Radegonde

T02 47 93 18 12,
amisduvieuxchinon@chinon-histoire.org.
You can visit the interior of the chapel all year by
appointment – enquire at the tourist office. €2.

The chapel sits in an elevated and rather remote
position, and is signed for pedestrians from place
St-Mexme, which lies at the eastern end of rue J.J.
Rousseau. From here a steep lane climbs behind
the two towers of the 10th- and 11th-century Eglise
St-Mexme and offers further signs to reassure you
that you're still on the correct route. Along the way
you'll pass a collection of troglodyte dwellings,
while the rooftops of the town gradually slip away
to your right. After about 1 km (and just when
you're convinced that the signage must be wrong)
you'll see ahead of you a rather overgrown
Romanesque portal, where a weathered plaque
identifies the site as both the Ermitage St-Jean and
Chapelle Ste-Radegonde. It was here that
sixth-century hermit Jean le Recluse or Jean de
Chinon established his cell in a cave, where he was
visited by King Clotair I's German-born wife

Few hints of what lies within.

Radegonde, who left the royal court to found the
monastery of Ste-Croix in Poitiers. The portal of the
little chapel leads to an open space with railings
and another gate; beyond is a troglodytic nave
with a 19th-century statue of the Saint and a small
altar set within a dome-like apse. Another bay
contains a second altar, another much earlier
statue and some 17th-century wall paintings.
Beyond lie caves enlarged from those of the
hermit, plus a series of passages which pass a
17th-century oratory to reach 26 steps descending
to an ancient well. According to legend its waters
have healing powers – but only if drunk at
midnight on the Summer Solstice.

Bourgueil

Maison des Vins de Bourgueil & Abbaye de Bourgueil

18 place de l'Eglise, T02 47 97 92 20, vinbourgueil.com.
Welcomes visitors all year though opening times vary.
Abbaye de Bourgueil, T02 47 97 84 92, abbaye-st-pierre-bourgueil.ifrance.com.
Every afternoon 1400-1730.

Chinon's long-standing wine producing rival dozes below the vast Forêt de Benais, within the heady embrace of its 1300-ha AOC vineyards. If you're keen to sample a selection of the celebrated Reds (or Rosés) whose predecessors inspired the likes of Rabelais, Ronsard and Balzac, simply visit the Maison des Vins de Bourgueil. In addition to the 80+ variations normally stocked, each week the centre spotlights four producers, with tastings for visitors and potential purchasers (don't feel compelled to buy a case, as each of the wines is available by the bottle). Closely linked to the wine tradition is Bourgueil's 13th- to 18th-century Benedictine Abbey (founded to the east of the village around 990 by Duchesse d'Aquitaine Emma de Blois. In time it became hugely important, administering priories and parishes stretching from Charente to the Ile de France. Today the site remains a convent but you can visit a large building dating from 1750 which has preserved not only its vast vaulted refectory but also a graceful, monumental stone and wrought-iron staircase worthy of a great chateau and claimed to be unique in France for its broad flights having no visible supporting masonry. Upstairs in the former monks' quarters is a museum documenting rural life up until the early 20th century. The monks themselves, who established the local wine growing tradition, are said to have planted the first Cabernet Franc vine in the abbey's Gothic cloister in 1089.

What the locals say

We find the local people incredibly friendly and warm, proud of their area and heritage, and still very knowledgeable about how things were in years gone by. My favourite restaurant is l'Helianthe at Turquant (restaurant-helianthe.fr). The cuisine is that of the 1920s, all local foods and wines, served beautifully – *Pot-au-Feu* of Loire fish, *Joue de Porc*, plus old-fashioned vegetables. Bourgueil's Tuesday market has a wonderful array of produce and lots of real characters. Visit the pâtisserie Fabrice Metry on place des Halles, which makes the famous Gallette Bourgueilloise, a creamy sponge cake – it's delicious and very filling and goes down well with a good coffee. And their chocolates are wonderful. Langeais' Sunday market is held at the foot of the chateau. Just opposite is a *chocolatier* and coffee shop … a *chocolat chaud* here is just the ticket on a chilly morning!

Jean Brookes, Les Mortiers self-catering gîtes, Parçay-les-Pins.

An 18th-century architectural tour-de-force.

Richelieu

With its geometrical, grid-like plan and moated ramparts, Richelieu evokes something of the spirit of the *bastide* villages of Aquitaine. The town was designed and constructed between 1631 and 1642 for the all-powerful Cardinal de Richelieu by royal architect Jacques Lemercier, whose Italian influences are clearly visible around the town. Grand'Rue, for example, is lined with the elegantly understated façades of 28 *hôtels-particuliers* (prestige townhouses) and links the place des Réligieuses with the market square of the place du Cardinal. The 17th-century market hall feels much older, its vast slate roof supported by a dark forest of oak and chestnut timbers. From one of the nearby bar tables you can join the locals in relaxed contemplation of events unfolding in the sunny square, on whose opposite side the classically styled Eglise Notre-Dame seems to offer nothing more exciting than four niche figures and a pair of tall, slender spires. Inside, though, it's vast and surprisingly airy, with decorative stonework which would not look out of place in Vicenza, and while the upper windows are largely clear, the side aisles contain some rich and exuberant coloured glass.

The Cardinal surveys the town he created.

Parc du Domaine de Richelieu

5 place du Cardinal, T02 47 58 10 09, parc-richelieu.fr.
Mar-Sep daily 1000-1900, Oct-Nov daily 1000-1800, Dec-Feb daily 1000-1700. Closed 25 Dec and 1 Jan. Free. Bicycles and boats available for hire – enquire at the shop just inside the entrance.

After Louis XII's generous elevation of Richelieu's estate to the status of a full dukedom the cardinal resolved to create the grandest chateau in all pre-Versailles France right here. The 475-ha park remains, complete with canals, bridges, rose gardens, an orangery, a pavilion (la Dôme) and appropriately monumental gates. Cruelly, though, the chateau was demolished during the 19th century and its materials plundered, in much the same way that the cardinal dismantled large portions of the Château Royal de Chinon (see page 191) for use in the construction of Richelieu – something to ponder during a gentle, shaded stroll or an idle punt, for which the park is just about perfect on a hot day. Don't miss seeing the rose gardens, which you'll find on your left at the far end of the avenue beyond the palatial main entrance gates. Notice, too, the cardinal's statue outside, contemplating the town he created, rather than what has not survived. Fortunately, some of the chateau's furnishings and works of art seized during the Revolution found their way into the collections of the Fine Arts Museums of Tours (see page 172) and Orléans (see page 87), where they remain on public display.

Sleeping

Château des Arpentis €€€
St-Règle (a few km east of Amboise off the D31), T02-47 23 00 00, chateaudesarpentis.com.
Located in a former Seigneury, Arpentis was fully restored in 2007 and offers luxury accommodation near Amboise. All the rooms, charmingly decorated with murals and tapestries, are different and a family room is available under the eaves. Price includes breakfast.

Hôtel Restaurant l'Aubinière €€€
29 rue Jules Gautier, St-Ouen-les-Vignes (5 km north of Amboise), T02 47 30 15 29, aubiniere.com.
Open all year. An absolutely lovely 3-star hotel with bright and spacious rooms furnished in a comfortable contemporary style. Each has a different character and the Pivoine room has the luxury of a comfy sofa. Treat yourself to a meal in the excellent restaurant which serves refined and delicious French cuisine (closed Mon and Tue midday, Sun evening Oct to May).

Le Fleuray €€€
Fleuray (15 km northeast of Amboise; follow D952 east on north bank, turn onto the D74, direction Cangey), T02 47 56 09 25, lefleurayhotel.com.
Well positioned close to Amboise, Blois and Tours, this is a family-friendly country house hotel and restaurant with welcoming, beautifully appointed rooms. Each room has views over the gardens and the elegant restaurant also has a shaded garden terrace where you can enjoy French cuisine with a contemporary twist (vegetarian menus also provided).

Le Manoir St Thomas €€€
1 Mail St-Thomas, T02 47 23 21 82, manoir-saint-thomas.com. Closed Mid-Nov to mid-Dec and Jan.
Originally a 12th-century priory, the hotel in the centre of Amboise has undergone many changes but still retains several historic architectural features. Some of the rooms include spacious suites with comfortable lounge seating and separate, stylish bathrooms.

Le Blason €
11 place Richelieu, T02 47 23 22 41, leblason.fr.
A hotel in the centre of Amboise with a charming half-timbered façade and quaint interior. The rooms are bright, well furnished and have modern fittings, though the bathroom in our small double room was tiny. In summer ask for an air-conditioned room on the top floor. There's secure parking for cars and bikes about 100 m from the hotel.

Art-Thé €€
8 place Michel Debré, T02 47 30 54 00.
Chambres d'hôtes above a salon de thé opposite the chateau entrance. Steep stairs take you to

A home from home.

two double rooms and a family room, all simply furnished and surprisingly spacious. Rooms at the front have a view of the chateau. Breakfast is served in the salon or on the terrace in fine weather.

Manoir du Parc €€€
8 av Léonard de Vinci, T02 47 30 13 96, manoirparc.com.
Just a few minutes' walk from the chateau and Clos Lucé, you can stay in a charming manor house, a luxurious tree house or a suite with a jacuzzi and hammam. All the accommodation is beautifully furnished and well-equipped. There's a heated swimming pool in the enclosed gardens and free Wi-Fi and parking. The tree house (for 2 people) costs about €1400 per week in peak season (breakfast, linen and housekeeping included).

Villa Mary €€
14 rue de la Concorde, T02 47 23 03 31, villa-mary.fr.
Restored in 2005, this charming townhouse offers very comfortable accommodation in 4 bedrooms, all tastefully decorated with *toile de jouy* in classic French style. Families (up to six people) are easily accommodated in adjoining rooms. Two of the rooms have views over the Loire. There's also a relaxing salon and a garden.

Campsites
Camping Municipal de L'Ile d'Or
100 rue de l'Ile d'Or (on the island), T02 47 57 23 37 (Apr-Sep) or T02 47 23 47 18, campsite-amboise.com.
Spread over 4 ha, there are 400 mostly shaded pitches (with or without electricity). The island enjoys fantastic views over the chateau. Friendly welcome and activities provided for children in the summer. Internet access (payable) during office hours.

Chenonceaux

See also listing for Château de Chissay in the Blois chapter, page 139.

Hotel du Bon Laboureur €€€
T02 47 23 90 02, bonlaboureur.com.
Closed mid-Nov to mid-Dec.
Originally an 18th-century posthouse, this hotel and gastronomic restaurant has grown to include five separate buildings, throughout which are dotted the hotel's beautifully appointed bedrooms. All 25 rooms have a completely different character though all are very comfortably furnished and most open out onto the gardens. Weather permitting, breakfast is served in the gardens until a very leisurely 1100.

Hôtel La Roseraie €€
7 rue du Docteur Brettoneau, T02 47 23 90 09, hotel-chenonceau.com.
An attractive ivy-clad hotel just a short walk from Chenonceau. There are plenty of well-kept rooms to choose from, each with its own (mostly floral) character. Expect a warm welcome from your hosts, who also have a restaurant and a lovely garden with a swimming pool at your disposal. Free Wi-Fi and private parking.

Tours

Domaine de la Tortinière €€€
Les Gués de Veigné, Montbazon (10 km south of Tours), T02 47 34 35 00, tortiniere.com.
The chateau and its restaurant are set in parkland overlooking the River Indre. All the rooms are beautifully presented, 11 of which are in the chateau itself, others are in estate buildings close by. Suites in the turret have amazing views towards the river. Children welcome.

Hôtel du Manoir €€
2 rue Traversière, T02 47 05 37 37, site.voila.fr/hotel.manoir.tours.
Map: Tours, F3, p170.
A small hotel with off-street parking (€6 per night) situated close to the station and near the cathedral quarter. Furnished with antiques, the rooms are pleasant, though a little dated.

Breakfast with home-made produce is served in a vaulted room. Free Wi-Fi.

Hôtel du Théâtre €€
57 rue de la Scellerie, T02 47 05 31 29, hotel-du-theatre37.com.
Map: Tours, D2, p170.
The hotel entrance is via a doorway opposite the Grand Théâtre and some rather steep and narrow stairs. The interior is intimate and welcoming with pleasant rooms off an inner courtyard. Request a room at the back for a peaceful night. Free Wi-Fi.

Hôtel L'Addresse €€
12 rue de la Rôtisserie, T02 47 20 85 76, hotel-ladresse.com.
Map: Tours, B3, p170.
In the heart of the place Plumereau district, this discreet hotel offers contemporary styling and modern comfort in a traditional building complete with beams and breakfast room with exposed stone walls. Some of the rooms have French windows with small balconies overlooking the half-timbered buildings on the street.

Hôtel Ronsard €€
2 rue Pimbert, T02 47 05 25 36, hotel-ronsard.com.
Map: Tours, D2, p170.
Close to the cathedral, the restaurants on rue Colbert, and the antique shops lining rue de la Scellerie, the Ronsard has 20 renovated and nicely decorated rooms, all with a/c and Wi-Fi. Parking (payable) is 5 minutes' walk away at the Vinci Gare.

Le Petit Nice Bed and Breakfast €€
7 Elisabeth Genin, Rochecorbon (8 km each of Tours), T02 47 52 87 26, le-petit-nice-rochecorbon.com.
Comfortable and quiet rooms are directly off the small courtyard of this family home hidden away at the end of a narrow lane with troglodyte dwellings and wine caves. Breakfast is taken on the terrace or in the sun room according to season.

Camping
Parc de Fierbois
Ste-Catherine de Fierbois (28 km south of Tours), T02 99 73 53 57, top-tree-houses.co.uk.
Nature lovers may like to try living in the trees in your very own treehouse 5-6 m above the ground with a view of the forest and lake.

Hotels like Le Diderot in Chinon offer a taste of gracious living.

Le Grand Monarque €€€
3 place de la République, T02 47 45 40 08, legrandmonarque.com.
Converted from an old post office and a 19th-century mansion, the hotel offers a range of 'standard', 'comfort', 'luxe' and 'prestige' rooms comfortably furnished with antiques. Some of the better rooms have beamed ceilings and exposed *tuffeau* stonework. Secure parking costs €10 per night. There is a secluded garden terrace, *bistrot* menu for lunch and an elegant dining room.

Hôtel de Biencourt €€
7 rue Balzac, T02 47 45 20 75, hotelbiencourt.com.
On a street just off the main square and metres away from the chateau entrance, the Biencourt has nicely furnished rooms, some of which are in an old school building to the rear. Breakfast can be taken on the patio in good weather.

Troglododo €€
9 chemin des Caves, T02 47 45 31 25, troglododo.fr.
Charming chambres d'hôtes rooms in an authentic troglodyte home situated in Honoré de Balzac's beloved 'Vallée du Lys'. The rooms open out onto a lovely sunny terrace with views over the valley.

Campsites

Camping de la Confluence
Route du Bray, Savonnières (13 km from Azay-le-Rideau), T02 47 50 00 25, tourisme-en-confluence.com.
May-end Sep.
Three-star campsite on the banks of the River Cher just a few minutes' drive from Villandry and with easy access, by bicycle or car, to Tours. Super facilities in a pleasant shady setting.

Camping Huttopia Rillé
Lac de Rillé (33 km north of Azay-le-Rideau), T02 47 24 62 97, huttopia.com.
Apr-Nov.
Enjoy the pleasures of a peaceful camping holiday around the shores of the Lac de Rillé nature reserve. An eco-friendly site where you can choose from a comfortable Canadian ridge tent under the trees, a wooden Huttopia hut on stilts, or a charming *roulotte* (gypsy caravan).

Le Manoir de Restigné €€€€
15 rue de Tours, Restigné, Bourgueil (21 km north of Chinon), T02 47 97 00 06, manoirderestigne.com.
Stay at Restigné in 18th-century style and elegance, savour local wines in the cosy bar (open to non-residents) and dine in the exceptional Le Chai restaurant. If all this isn't enough, there's a relaxing spa and fitness suite. Most suited to couples.

Hôtel Diderot €€
4 rue de Buffon, T02 47 93 18 87, hoteldiderot.com.
Charming hotel in a pretty courtyard setting a few hundred metres from the medieval quarter and the chateau. Welcoming hosts make this more of a home-from-home experience and breakfast is served with a large choice of home-made jams.

Logis St Mexme €€
115 rue Jean Jacques Rousseau, T02 47 95 56 14, logis-saint-mexme.fr.
Old abbey buildings have been renovated to provide two delightful and spacious chambres d'hôtes guest rooms. One overlooks the garden, the other has its own lounge area and enjoys views to the abbey.

Le Closet des Moustiers €€
Couziers (16 km west of Chinon), T02 47 95 95 09, leclosetdesmoustiers.com.
Guests are welcomed in this 18th-century former farmhouse. Now beautifully restored, it offers two charming chambres d'hôtes rooms in peaceful surroundings but not far from a host of historic sites and attractions. Breakfast includes home-made jam and is served in the garden when possible.

Eating & drinking

Amboise

L'Alliance €€€
*14 rue Joyeuse, T02 47 30 52 13,
lalliance-amboise.fr.*
Thu-Mon 1200-1400 and
1900-2100, Tue-Wed 1900-2100.
Closed 1 Jan to mid-Feb.
Inspired by the market, the
terroir and the seasons, the
young proprietors have
established a big reputation
for their stylish cuisine. In
summer, the shady terrace is
a delight; the dining room is
bright and contemporary.

Le Pavillon des Lys €€€
*9 rue d'Orange, T02 47 30 01 01,
pavillondeslys.com.*
Every evening except Tue and
also for lunch on Sat and Sun.
Closed end Nov-early Feb.
This charming 18th-century
house has three dining rooms
and a terrace for sunny weather
with a view towards the chateau.
The chef, who was born in
Amboise, creates exquisite dishes
using seasonal fresh produce.

L'Amboiserie €€
*7 rue Victor Hugo,
T02 47 30 50 40.*
Mid-Feb to end Dec daily,
closed Tue and Sun evenings
and Wed.
At the foot of the chateau walls
and not far from Clos Lucé,
L'Amboiserie offers a good
variety of dishes or fixed price
menus including grills, salads
and a gourmet selection of

galettes. Choose to dine on the
colourful terrace on sunny days.

Chez Bruno €€
*40 place Michel-Debré (opposite
the chateau), T02 47 57 73 49.*
1100-2230, closed Sun evening
and Mon, also Tue in winter.
Wine bar and bistro with an
inviting display of local wines
which you can taste and buy.
There are several tables on the
pavement terrace with views to
the chateau opposite. Serves
tasty bistro-style regional dishes
in its small restaurant.

Bigot €
*Place du Château, T02 47 57
04 46, bigot-amboise.com.*
Daily during the summer.
Salon de thé serving delicious
light meals all day. Choose from
a large selection of salads,
omelettes and savoury flans
but be sure to leave room for
one of their irresistible cakes.
There's a delightful tea room or
you can enjoy chateau views
from a table outside.

La Scala Amboise €
*6 quai Géneral de Gaulle, T02 47
23 09 93, lascala-amboise.fr.*
Apr-Sep daily, lunch
and evenings, Oct-Mar,
closed Mon.
Situated opposite the tourist
office and the river bank, this
Italian restaurant with a movie
theme provides a warm
welcome and efficient service
from friendly staff in its stylish

dining room or vast terrace.
Choose from pizzas, pastas,
bruschettas and meat dishes, all
at reasonable prices. (La Scala
restaurants appear throughout
the region, though not all have
the same quality and service.)

Cafés & bars
Café des Arts
*32 rue Victor Hugo,
T02 47 57 25 04, cafedesarts.net.*
Daily except Tue.
Friendly bar between the
chateau and Clos Lucé where
you can pause a while and gaze
up at the chateau walls. You may
catch a musical soirée here or
simply be tempted by their
generous snacks. They also offer
basic accommodation for
travellers on a budget.

Le Shaker
*3 quai Francois Tissard, L'Ile d'Or,
T02 47 23 24 26.*
Daily 1800-0300 (-0400 at
weekends), closed Mon in low
season and throughout Jan.
Cocktail bar with the definitive
view of the chateau from its
terrace – best just before sunset.
Cross the bridge from the main
town and descend the steps to
the right. The barman is a world
champion cocktail maker and
has 140 for you to choose from.

Au Soleil Levant €€€
*53 rue Nationale, Monnaie
(16 km northeast of Tours),
T02 47 56 10 34,
touraine-gourmande.com.*
Closed Sun evening and Mon.
Unpromising location but a real
find for those seeking refined
regional cuisine. The menu
changes according to season.

Rive Gauche €€€
*23 rue du Commerce, T02 47 05
71 21, toursrivegauche.com.*
Map: Tours, C2, p170.
Daily from midday.
Much celebrated Michelin-
starred restaurant in the heart of
Tours. Non-diners can enjoy the
atmosphere from 1800-0200 in
the wine and cocktail bar.

Au Martin Bleu €€
*4-6 place des Aumônes, T02 47
05 06 99, aumartinbleu.com.*
Tue-Sat 1200-1430 and
1930-2230.
Map: Tours, E4, p170.
Chef Florent Martin runs one
of the few remaining restaurants
to use Loire river fish and eels,
caught by local fishermen.
With other Tourangelle
dishes and regional wines to
complement the food, the
menu is irresistibly regional.

Comme Autrefouée €€
*11 rue de la Monnaie, T02 47 05
94 78, commeautrefouee.com.*
Closed end Aug-early Sep.
Map: Tours, B2, p170.
The *fouaces* were small pieces of
bread dough that were used to
test the temperature of the oven
and when cooked are rather like
pitta bread. They were
traditionally eaten with local
rillettes or *rillons*. You can watch
them being cooked then help
yourself (they are accompanied
by various garnishes).

La Chope €€
*25 bis av de Grammont,
T02 47 20 15 15, lachope.info.*
Daily 1200-1400 and 1930-2300
(2200 Sun). Closed 24-25 Dec
and for 2 weeks end Jul to
mid-Aug.

Map: Tours, E5, p170.
Seafood brasserie decorated in
belle époque style with deep
red velvet upholstered bench
seats, large mirrors and glass
wall lights. The menu has a wide
choice of fish and seafood and
there's an eclectic wine list.

Le Petit Patrimoine €€
58 rue Colbert, T02 47 66 05 81.
Closed Sun and Mon.
Map: Tours, D2, p170.
It's easy to pass by this modest
looking restaurant but if you are
looking for authentic regional
dishes, reserve your table or be
disappointed. The menu draws
on the whole range of
Tourangelle produce to delight
your senses.

Al fresco dining in Montrichard.

Cafés & bars

Aux Delices de Michel Colombe
1 place François Sicard, T02 47 20 37 03.
Map: Tours, E2, p170.
Artisan *chocolaterie, pâtisserie* and salon de thé in wonderful, old-fashioned premises on the corner of the square. Here you'll find regional specialities such as macaroons and *Nougat de Tours*, but in a mini version that's just perfect to have with afternoon tea.

Bar Le Tourangeau
36 place Grand Marché, T02 47 66 25 13.
Mon-Sat 0900-0200, Sun 1500-0200.
Map: Tours, B3, p170.
A friendly bar-brasserie, between place Plumereau and Les Halles, frequented by locals. A great place to go after visiting the market.

Café du Vieux Mûrier
11 place Plumereau, T02 47 61 04 77.
Map: Tours, B2, p170.
Situated on the ever-popular place Plumereau, this bar is named after the mulberry tree which grows in front of its half-timbered façade. A great place to watch the tourists perambulating round the square.

Le Molière
1 rue Corneille (on corner with rue de la Scellerie), T02 47 20 48 71.
Map: Tours, D2, p170.
This faded belle époque café opposite the Grand Théâtre is frozen in time, offering great coffee in a late 1950s French *nouvelle-vague* ambiance.

Les Frères Berthom
5 Rrue du Commerce, T02 47 20 01 66, lesfreresberthom.com.
Map: Tours, C2, p170.
Busy bar serving wide range of beers and popular with young people especially in the early evening. The terrace is often full but it's worth taking a look at the interior anyway.

Scarlett
70 rue Colbert, T02 47 66 94 09.
Daily (except Sun) until 1900.
Map: Tours, D2, p170.
Bijou tea room with an immense range of teas to choose from, plus cakes and pastries, coffee and hot chocolate.

The Pale Irish Bar
18 place Foire-le-Roi (on corner with rue Colbert), T02 47 64 80 56, thepale.eu.
Daily 1400-0200.
Map: Tours, E2, p170.
Friendly Irish pub with pool table, darts, big screen and plenty of outdoor seating. Regular music nights first Thursday in the month with a jazz or Irish flavour.

Villandry

L'Etape Gourmande €€€
Domaine de la Giraudière, T02 47 50 08 60, letapegourmande.com.
Mid-Mar to mid-Nov daily 1200-1430 and 1930-2100.
A true rural experience in a working 17th-century courtyard farm in the hands of convivial hostess Béatrice de Montferrier. The rustic cooking centres around goat's cheese produced at the farm. Dishes may include sautéed *piccata de veau* with local mushrooms, roast suckling pig and a *nougat glacé* made with goat's cheese.

L'Epicerie Gourmande €
6 rue de la Mairie, T02 47 43 57 49, epiceriegourmande.com.
Daily in summer.
Light meals with vegetarian choices served in a cosy dining room with a low, beamed ceiling, slate-top tables and a large fireplace. On sunny days there are tables outside on the pavement. Choose from galettes with gourmet ingredients or plates of *charcuterie* or cheeses with salad and a baked potato.

Errard €€€
2 rue Gambetta, Langeais,
T02 47 96 82 12, errard.com.
Daily high season, Oct-May.
Closed Sun evenings, Mon
and Dec-Jan.
Classic French cuisine starring
seasonal Touraine produce
served in the rather old-
fashioned dining room of this
former posthouse.

La Maison Tourangelle €€€
6 route Grottes Pétrifiantes,
Savonnières, T02 47 50 30 05,
lamaisontourangelle.com.
Daily 1200-1330 and 1930-2130,
except Sat lunch, Sun evenings
and Wed. Closed for 2 weeks
late Aug, 2 weeks end Oct and
2 weeks mid-Feb.
A charming and refined
ambiance pervades this restored
priory with views to the River
Cher. The chef Frédéric Arnaud
and his team produce cuisine
that's defined by the region and
the seasons. You'll need to book
at least a month in advance to
enjoy its pleasures.

L'Aigle d'Or €€€
10 av Adelaïde Riché, Azay-le-
Rideau, T02 47 45 24 58.
Daily except Sun lunchtime
and Wed.
A short walk from the main
square, this is where you'll find
tasty traditional dishes in a
pleasant dining room, or garden
at the rear, with excellent service.

Phone ahead and reserve a table
to avoid disappointment.

L'Auberge du XIIème Siècle €€€
1 rue du Château, Saché,
T02 47 26 88 77.
Closed Sun evenings,
Mon and Tue lunch.
A few steps from the chateau
and Musée de Balzac, this is
reputed to be one of the oldest
inns in France and was often
visited by the writer on his visits
to Saché. Classic recipes adorn
the menus (€32-70) which are
accompanied by a selection of
local wines. Phone ahead to
reserve your table and check the
restaurant is open as they take
frequent breaks.

A taste of Vieux Loches.

Au Coin des Halles €€
9 Rue Gambetta, Langeais,
T02 47 96 37 25.
Daily Jul-Aug, closed Thu lunch
and Wed low season.
Just a few steps from the
chateau, you'll find a refreshing
bistro-restaurant menu with an
inspiring selection of local dishes
plus a few from further afield. At
lunchtimes (not Sun), try the
'Menu Express' with a *plat du jour*,
excellent value at €15-18. The
terrace is lovely on sunny days.

Le Moulin Bleu €€€
7 rue du Moulin Bleu,
Bourgueil, T02 47 97 73 13,
lemoulinbleu.com.
The 15th-century windmill is a
landmark on the north bank of
the Loire near Bourgueil. The
views over the vineyards from
the terrace are spectacular and
quite romantic. On sale is the
local speciality *Confiture
d'oignons* (onion relish), superb
with game or paté.

Auberge La Lande €€
24 rue La Lande, Bourgueil,
T02 47 97 92 41.
Wed-Sun 1200-1400 and
1900-2100.
Not particularly attractive from
the road but this restaurant is
actually a charming house and
inside it's rather like eating in
someone's dining room. The
traditional cuisine and discreet
service are both excellent.
There's a selection of local wines,
plus some from further afield.

Entertainment

Tours

Cinema

Studio

2 rue des Ursulines (cathedral quarter), T02 47 20 27 00, studiocine.com.
Daily 1400-2200.
Shows international films in their original language (sub-titles in French).

Music & dance

Festival Jazz en Touraine

Montlouis-sur-Loire, T02 47 45 85 10 (tourist office), jazzentouraine.com.
Early Sep.
Even though it's called a jazz festival, you can expect various musical styles like salsa, electro, gypsy jazz and the blues in this well-established late summer revelry.

Opéra de Tours

Grand Théâtre, 34 rue de la Scellerie, T02 47 60 20 20, operadetours.com.
Stages a programme of operas, orchestral performances and recitals.

Tours sur Loire

Place Anatole Wilson, next to Pont Wilson, T02 47 70 37 37 (Tourist Office).
May-Sep.
On the banks of the river near the *embarcaderie* (boat trips) you can see numerous music and other cultural events, including open-air cinema. You'll find a shady terrace with tables (where food and drink is served) set around the stage and you can also enjoy river views.

Nightlife

La Café Chaud

33 rue Briçonnet, T02 47 05 64 45.
Mon-Sat 2100-0400 (club opens at 2300, closed Sun); Sun, 2200-0400.
A café and cocktail bar with a club called Métro downstairs. The drink price includes entry to the club. Popular with students.

Le Pacio

1 place de la Résistance, T02 47 20 56 89.
Mon-Sun 2300-0500 Wed, Thu and Sun free entry, Fri, Sat €8 with a drink.
A large dance floor with varied music though good if you like 80s pop.

A night at the opera, in Tours.

Shopping

The main shopping street in Tours is rue nationale where you'll find all the principle chain stores such as Galeries Lafayette and Monoprix. Just a few steps away, rue de la Scellerie has independent boutiques and interior design shops, and for foodies a wonderful *chocolaterie*, Mediterranean delicatessen and salons de thé. The indoor market at Les Halles is full of mouth-watering aromas and tempting displays and if this is not enough, visit one of the evening food markets in Tours or one of the nearby towns.

Art & antiques

There are several antique shops on rue de la Scellerie and every first Sunday in the month the street stages an all-day outdoor market. A good opportunity to seek out a few unusual souvenirs.

Food & drink

Briocherie Lelong
13 place du Général Leclerc, T02 47 05 57 77.
Established since 1907, this is the only genuine *briocherie* in France. Join the queue to savour the unique taste of fresh brioche – small or large (€0.80-2.40), plain or chocolate, they're all delicious.

La Chocolatière
2 and 4 rue de la Scellerie, T02 47 05 66 75, la-chocolatiere.com.
Artisan *chocolatier, pâtissier* and salon de thé. Producers of regional specialities such as the Nougat de Tours and the Muscadine.

Hardouin Le Charcutier
le Virage Gastronomique, Vouvray (on the RN152, 10 km from centre of Tours), T02 47 52 60 24, and 8 rue de la République, Vouvray, T02 47 52 65 33. Also at the Duc de Gascogne, Les Halles, place Gaston Paillhou, Tours, hardouin.fr.
Traditional *charcutier* producing *rillons, rillettes*, terrines, sausages and string *andouillettes*, flavoured with wines from Vouvray.

Markets

Les Halles
Place des Halles.
Daily 0700-1930, Sun and bank holidays 0800-1300.
This large covered market is a gastronomic delight and a feast for the eyes. You will find food and wine from throughout the Touraine region and it's a great place to pick up the ingredients for a hearty picnic.

Flower Market
Boulevard Béranger.
Wed and Sat all year.
The second largest flower market in France after Grasse stretches in a ribbon of colour along the centre of the Boulevard. You can buy cut flowers, arrangements, herbs and vegetable plants, plus a huge variety of shrubs and perennials.

Evening Food Lovers Market
Place de la Résistance.
1600-2100, 1st Fri each month,

Evening Street Market
Central Loches.
Jul-Aug 2nd Thu, 1800 to midnight.
Festive evenings where you can buy direct from producers and see craftsmen at work. Enjoy music and street entertainment in the heart of this historic town.

Atelier-galerie Hair
1 rue des Marais, Thizay (10 km west of Chinon), T02 47 95 90 01, charles-hair.com.
Ceramicist Charles Hair works from his studio in Thizay and has work on display in the Musée Pincé in Angers, and several galleries in Paris. He produces unique contemporary items and beautiful, delicately coloured celadons.

Tip…

On Fridays from June to September (1800-2400), look out for *Marchés Gourmands* in Bourgueil, Langeais, Chateau-la-Valliere, Neuillé-Pont-Pierre and Azay-le-Rideau (Saturday) where you can buy and taste local produce. Markets are held in rotation in each town.

Traditional street markets are as colourful as ever.

Activities & tours

Balloon flights
Here is a small selection of companies in Touraine offering balloon flights.

Au Grès des Vents
T02 54 46 42 40,
au-gre-des-vents.com.
Departures from Cheverny with launch sites here and at Chambord, Blois, Fougères, Chaumont and Chenonceau.

Balloon Revolution
T02 47 23 99 63,
balloonrevolution.com.
Based in Amboise, the company offers a personalized service with individual, couple or group tickets.

Touraine Montgolfière
T02 47 56 42 05,
touraine-montgolfiere.fr.
Launching from sites throughout the Touraine, there are three ticket types, giving greater flexibility as to when you take your flight.

Boat trips
River Cher
Traditional river boat cruises in a *toue* (flat-bottomed boat with cabin) are a great way to discover the river and encounter its wildlife and scenery. Some trips include passage under the arches of the Château de Chenonceau – the *Gabare* and the *Belandre* both depart from the Maison Eclusière in Chisseaux.

River Loire, Candes-St-Martin
Embarcadère, Candes-St-Martin,
T02 47 95 80 85, loireterroir.com.
The traditional style flat-bottomed boats *La Belle Adèle* (with disabled access) and the *Amarante* sail from this picturesque village near the confluence of the Loire and Vienne rivers. Trips have different themes, such as wine, cooking, fish or birds, or you can enjoy a sunrise or sunset picnic.

River Loire: Rochecorbon
56 quai de la Loire, Rochecorbon,
T02 47 52 68 88, naviloire.com.
€9, €6 under 12s.
Cruises of the Loire (duration 50 mins) with a lively commentary aboard the 66-seater *St Martin-de-Tours*. Occasional birdwatching trips with a guide. It is strongly recommended that you book your seats in advance.

Crafts
Societé Cooperative Agricole de Vannerie de Villaines
1 rue de la Cheneillère,
Villaines-les-Rochers,
T02 47 45 43 03, vannerie.com.
Tours of the workshop with basket makers at work and an interesting audiovisual presentation (English version on request). The village has the largest number of basket workers in France and there are other studios where you can browse and buy wickerwork products for just about any use. Several workshops run courses.

Follow the self-guided trail to learn about the many facets of basket making.

Cycle routes & hire
There are four *Loire à Vélo* routes to follow in the Touraine area (leaflets are available in English from a tourist office or downloadable, French only, from the website loire-a-velo.fr). See full details for *Loire à Vélo* on page 69.

Cyclopolitain
Rue de Châteauneuf, Tours,
T09 53 99 74 63,
cyclopolitain.com.
Electric tricycles with a chauffeur called a *Cyclonaut*. This is being promoted as the new, ecological way to travel in and around Tours – plus you have your own personal tour guide. 30 minutes for 2 people costs €18.

Detours de Loire
35 rue Charles Gille, Tours,
T02 47 61 22 23,
locationdevelos.com.
The best place to hire touring bikes, tandems and accessories. They do a useful delivery and pick-up service throughout the Loire Valley, luggage transfer and just about anything else connected to having an enjoyable cycling holiday. They have a selection of self-guided tours or will customize a tour especially for you. Adult bike hire for one week costs from €59. Dropping off the bike at another

location will add a small charge to the rental.

Food & drink
Chocolaterie Bigot
Place du Château,
Amboise, T02 47 57 04 46,
bigot-amboise.com.
Master chocolate makers since 1913, Maison Bigot give demonstrations and tastings on a *visite gourmande* by appointment only (Mar-Oct).

Musée de la Poire Tapée
7 chemin de la Buronnière,
Rivarennes (about 10 km west of
Azay-le-Rideau), T02 47 95 45 19.
The *poire tapée* or dried pear is a speciality of Rivarennes. An audiovisual presentation in three languages explains the history and different stages of production followed by a tasting. You pay a small charge for the tasting so do not feel obliged to buy, though it is difficult to resist.

Spa & wellbeing
Les Bains Douches
Impasse du Sanitas,
Loches, T02 47 59 12 12,
les-bains-douches.fr.
Offers original treatments for face and body with great two- or three-day packages that will leave you feeling restored and relaxed.

Domaine des Thomeaux
Hôtel & Spa
12 rue des Thomeaux, Mosnes (10
km east of Amboise), T08 25 37
00 00, domainedesthomeaux.fr.
The Domaine is a great place to recharge your batteries with the focus on relaxation. A full day of luxury and pampering, alone or with a partner costs between €100 and €210.

Relais du Plessis
Route de Thuet, Richelieu,
T02 47 58 75 50, relaisduplessis.fr.
The spa's philosophy is inspired by the principle of the five elements – air, water, light, plants and minerals. Drawing on natural resources, they offer a range of hydrotherapy techniques, massage and beauty treatments.

Swimming
Remember that bathing is forbidden in the Loire and in the Cher below Tours for safety reasons.

Centre Aquatic du Lac
275 av de Grammont,
Tours, T02 47 80 78 10,
vert-marine.com/centre-
aquatique-du-lac-tours-37.
Superb, modern complex just outside the centre of Tours with a 50-m heated outdoor pool, training pools, recreation pool, solarium and spa facilities.

Wildlife
Aquarium du Val de Loire
Les Hauts Boeufs, Lussault-sur-
Loire, T02 47 23 44 57,
aquariumduvaldeloire.com.
Open all year. €13,
€9 children (4-14) .
Aimed at families, the aquarium boasts 2 million litres of water (fresh and salt) and over 40 pools where you can discover the giants that populate the Loire such as a monster catfish, as well as all the iconic species from rivers and oceans throughout the world.

Transport

Echoes of the great age of travel.

Wine tours

Caves des Producteurs de Vouvray
38 La Vallée Coquette, Vouvray, T02 47 52 75 03, cp-vouvray.com. Daily 0900-1230 and 1345-1900 (15 May-15 Sep 0900-1900).
A good introduction to the Vouvray wine-making area and the secrets behind the sparkling *Fines bulles de Vouvray*. Taste a selection of Vouvray and Loire wines, purchase wine and regional products in the shop and visit a small exhibition of cooperage tools. Regular guided tours in English every day (May-Sep).

Cheese & wine tour
T02 47 50 64 42, riverloire.com.
A half-day package including a private tour through the famous wine caves at Rochecorbon followed by a tasting of the most important wines of the region accompanied by selected local cheeses. Every day from the Amboise and Tours areas.

Route des Vignobles Touraine-Val de Loire
vinsdeloire.fr
Wine enthusiasts can follow the special Loire Valley wine route through the vineyards of Touraine. The route passes through Vouvray and Montlouis-sur-Loire, then south of Tours along the Indre valley, ending with a circuit round Bourgueil and the Chinonais. Guides are available from tourist offices and the routes are clearly signed. Wine producers displaying the *caves touristiques* signs have regular opening hours and offer wine-tastings to visitors (groups by arrangement).

Train
There are good daily services to major tourist sites on the TER trains (ter-sncf.com/centre) departing from the main station in Tours. Château de Chenonceau rail station has 3 return trips a day (30 mins); the station is just 50 m from the château. Frequent trains from Tours to Amboise are 20 minutes.

Bus
The Fil Vert bus services (T02 47 31 14 00, tourainefilvert.com) to Chenonceau and Amboise operate all year. Azay-le-Rideau, Villandry and Savonnières (Jun-Oct) are best served during the school holidays. Catch all these services from the Halte Routière in front of the station on place du Général Leclerc in Tours. Bus journeys within Tours on the Fil Bleu (filbleu.fr) cost €1.25 for a single journey (*ticket à l'unité*) or €3.20 for one day (*une journée*). Buy your ticket from the driver when you get on the bus and stamp it in the yellow machine at the start of your journey. Each bus stop has a useful route map. The buses to the airport leave the city 2 hours before the flights to London and depart from the airport 20 mins after flight arrivals.

Taxi
Alphacars (T02 47 05 30 49) operate a shuttle service between the airport and Tours city centre (€5 one way).

Contents

Anjou

Troglo homes, like this one in Montsoreau, are newly chic.

Introduction

What to see in…

…one day
Begin in Angers, if possible taking in a Saturday morning **market**. Visit the **Château d'Angers** and climb to the ramparts, before seeing the **Teinture de l'Apocalypse**. Lunch just across the river in **La Doutre**, then visit the **Eglise de la Trinité** and the **Musée Jean Lurçat**. Round it off with a boat trip on the river and an evening meal on **place du Ralliement**.

…a weekend or more
With a second day, you'll have time to visit the **Château de Saumur**, then discover the old town, lunching on the quayside. If you love horses, the National Riding School (home of the **Cadre Noir**) is not to be missed; alternatively, visit the Plantagenêt tombs in the **Abbaye de Fontevraud** before strolling around nearby **Montsoreau**, climbing through the narrow lanes to see troglodytic houses and a perfect view of the chateau. Head back to Saumur for dinner in **place St-Pierre**.

Among the ancient territories of Anjou, known to the Romans as Andegavia, lie elegant chateaux such as Saumur, Montreuil-Bellay, Montgeoffroy and Brissac, many of them less visited than more familiar sites further upstream. The arduous hand quarrying which provided their smooth, pale stone also created countless troglodytic homes, while larger caves provided the perfect environment for storing wine and growing mushrooms. Anjou, too, has its own renowned AOC vineyards and also creates the world-famous Cointreau liqueur, not to mention lesser-known gastronomic delicacies like *pommes-tappées* – oven-dried apples from its productive orchards. The Loire, of course, is never far away and is joined by important tributaries like the Maine, Sarthe and Vienne, bringing a contemplative quality to the landscape. Here and there many sacred sites were established long ago, the most influential of them all lying below the Loire and close to Saumur at the Abbaye Royale de Fontevraud, where Henry II and Eleanor of Aquitaine lie buried. Finally there's the city of Angers, home of some of the Loire Valley's greatest historical treasures, perhaps the most precious of all being the monumental Apocalypse Tapestry created in 1375 and now lovingly preserved within the mighty chateau of the Dukes of Anjou.

An equine love affair continues in Saumur.

Saumur

Seen from across the Loire, Saumur looks like the definitive riverside town, presided over by its romantic chateau. The historic heart of the town holds many surprises, and repays a little patient exploration. It's also a fine place in which to dine, and will delight lovers of specialist (and very French) boutiques. Saumur's National Riding School (Ecole Nationale d'Equitation) is world famous, and welcomes visitors for a peep behind the scenes. Nearby lie the AOC wine-producing areas for which Saumur is famous (you'll also find many others a little further afield, including the renowned vineyards of the Château de Montreuil-Bellay, set high above the valley of the River Thouet). But what lies beneath the local landscape can sometimes be just as interesting, particularly around the rose-producing town of Doué-la-Fontaine, where you can explore vast, troglodytic, cathedral-like cave systems created by quarrying the distinctive yellow *falun* sandstone – and there are plenty of similar sites to discover nearby. Elsewhere lie more conventionally beautiful sites – at Montsoreau, for example, you can shop for bargains in one of the monthly flea markets held on the banks of the Loire, while nearby is Fontevraud's famous abbey, one of the most important historical sites in Europe.

Echoes of a cultured past in Saumur.

The Loire divides Saumur neatly in two – or three, counting the slender Île Offard anchored midstream. The *rive droite* handles most of the commercial activity while the historic quarter, on the southern bank, remains largely untouched by modern development. The pale stone façades of 'Saumur la Blanche' are a picture of unified elegance. Along the quayside lie landmarks like the 16th-century Gothic Hôtel de Ville and the magnificent Palladio-style theatre which is also home to the Maison du Vin, presenting the area's many fine wines. Saumur holds the prestigious Ville d'Art et d'Histoire label, and works hard to preserve its wealth of historic architecture. In place St-Pierre, for example, medieval half-timbered façades stand tall beside their *tuffeau* neighbours, including the 12th- to 17th-century Eglise St-Pierre. The medieval square is the most atmospheric of settings for diners at the café and restaurant tables, and a similar spirit accompanies shoppers in the heart of the old town. To the west of the town lies the Ecole Nationale d'Equitation.

Château-Musée de Saumur

T02 41 40 24 40, ville-saumur.fr.
1 Apr-30 Sep Tue-Sun 1000-1300 and 1400-1730.
€3, under 11s free. Guided visits available in English during Jul and Aug.

Looking only marginally less fanciful than the illustration in *Les Trés Riches Heures du Duc de Berry* (1410), an illuminated manuscript which came to define the power and elegance of medieval France, Saumur's chateau is a romantic, fairy-tale vision made real, and surveys the surrounding landscapes proudly from a commanding position on a limestone plateau high above the southern shores of the Loire. Not surprisingly, the chateau is the latest in a succession of strongholds to occupy the site, among the earliest having been that built by Comte de Blois Thibaud le Tricheur during the 10th century. It subsequently passed to Comte d'Anjou Foulques Nerra and his successors the

Essentials

❷ **Getting around** If you're based in or near Saumur, you'll almost certainly need your own transport, be it bicycle (the *Loire à Vélo* route runs along this beautiful stretch of the river with easy circuits to villages, attractions and the vineyards) or car. The *Corniche Angevine* (best driven east to west) between Savennières and Chalonnes-sur-Loire, takes you through the heart of the wine-growing areas.

❷ **Bus station** Agglobus (agglobus.fr) operates from the main bus station at Pôle Balzac. There's an information and ticket office at 19 rue Franklin Roosevelt (near the tourist office).

❷ **Train station** The Gare SNCF is on the north bank on avenue David d'Angers. The TER service serves most of the other Loire Valley towns (except on Sun).

❷ **ATMs** Rue Beaurepaire or rue d'Orléans, near the tourist office.

❷ **Hospitals** Route de Fontevraud, T02 41 53 30 30.

❷ **Pharmacies** Pharmacie du Centre, 25 rue Franklin Roosevelt, T02 41 51 11 63.

❷ **Post offices** Rue Volney, T02 41 50 33 53 and 5 avenue David d'Angers, T02 41 50 98 63.

❷ **Tourist information offices** 30 place des Fontaines, Doué-la-Fontaine, T02 41 59 20 49, ot-douelafontaine.fr; Maison du Parc, 15 avenue de la Loire, Montsoreau, T02 41 38 38 88, parc-loire-anjou-touraine.fr; place de la Bilange, Saumur, T02 41 40 20 60, saumur-tourisme.com.

A commanding view for a fairytale castle.

Around the region

Plantagenêts, before being seized by Capetian King Philippe II (Philippe-Auguste). In 1227 the fortifications were further strengthened by Louis IX, the exterior gaining an air of sophistication by the addition, by Louis I d'Anjou, of four octagonal towers during the 14th century. A century later, René I d'Anjou greatly improved interior living quarters. During the 16th century visionary Italian architect Bartolomeo added defensive perimeter bastions in a star shape, a full century before such systems became the trademark of France's greatest military engineer Sébastian Le Prestre de Vauban. After a period as the residence of Saumur's Governors, under Napoléon the chateau became a prison, holding for a while the notorious Marquis de Sade. It then served as a barracks and is currently nearing the end of a long campaign of renovation which will soon find the interior opened to visitors. For now, though, you can visit the Equestrian Museum collections displayed in a temporary setting.

Eglise St-Pierre

Place St-Pierre, T02 41 51 31 59.
Summer 0800-1900; winter 0800-1700. Free.

Looming assertively over place St-Pierre, the stylistic weirdness of the western façade is hard to ignore. Records from Fontevraud (see page 219) show the presence of a church dedicated to St-Pierre in 1109. At first the location, on a flood plain of the Loire, caused few problems, even after the structure's enlargement around 1180. In 1673, though, alarming cracks appeared in one of the main western buttresses. Since the culprit was the unstable geology, repairs proved ineffectual and in 1674 almost the entire western façade suddenly collapsed, taking with it part of the nave vault, while somehow leaving the organ intact. Saving the remainder of the building from destruction required urgent rebuilding works which saw an Ionic stage piled above a Doric one in a deliberate Counter Reformation gesture which has divided opinion ever since. The central tower remained unfinished for five centuries, but was finally crowned by a slightly twisted spire in 1775. Seven years later it was destroyed by lightning and would not be replaced until 1986. Although sinking foundations have continued to cause problems ever since, the will to save the church remains as strong as ever. The 12th- and 13th-century interior is topped with Angevin Gothic vaults. Above the arcades is a series of carved corbels similar to those in the cathedral of Angers (see page 280) and which include depictions of wine-making. The 15th-century stalls, too, are worth a closer look to see the humorous carved figures below the misericords. Before leaving take a look at the Romanesque south portal, whose foliated decoration includes acanthus and palm leaves on the capitals, plus vine leaves on the archway.

Musée de la Cavalerie

Place Charles de Foucauld, T02 41 83 69 23, museecavalerie.free.fr.
Mon-Thu 0900-1200 and 1400-1700, Sat-Sun 1400-1800. Free.

One of the region's more remarkable museums opened its doors in 2007. The collections fill three exhibition halls of the former *manège* (riding school) of the Cadre Noir. The first hall presents a comprehensive overview of the French mounted cavalry between 1445 (the year in which Charles VII established what amounted to the first national army) and the time of Napoléon III (mid-19th century). The imagery in period illustrations and paintings varies from grandly ceremonial to shocking scenes from the fields of battle. Naturally, there are well-preserved regimental uniforms, and full-size equine models. The second hall continues the story up to the Franco-Prussian War of 1870–1871 (which proved to be Western Europe's final major cavalry engagement) and the exploits of the now more familiar armoured cavalry, whose story continues to unfold today (the French armoured cavalry continues to make history in the world's conflict zones). The third hall houses a vast library and a centre for military research along with a temporary exhibition area.

Countless quays tell of once-important river navigation.

Five of the best

Anjou chateaux

❶ **Château d'Angers** For its rampart walks and Apocalypse Tapestry. (Page 228).

❷ **Château de Brézé** For its hidden troglodytic underworld. (Page 222).

❸ **Château de Brissac** For its gardens, vineyard and canal. (Page 237).

❹ **Chateau de Montgeoffroy** For its perfect 18th-century interiors. (Page 234).

❺ **Château de Saumur** For its elevated river views. (Page 215).

A sense of occasion in Saumur.

Ecole Nationale d'Equitation/le Cadre Noir

Av de l'Ecole Nationale d'Equitation, Terrefort, T02-41 53 50 60, cadrenoir.fr.
15 Feb-3 Apr and 18 Oct-6 Nov with guided visits (duration 1 hr) at 0930, 1100, 1400 and 1600, 6 Apr-16 Oct with guided visits every 30 mins except lunchtimes and mornings, when there is a public presentation. Closed Sat pm, Sun, Mon am and bank holidays. €7, €6 concession, €5 under 12s. Public presentations, where the public are invited to attend the dressage training (€16), start at 1030 (ticket office opens 0930). Advance booking advisable.

Musée des Blindés

1043 route de Fontevraud, T02 41 83 69 95, museedesblindes.fr.
Daily all year, although times vary (Jul and Aug 0930-1830). €7, €4 children (7-15), €19 family.

This huge collection contains examples of just about every variant of military tank imaginable. The displays (in huge, unheated halls) are grouped according to period and nationality, and include restored French, British, German and Eastern Bloc vehicles. There's even a section relating to French Resistance fighters. Alongside the tanks you'll find military motorcycles, armoured cars, personnel carriers, cannon and the Jeep used by Général Leclerc. And if you're still unable to track down that elusive armoured vehicle from your childhood Dinky-Toy collection, there's also an extensive display of scale models – plus the inevitable gift shop. Finally, you can see vehicles undergoing restoration in the museum workshops. In short, welcome to petrolhead paradise.

Dolmen de Bagneux

56 rue du Dolmen, Saumur, T02 41 50 23 02, saumur-dolmen.com.
Apr-Sep 0900-1900. Closed Wed except Jul and Aug. €3.50, €2 childre (6-16 yrs).

France's largest dolmen also sits in the most bizarre of settings, amid a clump of trees, flowerbeds and gravel paths tucked away behind a brasserie on the outskirts of Saumur. Here you'll find an 18-m-long main chamber, whose antechamber stones take the total length to over 23 m. The topmost stones, over 5 m wide, are thought to weigh over 500 tonnes and were manoeuvred into their present positions around 5000 years ago. No human remains were discovered when the site was the scene of major excavations back in 1775, suggesting that this was not a burial chamber. Now there's a display of prehistoric flint and stone tools found here and (mostly) elsewhere.

If you're taken with the monument then you may be able to purchase it, along with the brasserie, which, at the time of writing, was for sale.

Abbaye Royale de Fontevraud

T02 41 51 73 52, Fontevraud-l'Abbaye (15 km southest of Saumur), abbaye-fontevraud.com. Daily except 1 Jan, 1 May, 1 and 11 Nov and 25 Dec, 0900/1000-1730/1830 according to season. Jan-Apr and Nov-Dec, €6.50, €4.50 18-25 years; May-Oct €7.90, €5.90 18-25 years. Under 18s free.

France's largest and best-preserved monastic settlement lies below the confluence of the rivers Loire and Vienne, and was founded by 11th-century hermit (later Pope Urban II's emissary) Robert d'Arbrissel. From the very outset it was unconventional, bringing together on a single site independent communities of brothers, nuns, lay-sisters, lepers and invalids, each with their place of worship and attendant infrastructure. In 1119 it was visited by Pope Calixtus II and also enjoyed royal patronage from the Plantagenêt dynasty (half the abbesses, too, were of royal birth). In 1561, however, Fontevraud was desecrated by Huguenots, and then again in 1792 and 1793 by Revolutionary forces. But the ultimate indignity came by order of Napoléon, who in 1804 decreed that Fontevraud should become a prison. Amazingly, it remained so until 1963, but the entire site has now been restored, recovering much of its former gravitas and beauty.

The main abbey church is breathtaking in both length and width. Instead of conventional vaults, it employs a series of domes more typical of Aquitaine. Note also the dignified tomb figures of Henri II, Alienor d'Aquitaine, their son Richard, Coeur-de-Lion, plus Isabella d'Angoulême, wife of King John of England. South of the nave are huge, beautifully restored cloisters and, beyond, the 45-m-long refectory, all Romanesque apart from a Gothic vault added in 1515 to replace the original timber roof. Don't miss visiting the 12th-, 15th- and 17th-century Gothic **Eglise St-Michel** (signed from near the Abbey entrance), whose beautiful gilded altarpiece was transported here from the abbey in 1621.

Fontevraud's medieval designer kitchens

When they were constructed during the 12th century, France's sole surviving Romanesque kitchens would have represented the last word in contemporary design – even today there can't be many cooks who can boast their own smoke-room for preserving meats and fish. The architect conceived an octagonal plan and topped the building with a spire-like hood around 27 m in height. The present highly distinctive, steeply pitched Byzantine-style replacement was added during major restorations in 1904. Note the fish-scale stone cladding and a group of slender, decorative chimneys similar in style to those found at the Château de Chambord (see page 121). In order to minimize the ever-present risk of fire, Fontevraud's great kitchens were constructed in stone and originally stood separately from the main building. At some point, though, it acquired eight adjoining buildings, three of which were demolished during the 16th century when the kitchens were united with the refectory. Clearly the very model of efficiency, the kitchens fed around 800 residents each day during the height of Fontevraud's activity.

Fontevraud is (and always was) a world apart.

St Martin of Tours

During the fourth century Tours was the home of France's most celebrated evangelist, St Martin, who founded the country's second monastery just outside the city at Marmoutier, and who was elected Bishop of Tours in 371. His death at Candes-St-Martin (in western Touraine) in November 397 sparked a major religious dispute, as the people of Tours and Poitiers (where Martin had previously been a disciple of Bishop Hilary) vied to keep his precious remains. The Tourangeaux slipped the body through a window in Candes' church in the dead of night, then carried it back on the Loire – it's said that as he passed the stark autumnal trees burst miraculously into leaf again. From this moment Tours became a great pilgrimage centre as crowds sought the healing powers attributed to the Saint's relics, which were by the 12th century entombed in a great Romaneque Basilica dedicated to him. The tumultuous events of the Revolution spared only the Tour Charlemagne and Tour de l'Horloge of the building (see page 174). The Saint's mortal remains still lie nearby, however, in the 19th-century Basilique St-Martin.

Collégiale de Candes-Saint-Martin

Candes-Saint-Martin (14 km upstream from Saumur), T02-47 58 90 21, collegialedecandes.fr. Daily except Jan 1 0900-1200 and 1400-1800. €2, supplement for guided visit €2.

In 387 Saint Martin established a priory at Candes (one of six parishes founded by the Saint) overlooking the confluence of the Loire and the Vienne. Previously Christianity had been confined to larger towns, so converting comparatively remote rural areas would have been a very different undertaking. In 848 the priory was incorporated into the Bishopric of Tours and became a collegiate church. Approach the western façade today and you'll see clear signs of the 15th-century fortifications deemed necessary to respond to the turmoil of the Hundred Years' War. Purely decorative, though, are two levels of statuary which, unusually, find both saints and apostles standing shoulder-to-shoulder. Step into the porch, constructed around 1250, and you'll find more many fine sculptures, whose marked stylistic variations reflect the 50-year period over which they were created. Inside the church feels impressively high, with immense incised piers rising to Angevin (or 'Plantagenêt') Gothic vaults of equal height for both the nave and side aisles, the architect clearly having been inspired by the Cathédrale Saint-Pierre further south in Poitiers. The transepts and choir, though, retain a Romanesque spirit, their construction having begun around 1180. To the left of the choir is a narrow passage leading to the Chapelle St-Martin, in which the Saint passed away in 397. The subsequent spiriting-away of his body to Tours is represented in a stained glass window. Other curiosities include a well sunk in the south transept during the 15th-century fortification works and the interestingly decorated Chapelle St-Michel, concealed above the entry porch and accessible via a steep staircase.

Château de Montsoreau

Passage du Marquis de Geoffre, Montsoreau (14 km upstream from Saumur), T02-41 67 12 60, chateau-montsoreau.com. May-Sep daily 1000-1900, Apr and Oct to mid-Nov daily 1400-1800. €8.30, €6.80 students and 14-18 years, €5.20 children (5-14), €25 family tarif (2 adults, 2 children).

Throughout history this chateau's setting, at the confluence of the Loire and the Vienne, would have been of great strategic importance. From the banks of the Loire the chateau appears stern and forbidding, but approach it from the village on the hillside behind and you'll see a much less austere (but still impressive) countenance. In many ways this dual personality mirrors that of the location, readily defensible by the river-fed moats which once surrounded the chateau yet severely compromised by the substantial landmass rising behind it. The name comes from 'Monte Sorello', stronghold of the Comte d'Anjou's ally Guillaume de Montsoreau. The site was placed under siege by Henri II in 1152, although most of what is visible today dates from the 15th century. Its builder was Jean II de Chambes, Councillor to Charles VII.

During the 19th century the chateau achieved a degree of celebrity when it inspired Alexandre Dumas' historical novel *La Dame de Monsoreau*, which followed *La Reine Margot*. Today, after renovations to combat the effects of years of decay, the exterior, with its fine Renaissance *escalier* and bas-reliefs of the Chambes family's heraldic arms, is once again pristine. Some 18 rooms are visitable and devoted to *Les Imaginaires de la Loire* – family-friendly animated displays recounting the Loire's history, navigation and trade, plus the story of the Dumas novel, and, of course, the chateau itself.

The Château de Montsoreau reveals its gentler side.

Around the region

Château de Brézé

Brézé (11 km southeast of Saumur), T02 41 51 60 15, chateaudebreze.com.
Feb-Mar Tue-Sun 1000-1800; Apr-Sep daily 1000-1830, Oct-Dec Tue-Sun 1000-1800. Closed 25 Dec. €11, €6 children (6-18).

For those approaching via, say, a hot air balloon the extraordinary situation of this 11th- to 14th-century chateau would be clear in an instant. The rest of us, though, have to wait until we're beyond the courtyard and suddenly confronted by a bridge spanning the 18-m-deep abyss surrounding the central buildings. The obvious defensive value provided by the moat's great depth was essential, since a gentle hilltop location meant that it would always remain dry. The excavations, which left the chateau perched on a huge pillar of the pale, *tuffeau* limestone from which the building is also constructed, didn't stop there. As you'll discover during the course of a visit, there's as much nibbled-away at below ground as there is built above it, in the form of the medieval troglodytic village of La Roche. This cave-like complex includes grain stores, silkworm caves, wine cellars, stables and a prison, the whole thing connected by a network of passageways.

The chateau above can trace its own history back to 1063 but the main fortifications date from the 15th century. The Renaissance injected an element of sophistication in time for a visit in 1565 of Charles IX and his mother Catherine de' Medici, and the style was chosen (alongside neo-Gothic) for the extensive enlargement works of the 19th century. The Second World War saw Brézé under German occupation, although today the interiors have been comprehensively restored to their 19th-century elegance. Particularly impressive are the kitchens, whose vast array of copperware gleams proudly.

A little of the Château de Brézé's mystery is revealed.

The curious world of Boule de fort

Curiously, the region's most widely played ball game (and said to have been invented, or at least played, by the Plantagenêts) is almost invisible to most visitors to the Loire. The Anjou area alone has over 300 *Boule de fort* clubs (each with an average 120 members) devoted to this relative of *pétanque*, a game played in dusty village squares throughout France. The Loire version, however, takes place indoors on a slightly concave *piste* some 23 m long and 6 m wide, its smooth surface kept that way by the players wearing carpet slippers. The game uses wooden balls or *boules* weighing up to 2 kg, whose rolling surfaces are smooth iron hoops; the remaining areas, like the non-spherical balls normally used on bowling greens elsewhere, are slightly flattened. One ('*fort*') side is also weighted. When thrown, the balls therefore refuse to run straight, instead curving smoothly until they finally come to rest on their heavier side. Players aim towards a small jack (*le maître* or *petit*), the game requiring great skill and gentleness, combined, when necessary, with more spectacular techniques like bouncing off the sides of the court to reach the target.

There are initiations into Boule de fort from 1800-2000 every Thursday during July and August at the Société la Cure, place Jeanne d'Arc, St-Hilaire-St-Florent (4 km downstream from Saumur), T02 41 67 31 76.

Château & Collégiale de Notre-Dame, Montreuil-Bellay

Montreuil-Bellay (15 km southwest of Saumur), T02-41 52 33 06, chateau-de-montreuil-bellay.fr. Apr-Jun and Sep to early Nov Wed-Mon 1000-1200 and 1400-1800; Jul-Aug daily 1000-1830. Guided tour of interior and gardens €8, €6 students over 15 yrs, €4 6-14 yrs; gardens only €4. The Collégiale (daily, 0900-1900) is accessible on foot to the right of the chateau entrance.

Approach from the north to see the chateau and its giant former chapel rising slowly and dramatically beyond a sea of vines, then descend to the banks of the River Thouet for the full impact of the elevated site. Originally settled by the Romans, its strategic value clearly appealed to Comte d'Anjou Foulques Nerra, who constructed a military stronghold during the early 11th century. Its subsequent occasionally turbulent career saw both Phillippe II and Louis VIII holding court here, although most of what is visible today dates from the 15th century. Subsequently, apart from accommodating female Revolutionary dissident prisoners, and serving as a makeshift hospital caring for First World War casualties, Montreuil has mostly remained a gracious and comfortable private residence. Just how comfortable is revealed in visits which also take in private gardens plus huge vaulted kitchens and cellars in which you can taste the chateau's own AOC wines.

The Gothic collegiate church, completed in 1484, was originally the chateau canons' chapel. Outwardly vast and rather austere, its interior feels lower than expected, with an air of sadness intensified by the walls' prominent black band bearing the arms of d'Harcourt family victims of the Revolution, while many windows have lost their stained glass and are partly filled in. Notice the Angevin vaults overhead, an ornate oratory to your left and a series of sculpted figures set within the nave's largely decorative piers. Among the interesting oil paintings adorning the interior is a charming depiction of Saints Claude, Ambroise and Louis by local artist Riavay, dated 1609. The nearby town is well worth exploring – be sure to follow the Escalier St-Pierre stone stairway down to the riverside.

Doué-la-Fontaine & Les Cathédrales Troglos des Perrières

Rue d'Anjou, Doué-la-Fontaine (17 km west of Saumur), T02 41 59 06 13, ville-douelafontaine.fr/perrieres/. Mid-Jun to mid-Sep daily, Apr-Jun and Sep-Oct Wed-Sun. You can follow a trail through the caves at any time (ask for an English translation

Antoine Cristal, pioneering wine-maker

Son of a wagoner from the Auvergne, Antoine Cristal was born in Turquant in 1837, and began his working life as a textile salesman. He was so successful that somewhere along the way he ended up purchasing the company which employed him and, with some shrewd investments, amassed a considerable fortune. In 1886 he purchased the Château de Parnay, near Saumur, and turned his talents to wine-making. Again he was extremely successful, selling wine to Parisian restaurants and even supplying the English court. At that time the local wines were almost exclusively white, but Cristal began a conversion to predominantly red wines, forerunners of what we know today as Saumur-Champigny. His highly experimental vineyard also developed a viticulture system known as *clos des murs*, which entailed constructing some 3 km of high walls aligned east-west. He then planted Cabernet Franc vines on the north side, where their roots would remain in the shade. The stems, however, were trained through a line of holes, allowing plants to flourish on the sun-warmed south side – the stone absorbed the heat during the day and slowly released it overnight. The walls survive, and Clos Cristal 'Les Murs' wines are still made exclusively from grapes picked along them, although the unique system seems too expensive for other vineyards to emulate.

Cristal was reputedly grumpy and ill-tempered, and never married, leaving the chateau to his niece. In a philanthropic gesture, although, he bequeathed his vineyard at Champigny to the Hospice of Saumur. Now a modern hospital, it still benefits from Clos Cristal Saumur-Champigny wine sales.

Clos Cristal, route de Cristal, Souzay-Champigny (7 km upstream from Saumur), T02 41 52 96 08, clos-cristal.com.

and activities for children) or join a guided tour at 1100, 1500 or 1700 according to season.

Apart from its popular zoological park, this slightly straggling village looks superficially to have little else of interest, but you'll be surprised by what lies (literally) below the surface. Doué sits on beds of *falun* – a coarse, golden stone highly prized throughout the fifth and sixth centuries for making sarcophagi. At the Cave aux Sarcophages you can take a guided visit to a group of caves from where around 35,000 sarcophagi were quarried, and which offered refuge during Viking raids. A potentially more atmospheric experience is on offer at Les Cathédrales des Troglos des Perrières (in a hamlet on outskirts of Doué), where an extensive network of subterranean former quarries can be visited freely, and whose tall, bottle-shaped forms suggest the Gothic *arc-brisé* (broken arch) of the great cathedrals. Here, though, it's a shadowy world whose sense of mystery is heightened by well-conceived lighting effects, many triggered by motion sensors. It can be disorienting, but following the arrows will take you safely back to your starting point. Here and there large areas of the yellow stone walls show bottle green discolouration, evidence of the caves' former use for commercial mushroom production. Adjacent to the site in a long, narrow opening in the landscape is a restored terrace of troglodytic dwellings. A final surprise is that Doué's *Arènes* are not in fact Roman, but were quarried during the 15th or 16th centuries; the amphitheatre still hosts events including the annual *Journées de la Rose*, which underline the area's position as Europe's premier rose producer. A staggering seven million plants are sold annually.

Eglise Prieurale Notre-Dame de Cunault

Cunault (14 km downstream from Saumur), chenehutte-treves-cunault.fr.
Daily 0800-1800 (2000 in summer). Free.

The church served an abbey founded by monks fleeing with the remains of St-Philbert from the Ile de Noirmoutier during Norman attacks in 847. Five years later they were obliged to seek refuge further afield in Burgundy, Cunault becoming a dependency of the Benedictine abbey of Tournus. After the Hundred Years' War the church ceased to be a priory and in 1749 was sold for use as a barn, but was restored during the 19th century. Today the squared-off western façade looks less than enthralling, but beyond is a massively buttressed 11th-century bell tower straddling the body of the 11th- to 13th-century church and topped with a later spire (or *flèche*). The tower's four bells are said to come from the Cathedral of Constantine in Algiers.

Above the entry portal is a finely sculpted tympanum depicting the Virgin in Majesty. The Romanesque interior is startling, with groin-style vaults suspended high above mostly rounded arches, although the slightly pointed final arches (built around 1170) hint at the arrival of Gothic. Both the pier capitals (well over 200 in all) and the transverse arches supporting the vaults are richly sculpted with stylized foliation and a wealth of characters, both human and demonic. Notice the massive construction of the side aisles, designed to resist the outward forces acting upon the nave from the heavy stone vaults. In the large raised ambulatory beyond the nave you'll find the carved and painted wooden shrine containing the remains of St-Maxcenceul, a devotee of St-Martin of Tours who brought Christianity to the area during the fifth century (see page 174).

Cunault has had a long and chequered history.

Angers

Throughout history its location at the meeting of several important rivers made Angers irresistible, not only to those who settled there, but also to outsiders intent on pillaging the fruits of the locals' labours. No wonder it came to possess the most formidable of all the Loire Valley chateaux, whose multi-coloured towers remain a potent symbol on the skyline. Inside is the world-famous Apocalypse Tapestry, a miraculous medieval survivor that contributed to Angers becoming officially a 'Ville d'art et d'histoire'. And it's impossible to stroll through the heart of the old town without being repeatedly halted in your tracks by a succession of architectural revelations. Exuberant art nouveau and belle époque buildings rub shoulders with sharp art deco – all mere newcomers compared to the medieval half-timbered 15th-century Maison d'Adam, the early Gothic Cathédrale St-Maurice and even older Romanesque and Carolingian-era survivors. Some of them provide the most atmospheric settings imaginable for fabulous collections of art and creativity. Add a vibrant, youthful society, a dazzling array of elegant shops and a wide choice of restaurants for every taste and you'll see why Angers is unquestionably one of the Loire Valley's essential visits.

The medieval Maison d'Adam, place Sainte-Croix, Angers.

Angers listings

● Sleeping
1 Camping du Lac de Maine *avenue du Lac de Maine*
2 Grand Hôtel de la Gare *5 place de la Gare*
3 Hôtel d'Anjou *1 boulevard du Maréchal Foch*
4 Logis de la Roche Corbin *3 rue de la Harpe*
5 Mercure Centre Gare *18 boulevard du Maréchal Foch*

● Eating & drinking
1 Crêperie du Château *21 rue St-Aignan*
2 La Ferme *2 place Freppel*
3 La Soufflerie *8 place du Pilori*
4 Le Bouchon Angevin *44 rue Beaurepaire*
5 Le Favre d'Anne *18 quai des Carmes*
6 James Joyce Irish Bar *40-42 boulevard Carnot*
7 Le Petit Comptoir *40 rue David d'Angers*
8 Origin'all Café *49 rue St-Julien*
9 Provence Caffé *9 place du Ralliement*

Château d'Angers & la Tenture de l'Apocalypse

2 Promenade du Bout du Monde, T02 41 86 48 77, angers.mouments-nationaux.fr.
2 May-4 Sep 0930-1830; 5 Sep-30 Apr 1000-1730. Closed 1 Jan, 1 May, 1 and 11 Nov, 25 Dec. €8, under 18s free. Audio guides available in 5 languages €4.50.
Map: Angers, p228.

With its 17 massive layer-cake towers of grey schist and pale limestone, there's no mistaking the most formidable of all the Loire Valley chateaux, constructed from 1230 onwards on a rocky spur overlooking the River Maine. Enter via a drawbridge on the landward side and turn right to a flight of steps signed to the ramparts, from

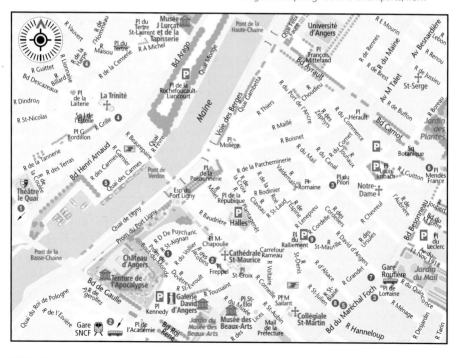

whose lofty walkways you'll see the large landscaped interior spread before you. Towering over the Logis Royal of the Dukes of Anjou (fire-damaged in January 2009 but expected to reopen for the 2010 season) is a Gothic chapel built around 1410 by Yolanda d'Aragon, wife of Louis II. Beyond are the *parterres* of a Renaissance-style garden, looking rather restrained after the swirling complexity of those outside in the former moat. Continue around the walkway for bird's-eye views of the 18th-century chateau governor's house, the city skyline and a full panorama across the river to La Doutre quarter and the pleasure port. The walkway was created during the late 14th century when all but one of the towers were lowered by around 10 m to install artillery terraces. The Tour du Moulin (windmill tower), though, retains its original height of 42 m, and you can climb to the summit via a series of steep, narrow staircases incorporated into the smoothly curving walls. The views are well worth the effort. When you descend, visit the cavernous interior of the Angevin Gothic chapel, whose medieval features include finely carved misericords, a set of still-colourful bas-reliefs, some large but rather faded wall paintings and vibrant stained glass remounted among modern panels.

The modern, purpose-built gallery for the **Tapestry of the Apocalypse** has an outward air of industrial austerity, but what lies within is quite simply exquisite. Enter the building and turn right through two sets of swing doors and you'll come face to face with the world's longest hand-woven tapestry, created by order of Louis I in 1375. Originally over 100 m long, it took 10 years to complete, and was displayed around the interior of the cathedral on great occasions. During the Revolution, although, it was cut into 74 separate panels and dispersed around the city to serve as horse blankets, doormats and other ignominious roles. In 1848, a local canon set about recovering and restoring them for posterity. The 600-year-old panels are now worn to half their original weight, but their imagery remains as powerful as ever. As your eyes grow accustomed to the low light levels necessary to preserve the colours, you'll be drawn

Essentials

❾ Getting around You can easily explore the city on foot but there are plenty of buses and a new tramway (still under construction at the time of writing). The P+Bus car parks (P+R for the tram) on the city outskirts have direct links to the centre. The *Corniche Angevine* (best driven east to west) between Savennières and Chalonnes-sur-Loire, will take you through the heart of the wine-growing areas.

⊖ Bus station COTRA (cotra.fr) buses operate from place Lorraine. Many services stop in front of the rail station and there is an information terminal on the concours.

❿ Train station Gare St Laud is 10 minutes' walk from the chateau.

❾ ATMs boulevard du Maréchal Foch and at the nearby central post office (see below).

⊕ Hospital 4 rue Larrey, T02 41 35 36 37. The *urgences* (accident and emergency) building is at 6 allée des Arcades, open 24 hours a day.

⊕ Pharmacies Pharmacie St Serge, 54 boulevard Ayrault, T02 41 87 76 47; several others between place du Ralliement and the cathedral.

❞ Post offices 1 rue Franklin Roosevelt, T02 41 20 81 62; 3 boulevard Henri Arnauld, La Doutre, T02 41 87 69 43; Gare St-Laud.

❶ Tourist information offices 7 place Kennedy, Angers, T02 41 23 50 00, angersloiretourisme.com; 8 place de la République, Brissac-Quincé, T02 41 91 21 50, ot-brissac-loire-aubance.fr; place de l'Hôtel de Ville, Chalonnes-sur-Loire, T02 41 74 91 54, loire-layon-tourisme.com.

The former moat now houses vibrant parterres.

closer, at which point you'll find the theme of each panel displayed on the rail beneath them. Less obvious are touches such as a small woven cross concealed beneath the horns of the Devil, or the style of stitching which means that a full mirror image is visible on the reverse of each panel.

At the far end of the gallery a glazed section of flooring reveals the excavated foundations of an earlier chapel, and further archaeological finds are visible beside the gift shop, accessible by crossing the garden area after leaving the gallery.

Cathédrale St-Maurice

Place Monseigneur-Chapoulie, T02 41 87 58 45.
Daily 0830-1900.
Map: Angers, p228.

The skyline of Angers is still satisfyingly dominated by the twin spires of its ancient cathedral, whose dedication comes from one of its predecessors, a modest fourth-century church which possessed a phial containing a few drops of the blood of St Maurice. Much of what we see today dates from the 12th century, including the mostly Romanesque western façade, which was begun around 1170. Gaze upwards and you'll see clear signs of a long evolutionary period which produced both Gothic and Renaissance features,

culminating in the tall spires added during the 19th century. The façade is unusually narrow, the reason for which is revealed inside, where the nave shows its Romanesque origins with its lack of side aisles. Notice the early vaults above, whose diagonal ribs rise much higher than the transverse arches between them, establishing the Angevin (or Plantagenêt) Gothic style. Note also the balcony-style gallery running the full length of the interior on often humorous carved stone corbels, plus paired Romanesque windows set within Gothic arches. Unlike the nave, the transepts and choir were rebuilt during the 13th century. The choir feels rather cold and remote, mainly due to a magnificently over-the-top baroque high altar (1758) and the dark timber stall panelling added in 1780, thereby obscuring much earlier wall paintings. The transepts, however, contain huge and very beautiful 15th-century rose windows.

Among the more impressive of the remaining interior features are a monumentally proportioned carved timber pulpit of 1855, and a colossal organ occupying almost the entire western wall. After peering in awe at the silverware in the Trésorerie to the right of the exit, cast a final glance at the exterior of the nave and ponder quite how it's still standing, without so much as a single flying buttress.

A rich tapestry of life revealed.

One of the cathedral's vast rose windows.

Collégiale St-Martin

*23 rue St-Martin, T02 41 81 16 00,
collegiale-saint-martin.fr.*
Jun-Sep daily 1000-1900, Oct-May Tue-Sun
1300-1800; closed 1 Jan, 1 and 8 May,
1 and 11 Nov, 25 Dec. €3, under 18s free.
The free audio guide is available in English
and is well worth having.
Map: Angers, p228.

This ancient collegiate church seems intent on
keeping a low and slightly austere profile amid the
bustle of the old town. Inside it's a medieval time
capsule, starting with a visibly out-of-square nave
which has its origins in a 10th- to 11th-century
Carolingian basilica. Note the simple, barn-like
timber roof and rugged stone walls above
round-arched arcades supported on heavy,
square-section piers. Continue towards the
transept crossing, where alternate layers of pale
stone and pink brick support a tall, stone-vaulted
lantern tower. Curiously, it doesn't light the
crossing, since the windows merely overlook
transepts which are almost as high as the tower.
Beyond the crossing is a much lighter Angevin
Gothic-vaulted choir dating from when the church
was enlarged during the late 12th century. What
looks like a left-hand side aisle is in fact the
Chapelle des Anges (Angel Chapel), a low, vaulted
passage with a touch of drama, courtesy of up
lighting for the carved pier capitals, and the
presence of an early inscribed slate memorial. To
the right of the choir is an 18th-century former
sacristy, now containing artefacts dating from the
fifth century. For a more atmospheric immersion
into the past, follow the nearby steps to the dimly
lit crypt, where you'll discover the excavated
foundations of both fifth- and ninth-century
sections of the church. The main body of the
building is also effectively a museum, displaying
fine examples of medieval statuary from the Anjou
region. Among the more miraculous survivors is a
Virgin and Child, probably dating from the 14th
century and discovered during excavations of the
south transept in 1931.

Musée des Beaux-Arts

14 rue du Musée, T02 41 05 38 00, musee.angers.fr.
Jun-Sep daily 1000-1830, Oct-May Tue-Sun
1000-1200 and 1400-1800, closed 1 Jan, 1 May,
1 and 11 Nov, 25 Dec. €4 (€6 to both permanent
and temporary exhibitions), under 26 years free.
Map: Angers, p228.

Your first glimpse of the magnificent (and
magnificently restored) 15th-century Logis de
Barrault tells you that this will be far from a typical
art gallery visit. Enter through the glitzy, glass-clad
entrance and you'll find the visitor reception desk
to your right, and beyond, a staircase (or lift)
leading to the permanent collections on the upper
floors, where you can wander through a
substantial body of works by 14th- to 16th-century
Renaissance French, German, Italian and Flemish
'primitive' painters. Accompanying them are
further 15th- and 16th-century Italian canvases
from Siena and Florence, a substantial body of
16th-century portraits and much more, all looking
perfectly at home in the atmospheric setting of
this supremely elegant Renaissance Gothic
building. The Logis has served as the town's
principal museum space since 1805, so don't miss
the opportunity of immersing yourself in the
Histoire d'Angers section (easily missed, the entry
is opposite the lift behind the reception desk)
when you descend to the ground floor. Although
inevitably accorded much less space than the fine
arts collections, many of the artefacts on display
here are in their own way equally moving, and
there's simply no better introduction to the
history and evolution of the city.

Musée des Beaux-Arts.

Galerie David d'Angers

33 rue Toussaint, T02 41 05 38 00, musees.angers.fr.
Jun-Sep 1000-1830; Oct-May 1000-1200 and
1400-1800. Closed Mon, 1 Jan, 1 May, 1 and
11 Nov, 25 Dec. €4, under 18s free.
Map: Angers, p228.

Tucked away in the Jardin des Beaux-Arts, a small
haven of landscaped park behind the Musée, is the
previously abandoned 13th-century Augustinian
abbey of St-Aubin, whose collapsed roof vaults
were replaced during the early 1980s with glazed
panels supported by a slender metal framework.
The resulting techno-Gothic space was opened by
François Mitterrand in 1984 and houses a collection
of sculptured busts, medallions and bas-reliefs
from the prolific output of celebrated locally born
figurative artist Pierre Jean David d'Angers
(1788-1856). Elsewhere, in important sites such as
Père Lachaise Cemetry and the Panthéon (Paris),
his vigorous sculptures seize your attention, but
here they're ultimately outgunned by the
distractions of the building to which they have
been consigned. Persevere, though, as the artist's
greatest works are assembled here, either as studio
studies or, in the case of bronzes, replicated from
the original moulds. Many of the personalities
represented were writers or political activists who
shared the artist's fierce commitment to the
campaign for human rights – look out for Balzac,
Chateaubriand, Goethe, Victor Hugo and many
other influential figures.

The pleasant park outside belonged originally
to the first abbey, founded around 534. Between
1834 and 1925 the site found its own place in
history when the Societé d'Agriculture, Sciences et
Arts d'Angers established a series of gardens as a
centre for research and education in fruit
production, which resulted in the famous Doyenne
du Comice – finest of all dessert pears.

Eglise de la Trinité

Place de la Laiterie, La Doutre, T02 41 87 18 77.
Daily, 0900-1200 and 1430-1730 (1830 Mar-Sep).
Map: Angers, p228.

This almost cathedral-size early medieval parish
church makes quite an impact among the
surrounding straggle of half-timbered façades in
the heart of La Doutre. But apart from an amusing
series of carved corbels grinning out from a simple
roll-moulding just above eye-level, the exterior
offers few clues as to what lies inside. The building
was constructed back-to-back with an earlier
abbey, so the entry portal is quite low-key, but
once inside the huge interior (completed around
1180) falls away impressively beyond an almost
full-width flight of steps. Tucked away to the left is
a smaller flight leading to an 11th-century crypt,
and a wall-mounted carved memorial to Renée
Sarazin, Abbess of the adjoining Abbaye du
Ronceray, 1493-1499.

Extensive restorations which have left the
church interior rather bare at least highlight the
wealth of features in the stonework. Most obvious
are the apse-like nave arcades created within the
immense thickness of the outer walls – look closely
and you'll notice that each arch is decorated with a
unique carved frieze. Above are Romanesque-style
(round-arched) windows framed within more
pointed Gothic arches, 'transitional' construction
features underlined by the same Angevin vaulting
found in the Cathédrale St-Maurice. Here, though,
the ribs are more complex and their central bosses
sit within unusual wheel-like motifs.

The replacement of medieval stained glass by
grisaille (pale grey) panels fills the nave with light,
unlike the smaller and lower choir, whose richly
coloured medallion glass preserves the mystical
effect which would once have given the church a
very different appearance. As you are about to
leave notice a beautifully carved timber
Renaissance spiral staircase, dating from the 16th
century, to your right.

Around the region

Musée Jean Lurçat et de la Tapisserie Contemporaine

4 bd Arago, La Doutre, T02 41 05 38 00, musees.angers.fr.
Jun-Sep 1000-1830; Oct-May 1000-1200 and 1400-1800. Closed Mon, 1 Jan, 1 May, 1 and 11 Nov, 25 Dec. €4, under 18 years free. The free audio guide is available in English.
Map: Angers, p228.

Few places can have seen more life (and death) than this former hospital constructed in 1175 by order of Henri II, and which for almost eight centuries provided care for the people of Angers – to your right as you enter is the apothecary's dispensary, with china and porcelain items from the 17th and 18th centuries. Like most large medieval buildings, it employed Gothic construction methods, but this Angevin variation, for all its practicality, is serenely elegant, with a striking lightness of form. Today the Hôpital St-Jean has been painstakingly restored to display *Le Chant du Monde* (The Song of The World) – 10 huge tapestries designed by the artist Jean Lurçat (1892-1966). Like the city's other great Apocalyptic tapestry nearby, the imagery is unsettling, and represents a highly influential artist's response to the shattering effects of the two world wars through which he lived. Ultimately, though, the panels offer a vision of hope for the future, and their stylized forms and vibrant colours leap from the black ground onto which they have been applied. The works, created by skilled weavers in three renowned workshops in Aubusson (Creuse), were begun in 1957 and took a further 10 years to complete.

The gallery space became a full museum when an adjoining former orphanage building was restored to display further textile works of art, whose permanent collections are supplemented by temporary exhibitions. Outside are the former hospital gardens, where, among other things, you'll discover the extravagantly decorated Renaissance Porte du Présidial d'Angers (the doorway of the former Court of Law).

Terra Botanica

Between Angers and Avrillé (exit 16 on the A11), T02 41 25 00 00, terrabotanica.fr.
Daily May-Aug, Easter and Nov holidays, Apr and Sep Fri-Sun. €17.50, €10 children (under 12), €50 family ticket (up to 5 people). The tramway Line A, due to open mid-2011, will stop at Terra Botanica.

This brand new attraction claims to be the first plant-based amusement park, so it will be quite at home in Anjou, a region long focused on horticulture and medicinal plants. Due to open in May 2010, the 110,000 sq m of gardens and lakes will contain nearly 40 different interactive family attractions to discover every aspect of plant life. Highlights look set to include a Voyage to The Centre of The Earth (in '4D', apparently) and the Botanic Odyssey, a journey retracing the steps of famous botanists.

Château de Montgeoffroy
Mazé, (34 km northwest of Saumur), T02 41 80 60 02.
Daily Apr-Nov, closes lunchtimes in low season. €9, €4.60 children.

Set amid woodland in the Authion Valley, this picture of 18th-century elegance was one of the last great chateaux of pre-Revolutionary France. Its Parisian architect was Nicolas Barré, who elected to retain two round towers and a chapel from the chateau's mid-16th-century predecessor for his client Maréchal Louis Georges Erasme de Contades, whose grandfather had acquired the estate in 1676. Erasme de Contades had not only been Governor of Strasbourg but had commanded the French army during the Seven Years' War, prior to the Treaty of Paris in 1763. Remarkably, the estate remains in the hands of his descendants, and its state of preservation is exceptional. The quality of the furnishings is likewise peerless, with many pieces signed by famous makers such as Garnier

Basses Vallées Angevines

The area to the north and south of Angers is known as one of Europe's richest and most beautiful natural wetlands. It's crossed by three rivers – the Mayenne, the Sarthe, and the Loir, which combine to form the Maine before entering the Loire. The vast flood plain and its meadows provide a stopover for thousands of migratory ducks and waders, and are the main breeding grounds in France of the corncrake. Walkers and cyclists can follow routes around the Ile St-Aubin Nature Reserve, which is just five minutes' north of Angers. The only access is by ferry from the Port de l'Ile, departure times varying according to season (and sometimes not at all during winter floods). The Ferme de l'Ile St-Aubin (Jun-Aug Tue to Sat 1430-1730), about 2-km walk from the ferry, has been converted from an old farm into an exhibition and education centre and is worth a visit to learn more about the area's natural heritage.

The Loire and its tributaries provide a haven for wildlife.

and Durand in exquisite rooms still hung with their original tapestries. You can also inspect documents bearing the signatures of Louis XV, Louis XVIII and Napoléon, tour the monumentally scaled (and comprehensively equipped) period kitchens and visit the estate stables and tack room. The 16th-century chapel is also interesting, with Angevin Gothic vaults decorated with carved and painted central bosses.

Château du Plessis-Bourré

Écuillé (15 km north of Angers), T02 41 32 06 01, plessis-bourre.com.
15 Feb-30 Mar and Oct-Nov Thu-Tue 1400-1800, Apr-Jun and Sep Thu pm to Tue 1000-1200 and 1400-1800, Jul-Aug daily 1000-1800.
€9, €5 children.

Looking every inch the dream period film location, this 15th-century chateau was constructed on the ancient manor estate of Plessis-le-Vent by Louis XI's Finance Minister Jean Bourré, whose personal wealth propelled it from plans to completion in less than five years (1468-1472). Along the way he added many of the defensive features employed at the Château de Langeais (whose construction he had overseen) including sentry walks, massive corner towers and, naturally, a drawbridge. The whole thing was then enclosed within a moat of lake-like dimensions. No doubt curious, the King visited in 1473, and was followed in 1487 by Charles VIII. In 1751, however, the estate was sold to the Ruillé family, one of whose number, Jean-Guillaume Ruillé, was among those executed during the Revolution in 1794. During the 19th century the chateau stood unoccupied until a notaire from Angers purchased it in 1851 to save it from destruction. In 1911 it passed to the Vaïsse family, who restored it and in whose hands it still remains. During the First World War Plessis-Bourré was requisitioned to serve as a hospital for treating casualties of the conflicts, whilst the Second World War found it, somewhat bizarrely, accommodating the American Ambassador to Poland.

The visit takes in both military features and later Renaissance additions, eloquently illustrating how a fortress evolved into an elegant country home.

The Château de Plessis-Bourré is a picture of medieval refinement, Anjou-style.

Château de Brissac

Brissac-Quincé (17 km southeast of Angers), T02-41 91 22 21, chateau-brissac.fr. End Mar-Jun and Sep-Oct Wed-Mon 1000-1215 and 1400-1800, Jul-Aug daily 1000-1800. Guided tour of interior and access to grounds €8.80, €7.80 concessions, €4.50 children (7-14), grounds only €4.

Billed as the tallest chateau in France, this seven-story giant certainly grabs your attention. Visits are in guided groups only, but once you've bought your ticket you can also wander freely around the surrounding landscaped parkland and among the estate's 28 ha of vineyards, established in the 15th century and with their very own AOC (Anjou Villages Brissac). The vines bask on a plateau above the Promenade du Pont Rouge footpath – follow the signs to *'la Vigne des 5 Siècles'* and you'll find them easily enough, along with romantic views of the chateau itself. Further on, in a peaceful woodland clearing, is a classical-style family mausoleum from the early 19th century. Below the vineyards lie the estate's palatial stables, a wing of which offers a reconstruction of times gone by, complete with full-sized (replica) horses and stereo effects which will have you glancing over your shoulder at the sound of approaching hooves.

Another footpath (la promenade de Gilles) circumnavigates the chateau beside a meander of the Aubance river, and offers the opportunity to visit an 18th-century underground canal. From most angles the chateau has a slightly uneasy blend of styles, with 17th-century French Renaissance piled high between two huge, feudal-looking towers which actually date from just two centuries earlier. Had they been replaced as planned by something more in keeping with the rest of the structure, things would have looked much more harmonious (but arguably less interesting). You can enjoy a wine-tasting session while waiting for the chateau tour. Tour highlights include Louis XIII's bedchamber, a 32-m-long grand gallery and a private belle époque theatre.

Château de Serrant

St-Georges-sur-Loire (19 km west of Angers), T02 41 39 13 01, chateau-serrant.net. 15 Mar-Jun and Sep Wed-Mon 0945-1200 and 1400-1715, Jul-Aug daily 0945-1715, Oct to 15 Nov Wed-Sun 0945-1200 and 1400-1715. €9.50, €6 under 18s. Guided tours only (1 hr), hourly throughout the day.

Here's another former fortress which, following the arrival of the Renaissance, mutated uncertainly into a gracious showpiece residence. The De Brie family had lived here since the 14th century, seemingly at ease until Charles de Brie decided to follow the Court fashion and rebuild the chateau in fashionable Italianate style. The works, though, proved far beyond his means, so were only partly executed. In 1636 the slightly raffish Guillaume de Bautru acquired the estate and took a renewed interest in his predecessor's project, following the original plans so that new work blended seamlessly into what had already been achieved. The chapel, however, was the work of the illustrious Jules Hardouin Mansart. When the family line ceased in 1749 the estate passed to Irishman Antoine Walsh, a wealthy shipowner from Nantes. The family built two pavilions, reworked interiors and laid out landscaped parkland, before the marriage in 1830 of Valentine Walsh de Serrant to the aristocratic Duc de la Trémoïlle. The subsequent restorations and refinements have continued ever since, now overseen by the present owners (and Trémoïlle family descendants) Prince and Princess de Merode. The interiors open to the public can truly be described as palatial, and because of the chateau's history of uninterrupted occupation, are the real thing, rather than a soulless 'in-the-style-of' recreation. The Renaissance 'stone-lace' staircase also qualifies as a unique architectural feature.

La Corniche Angevine

The Corniche lies at the extreme west of the Val de Loire UNESCO World Heritage Site and takes in the river's southern bank and flood plain, plus hills of limestone and coal deposits. As its name suggests, it's a great scenic drive, with exceptional views from the winding section between Rochefort-sur-Loire and Chalonnes-sur-Loire. However, the area is well worth a closer look to discover its industrial past, a wealth of wildlife and the Coteaux du Layon vineyards. The Corniche also attracts walkers and mountain bikers, who are well served with marked trails. At the panoramic viewpoint of La Haie Longue is a monument to the memory of aviator René Gasnier, who in 1908 flew for a distance of around 1 km (at an altitude of 6 or 7 m) in an aircraft of his own design. He went on to help establish the airport of Angers-Avrillé and to organize the first air races between Angers and Saumur. His body lies in the chapel overlooking the field in which he first took to the air and a replica of his aircraft can be seen in the Regional Air Museum at the airport.

For almost six centuries the area had a major coal mining industry, the last mine closing in 1964. You can't miss the chapel of Ste-Barbe des Mines, thanks to its prominent roadside location. The chapel, dedicated to the miners, is open to visitors by appointment (stebarbe.com). In the old mining village of Ardenay are the historic Moulins d'Ardenay, two of the many windmills which were once sited along the ridge. All along the rocky outcrop limestone was quarried to extract lime – in the 19th century the industry used up to three-quarters of the local coal production to fire the huge numbers of lime kilns (*fours à chaux*). Several examples remain to this day, although the methods were in use during the Roman occupation.

Chalonnes-sur-Loire lies at the confluence of the Loire and the small River Layon, which flows along a geological fault line responsible for shaping the landscape. The Layon also lent its name to sweet white wines made with Chenin, Cabernet Franc and Cabernet Sauvignon grapes – you can wander among the vineyards at St-Aubin de Luigné.

The hilly countryside is some of the most varied and challenging for cyclists in the Loire Valley and the network of over 200 km of signposted trails which leave from Chalonnes include tough climbs, forest paths and easier tracks through the vines.

Information: *layon.org for trails and places to visit; stebarbe.com for industrial history and geology; chateaudebellevue.fr, a vineyard you can visit at St-Aubin de Luigné; suronde.fr, another vineyard visit at Rochefort-sur-Loire.*

Rochefort-sur-Loire.

Sleeping

Château de Verrières €€€€
53 rue d'Alsace, T02 41 38 05 15, chateau-verrieres.com.
Very welcoming luxury chateau hotel set in its own grounds, though situated within Saumur just a short walk from the old quarter. The rooms are decorated in classic French style, apart from a contemporary suite on the top floor. Expect every comfort (including heated swimming pool and free Wi-Fi) in elegant surroundings.

Hôtel Adagio €€€
94 av du Général de Gaulle, T02 41 67 45 30, hoteladagio.com.
Comfortable hotel with modern, well-equipped rooms on the Ile d'Offard in the middle of the Loire. It's worth paying a little more for a spacious room with views of the Loire and the chateau. A buffet breakfast is served in the dining room overlooking the river. Free Wi-Fi.

Hôtel Anne d'Anjou €€€
32 quai Mayaud, T02 41 67 30 30, hotel-anneanjou.com.
On the banks of the Loire a short walk from the historic centre and at the foot of the chateau walls, this beautiful 18th-century mansion retains its charming period interior with a grand staircase and a trompe l'oeil ceiling. Rooms are comfortable, those overlooking the pretty courtyard being quieter.

Traditional style (with river views), Saumur.

Hôtel Le Mercure €€€
1 rue du Vieux Pont (on the Ile d'Offard), T02 41 67 22 42, mercure.com (hotel code 6648).
Large chain hotel in a quiet location offering comfortable rooms just 5 minutes' walk from Saumur centre. The best feature is the panoramic view across the Loire to the chateau from riverside rooms, the breakfast room and the bar.

Le Mascaron €€€
6 rue Haute St-Pierre, T02 41 53 36 68.
Closed Nov-May.
If you're looking for somewhere central with bags of character, this 16th-century logis set around a courtyard should suit. Situated in the heart of the old quarter, your own suite has a separate entrance off the street and successfully combines contemporary touches with medieval stone features and exposed beams. Private parking.

Château de Beaulieu €€€
98 route de Montsoreau, T02 41 50 83 52, chateaudebeaulieu.fr.
Closed Nov-Easter.
Enjoy bed and breakfast in this grand 18th-century chateau just 2 km from Saumur. Rooms are decorated in charming classic French style and your hosts offer an evening meal (€30-40), so you won't have to tear yourself away from the lovely terrace in the summer. There's also a heated swimming pool.

Ami Chenin €€
37 rue de Beaulieu, T02 41 38 13 17, amichenin.com.
Closed Nov-Jan.
Beautifully furnished rooms, a relaxing lounge and a dining room with an enormous fireplace, a beamed ceiling and a mezzanine level where guests can enjoy splendid breakfasts or evening meals (booking required). You'll get a warm welcome and a taste of the *art-de-vivre* in this former wine grower's house.

La Maison Cendrière €€
9 rue Cendrière, T02 41 53 36 68, lamaisoncendriere.com.
Charming chambres d'hôtes in a townhouse with a peaceful garden in the historic quarter. This enchanting place has four individually furnished rooms and a family suite, all enhanced with small personal touches.

Le Patio €€
31 quai Mayaud, T02 41 51 20 22, lepatiosaumur.fr.
This 17th-century former lodging house in the historic centre of Saumur is once again welcoming guests to its quiet, spacious and beautifully furnished rooms. Summer breakfasts are served in the pretty courtyard.

Le Lamartine €
483 rue Lamartine, T02 41 50 92 63, lelamartine.drgconseil.com.
Just five minutes' walk from the chateau, Le Lamartine is a classic Loire Valley house in pale *tuffeau* stone. There are three light and airy bedrooms, one with direct access to the garden (€65), and all with private bathrooms. Guests are welcome to use the garden and the above-ground pool.

Around Saumur

Hôtel de la Marine de Loire €€€
9 quai de la Loire, Montsoreau, T02 41 50 18 21, hotel-lamarinedeloire.com.
Charming marine-themed hotel in the centre of the village with contemporary and stylish rooms in shades of pearl blue and grey. Romantic 'cocooning' weekends and wellbeing packages are temptingly luxurious.

Hôtel La Demeure de la Vignole €€€
3 impasse de la Vignole, Turquant (3 km west of Montsoreau), T02 41 53 67 00, demeure-vignole.com.
Clinging to the golden *tuffeau* cliffs above the Loire, this 17th-century residence provides a unique range of charmingly finished accommodation, some of it in 12th-century troglodyte dwellings. It also has an amazing underground swimming pool and a fitness suite. Evening meals served Tuesday-Saturday (booking required). The hotel also has a luxury two-bedroom troglodyte gîte to let.

Hôtel le Bussy €€-€€€
4 rue Jeanne d'Arc, Montsoreau,
T02 41 38 11 11, hotel-lebussy.fr.
Situated in a quiet spot near the
chateau entrance, the hotel
enjoys a panoramic view over
the chateau and to the river
beyond. Rooms are spacious
and most have the great view
(ground floor rooms without
a view are a little cheaper).
Breakfast is served in the
troglodytic dining room or
on the terrace.

Le Domaine de Mestré €€
Fontevraud l'Abbaye (4 km south
of Montsoreau), T02 41 51 72 32,
bed-and-breakfast-mestre.
ic-sites.com.
The same family has lived here
since the 18th century, and you
certainly get a sense of timeless
charm, both inside the house
and in the surrounding mature
gardens and courtyard. The
rooms are spacious and
furnished in period style with
their own modern bathrooms.
Breakfasts, afternoon tea and
evening meals (€25 excluding

drinks) using local ingredients
are all served on pretty Limoges
porcelain. Free Wi-Fi.

Maison d'hôtes La Pinsonnière €€
225 rue du Château, Sanzier
Vaudelnay (4 km west of
Montreuil-Bellay), T02 41 59
12 95, la-pinsonniere.fr.
An old farmhouse with
courtyard, parts of which date
back to the 17th century, has
been renovated to provide four
themed guest rooms. The hosts
are dedicated to using local
products for the evening meals
(reserve in advance) and provide
organic toiletries in the rooms.
If you feel adventurous, book
the Mongolian yurt in summer.

Self-catering
Les Mortiers
Parçay-les-Pins (35 km north
of Saumur), T02 41 82 60 34,
frenchholiday.co.uk.
Private and peaceful gîtes in
converted 18th-century barns,
surrounded by unspoilt
countryside and well placed to
visit central Loire Valley sites.
Also has a lovely heated outdoor
swimming pool with a
space-dome for cooler days.
Prices range from €420 for a
one-bedroom gîte in low season
to €1180 for a larger one in
August. Price includes all linen,
broadband connection, gas
and electricity.

Boutique meets chic in fashionable Montsoreau.

Campsites

La Vallée des Vignes
*Concourson-sur-Layon
(4 km west of Doué-la-Fontaine),
T02 41 59 86 35,
campingvdv.com.*
British-run 4-star campsite with
all amenities and ideally placed
for visiting local attractions and
historic towns and sites.

Les Nobis
*Rue Georges Girouy, Montreuil-
Bellay, T02 41 52 33 66,
campinglesnobis.com.
Apr-Oct.*
A 4-star campsite in a shaded
riverside park at the foot of the
chateau walls and with on-site
restaurant, grocery, boat hire
and summer entertainment.

Angers

Hôtel d'Anjou €€€
*1 bd du Maréchal Foch,
T02 41 21 12 11, hoteldanjou.fr.
Map: Angers, p228.*
Individually styled rooms in
a charming centrally located
hotel with good access to
public transport and the main
sites. Rooms are air conditioned
and soundproofed, ensuring
a peaceful night's sleep.
Chauffeur available at any
time (charges apply), Wi-Fi
and parking available.

Mercure Centre Gare €€€
*18 bd du Maréchal Foch,
T02 41 87 37 20, mercure.com
(hotel code 6851).*

Map: Angers, p228.
Recently refurbished central
hotel within easy reach of
historic sites, shops and
restaurants. Enjoy chic city-
style rooms to international
standards with luxury beds
and bathrooms. Plentiful buffet
breakfasts and pleasant staff
always on hand. Free Wi-Fi and
(limited) secure parking.

Grand Hôtel de la Gare €€
*5 place de la Gare, T02 41 88
40 69, hotel-angers.fr.
Map: Angers, p228.*
In a smart crescent opposite
the rail station, the Grand Hôtel
offers good value, bright and
welcoming accommodation
just 10 minutes' walk from the
chateau. There are plenty of
cafés and restaurants nearby.

Logis de la Roche Corbin €€
*3 rue de la Harpe, T02 41 86
93 70, logisdelaroche.com.
Map: Angers, p228.*
Situated in La Doutre, not far
from cafés and restaurants in
this historic quarter of Angers,
you'll find a lovingly restored
17th-century townhouse behind
a high wall. It offers a suite for
two people, with a private
courtyard garden. With
18th-century period furniture,
it's refined and relaxing.

Campsite

Camping du Lac de Maine
*Avenue du Lac de Maine,
T02 41 73 05 03,*

*camping-angers.fr.
Closed mid-Oct to end Mar.
Map: Angers, p228.*
The 90-ha park on the edge of
the city provides all kinds of
activities, and even has a nature
reserve. You can walk or ride into
the city centre along the banks
of the river. This is an ideal family
base with all amenities –
patrolled bathing, bike hire and
free Wi-Fi are just a few of the
services on offer.

Around Angers

Le Cavier €€
*Route de Laval, Avrillé (6 km
north of Angers), T02 41 42 30 45,
lacroixcadeau.fr.*
Hotel and restaurant just 10
minutes from the centre of
Angers, yet in its own
magnificent setting around an
exceptional windmill. Rooms are
quiet and comfortable and
amenities include an outdoor
pool and private gardens.

Moulin de Clabeau €€
*Vauchrétien, near Brissac-Quincé
(19 km south of Angers), T02 41 91
22 09, gite-brissac.com.*
There are three chambres
d'hôtes rooms, including a family
room, in this restored water mill
on the Aubance, in the heart of
Anjou vineyards. The bedrooms
are delightful and the hosts,
whose family have lived in the
mill for centuries, are happy to
offer advice to help you make
the most of your stay.

Eating & drinking

Saumur

Auberge Saint-Pierre €€€
6 place St-Pierre,
T02 41 51 26 25,
auberge-saintpierre.com.
There's a medieval theme inside this popular restaurant with its bustling (in summer) outside terrace. The menu has entertaining illustrations and descriptions and house specialities include regional dishes such as smoked duck with *Rivarennes poires-tapées* (dried pears).

L'Orangeraie €€€
Les Feuquières, Château de Saumur, T02 41 67 12 88,
restaurant-lorangeraie.com.
Closed Sun evenings, Mon and Tue evenings in low season.

Enjoying pleasant surroundings within the confines of the chateau, the conservatory-style dining room and summer terrace offer diners impressive views of the chateau and the Loire. Expect refined regional dishes accompanied by a good selection of local wines.

30 Février €€
9 place de la République,
T02 41 51 12 45.
Closed Sun-Mon in low season, Sun lunch in summer.
Bright and friendly, this café's specialities are pizzas, salads and vegetarian dishes. It's a good spot for convivial terrace dining in summer.

Le Café de la Place €€
16 place St-Pierre,
T02 41 51 13 27,
cafedelaplace-saumur.com.
Mon-Sat.
Wine bar and bistro serving a tasty selection of hot dishes. Its large terrace is situated in the heart of the square, which has a great atmosphere on summer evenings. Inside is a cosy bar and a dining room with exposed beams. Occasional live music.

Le Panorama €€
Château car park,
T02 41 53 28 15.
Closed Mon in low season and 15 Dec-1 Feb.
Serves drinks and a large range of salads and hot meals in an informal and friendly setting. The terrace has a magnificent view of the chateau and the Loire below.

Cafés & bars
Barre de Chocolat
Grand'Rue, T02 41 83 06 77.
Tue-Fri 0930-1930, Sat 0900-1800, winter hours vary.
Sit at the counter and enjoy a real hot chocolate at this *chocolaterie* just off place St-Pierre.

Le Saint-Cloud
16 place Bilange, T02 41 51 25 81.
A street corner bar with terrace, where you can sample regional wines from €1.80 per glass. Note: there's a small surcharge for drinks on the terrace. Wi-Fi hot-spot.

The gastronomic menu is alive and well.

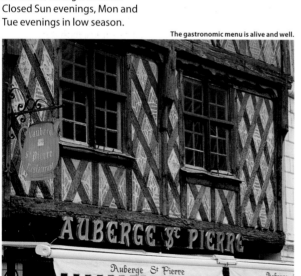

La Ferme €€€
2 place Freppel, T02 41 87 09 90, la-ferme.fr.
Closed Wed and Sun evenings.
Map: Angers, p228.
Traditional, hearty fare in a rustic setting designed to bring a little of rural France into the city. Expect menu classics like *Coq au Vin d'Anjou, Pot-au-Feu* (a traditional meat and vegetable casserole) and *cassoulets* all made with delicious local produce. Not one for vegetarians.

Le Favre d'Anne €€€
18 quai des Carmes, T02 41 36 12 12, lefavredanne.fr.
Tue-Sat.
Map: Angers, p228.
Chef Pascal Favre d'Anne worked alongside the celebrated contemporary chef Marc Veyrat in Annecy before receiving his own Michelin star at Angers in 2008. The creative seasonal menus are inspired by fresh produce from the *potager*, accompanied by local wines. There are fine views across the river to the chateau, and a refined, modern interior.

Le Petit Comptoir €€€
40 rue David d'Angers, T02 41 88 81 57.
Tue-Sat, closed early Aug, 1-5 May and late Jan.
Map: Angers, p228.

The red façade heralds a small but welcoming bistro with a relaxed atmosphere. Two chefs produce a classic repertoire with plenty of artistic creativity.

Provence Caffé €€€
9 place du Ralliement, T02 41 87 44 15, provence-caffe.com.
Tue-Sat.
Map: Angers, p228.
Popular, warmly lit restaurant in a prime location opposite the theatre. Large choice of fish dishes accompanied by seasonal vegetables in Provençal style. Reservation advised.

La Soufflerie €€
8 place du Pilori, T02 41 87 45 32.
Map: Angers, p228.
For something really different, choose from a vast choice of both savoury and sweet soufflés in this popular restaurant with a terrace that's perfect for summer evening dining. It's best to reserve during busy periods.

Le Bouchon Angevin €€
44 rue Beaurepaire, La Doutre, T02 41 24 77 97.
Closed Aug.
Map: Angers, p228.
A convivial wine bar and restaurant serving a limited but appealing menu of delicious traditional dishes, along with an excellent choice of regional wines. Reservations advised.

While you're here, why not?

Crêperie du Château €
21 rue St-Aignan, T02 41 88 53 87, creperieduchateau.fr.
Tue-Sun, closed Sun evenings and Thu evenings.
Map: Angers, p228.
A few steps from the chateau entrance, here you can savour real Breton crêpes and galettes with interesting fillings, accompanied by a selection of traditional French ciders.

Cafés & bars

James Joyce Irish Bar
40-42 bd Carnot, T02 41 87 76 87, jamesjoyce.fr.
Mon-Fri 1130-0145, Sat 1500-0145, Sun 1600-0145.
Map: Angers, p228.
A friendly pub with regular live music and decent food. Happy hour on Monday and Thursday 1900-2100.

Origin'all Café
49 rue St-Julien, T02 41 34 18 86.
Map: Angers, p228.
Just off Maréchal Foch, this tiny salon de thé has lounge seating and a friendly welcome. At the end of a long day try the thick and delicious hot chocolate.

Entertainment

Around Saumur

Festivals & events

Journées de la Rose

At Doué-la-Fontaine, city of roses and the European centre of production, the growers organize a spectacular display around the 14 July each year in caves carved from the local *falun* sandstone. €8, €3 children. Meals (including drinks), at €17 per person, are served from noon.

Les Estivales du Cadre Noir

Ecole Nationale d'Equitation, Saumur, T02 41 53 50 81, cadrenoir.fr.

In mid-July you can attend this traditional gala event of the Cadre Noir (National Horseriding School) to witness the skill and spectacle of the riders and their mounts.

Angers

Cinema

Les 400 Coups

12 rue Claveau, T02 41 88 70 95, les400coups.org.

Independent cinema with seven screens showing films in their original language, particularly those with novel themes or of aesthetic appeal.

Festivals & events

Festival d'Anjou

T02 41 88 14 14 (tickets), festivaldanjou.com.

From mid-June to the end of July, no fewer than 30 theatrical events take place in the open air amid stunning backdrops such as the Château de Brissac, Château du Plessis-Macé and Château de La Perrière. Tickets go on sale from mid-May from the tourist office on Place Kennedy, Angers.

Soleils d'hiver

This traditional festive market, illuminations and programme of events lights up Angers' town centre in the weeks before Christmas.

Music

La Casa de Cuba

23 bd du Maréchal Foch, T02 41 20 03 28, la-casadecuba.fr. Mon 1800-0200, Tue-Sat 1130-0200, Sun 1600-0200.

A Cuban bar serving cocktails and tapas plus a large helping of salsa and latin rhythm. Every Thursday there are salsa lessons, for the price of a drink.

Theatre

Théâtre Le Quai

17 rue de la Tannerie, T02 44 01 22 22, lequai-angers.eu.

Angers' new venue, situated on the right bank opposite the chateau, hosts year-round music and theatre events. In summer the plaza comes alive with open-air performances. You can idle away an hour or two while enjoying panoramic views from the restaurant terrace.

A French romance.

Shopping

Atelier de la Girouetterie
24 rue du Puits Venier, Le Coudray-Macouard (8 km south of Saumur), girouette.com.
Tue-Sat 1000-1200 and 1400-1730. Closed 24 Dec-6 Jan. Free.
Visit the weathervane workshop where you can see the intricate work and choose a unique and highly original souvenir from this artisan maker.

La Dentellerie
7 rue de la Tonnelle, Saumur, T02 41 67 23 01.
Tue-Sat 1000-1230 and 1430-1900.
This is a real treasure trove tucked away near place St-Pierre. Selling both antique and new items, La Dentellerie is packed with finely worked lace and precious fabrics. Anyone would be amazed by this shop; specialists will be enthralled.

Le Liegeur
28 rue de la Tonnelle, Saumur, T02 41 51 31 60, le-liegeur.com.
Tue-Fri 0915-1215 and 1430-1915, Sat 0915-1215 and 1445-1915.
A shop entirely dedicated to wine, with just about every accessory to suit the most passionate wine-lovers.

Les Puces de Montsoreau
Quais de la Loire, Montsoreau (12 km upstream from Saumur), T02 41 51 70 22 (tourist office), ville-montsoreau.fr.
0900-1800 on the 2nd Sun of every month.
Hunt for a bargain at this antiques and flea market held in an incomparable setting on the banks of the Loire. Prices are reasonable and afterwards you can cool off with a refreshing drink in a nearby bar terrace.

Poterie de la Rose Bleue
21 rue de la Croix de Fer, Doué-la-Fontaine (17 km west of Saumur), T02 41 59 86 83, rosebleue.fr.
Winter Tue-Sat 1400-1800; summer Tue-Sat 1000-1900, Sun 1400-1800.
A troglodytic pottery studio making practical and creative pieces.

Savonnerie Martin de Candre
Mestré, Fontevraud-l'Abbaye (15 km southeast of Saumur), T02 41 51 75 87, fontevraud.com.
As you enter the *savonnerie* boutique, you'll be immersed in the fragrances and colours of the traditional 100% vegetable soaps made here using the classic Marseille process.

Benoit Chocolats & Macarons
1 rue des Lices and 33 rue St-Aubin, Angers, T02 41 88 94 52, chocolats-benoit.com.
Tue-Sat 0930-1230 and 1400-1915, Mon 1500-1900. Closed Sun.
Handmade chocolates, confectionery, *macarons*, tea and very special hot chocolate and *pâtisseries*.

Giffard
Av de la Violette, Avrillé (6 km northwest of Angers), T02 41 18 85 00, giffard.com.
Fri 1400-1800.
In 1885 a pharmacist from Angers, investigating the refreshing and digestive properties of mint, invented a liqueur which he named '*Menthe Pastille*'. The same family is still producing fine liqueurs and cordials, which are ideal for cocktails and celebration drinks.

La Maison des Artisans
Maison d'Adam, 1 place Ste-Croix, Angers, T02 41 88 06 27, maison-artisans.com.
Tue-Sat 0930-1900, Mon 1400-1900. Closed Sun.
One of the most familiar sights in the historic heart of the city, built in the 15th century by a wealthy merchant, the Maison d'Adam now houses an interesting boutique selling original gifts and creations.

La Petite Marquise
22 rue des Lices, Angers,
T02 41 87 43 01, quernon.com.
Mon 1400-1900, Tue-Sat
0900-1900.

Small squares of blue chocolate, the *Quernon d'Ardoise* are made to look like the tiles of schist used on the rooftops of Angers. After the chocolate has melted in your mouth there's a crunchy nougatine almost as hard as the tiles themselves. Created in 1966, the award-winning Quernon has become a popular souvenir.

Maison du Vin d'Anjou
5 bis place Kennedy, Angers,
T02 41 88 81 13, vinsdeloire.fr.
1 Apr-30 Sep Tue-Sat 0930-1300
and 1400-1900,
Sun 1030-1300, Mon 1400-1900.
Winter open Tue-Fri and
Sat am. Free.

Visiting thousands of wine producers and sampling the diverse effects of *terroirs* and numerous grape varieties can be a time-consuming business. At the Maison du Vin in Angers (and next to the tourist office in Saumur) you can discover and taste many of the region's wines, and buy whatever takes your fancy, all in one place.

What the world has been eagerly awaiting: blue chocolate.

Activities & tours

Balloon flights
Montgolfières d'Anjou
T02 41 40 48 04, montgolfieres.fr.
All year, on reservation.
Flights over the Loire, chateaux and vineyards of Anjou, particularly beautiful at sunset.

Boat trips
Loire de Lumière
La Gare, La Menitre, T02 41 45 24 24, loiredelumiere.com.
Departures from St-Rémy-la-Varenne May and Sep 1500 and 1630, Jun-Aug 1500, 1630 and 1800. €8, €5 children (5-16).
These trips are particularly known for birdwatching and seeing the wild side of the Loire. Sailings on Wednesday afternoons are accompanied by an expert from the Ligue pour la Protection des Oiseaux League for the Protection of Birds).

Maine Anjou Rivières and the Hirondelle
Le Moulin, Chenillé-Changé (on the Mayenne, 39 km north of Angers), T02 41 95 10 83, maine-anjou-rivieres.com.
If you'd prefer to explore the 250 km of region's waterways yourself, you can hire a boat from €36 per person per day (based on one week for two people, no licence required). The company also runs the *Hirondelle* cruises from la Doutre in Angers, providing a simple 90-minute guided trip, a meal on board or a themed evening.

Saumur-Loire
Quai Lucien Gautier, Saumur (in front of the Mairie), T06 63 22 87 00, bateaux-nantais.fr.
Cruises from May to September, either to see the wild river and birdlife or for a romantic sunset trip. From €9, €4.50 children.

Cycling & cycle hire
Loire à Vélo
There are seven routes to follow in the Anjou area, with leaflets available in English from a tourist office or downloadable (French only) from the website (loire-a-velo.fr). See full details for *Loire à Vélo* page 69.

Cycles Cesbron
2 av Gallieni, Les Ponts-de-Cé (6 km south of Angers), T02 41 44 87 44, info@cyclescesbron.
Tue-Sat 0900-1200 and 1330-1900 (1800 Sat).

Détours de Loire
1 rue David d'Angers, St-Lambert-des-Levées, Saumur (on right bank), T02 41 53 01 01, locationdevelos.com.
Apr to mid-Oct daily 0930-1230 and 1630-1830.

Vélo Passion
102 rue Ligérienne, La Daguenière (11 km east of Angers), T02 41 69 07 76, velopassion2@wanadoo.fr.
Apr-Sep Tue-Sat 0900-1200 and 1400-1900 (1800 Sat).

Food & drink
Carré Cointreau
Bd des Bretonnières, Saint-Barthélèmy-d'Anjou (5 km east of Angers), T02 41 31 50 50, cointreau.fr.
Tasting (Tue-Sat 1100-1800 except public holidays) following an initiation in the art of cocktails by the barman. Guided visits to the distillery €9.50 (times vary). The visit includes an insight into the manufacture of Cointreau in the distillery and an incredible exhibition of objects, film and images associated with the celebrated liqueur. This is followed by a tasting in the bar with some original serving ideas.

Le Musée du Champignon
Route de Gennes, St-Hilaire-St-Florent (4 km downstream from Saumur), T02 41 50 31 55, musee-du-champignon.com.
Mar to mid-Nov.
Mushroom culture in a strange and mysterious world. Guided visits available.

Le Saux-aux-Loups
Route de Saumur, Montsoreau, T02 41 51 70 30, troglo-sautauxloups.com.
Mar-Nov.
Learn about geology and mushroom-growing techniques in these immense underground galleries which have been worked since the Middle Ages. On-site restaurant and boutique.

We are the champignons.

Mushroom-growing around Saumur

Mushrooms have been cultivated in the troglodytic caves carved from the soft *tuffeau* stone in Saumur and the Loire basin for over a century. The scale of production is staggering, representing about 60 percent of the French market (making this the leading producer in Europe).

The most common variety is the small, white *champignon de Paris* (button mushroom) but producers grow more exotic fungi like the shiitake and oyster mushrooms.

Le Troglo des Pommes-Tapées
Le Val Hulin, Turquant,
T02 41 51 48 30,
letroglodespommestapees.fr.
Mid-Feb to mid-Nov. An adult visit with a tasting costs €5.50.
Visit the museum and taste the celebrated *pommes tapées*, dried apples with a wonderfully sweet and concentrated flavour (some are soaked in local wines).

Golf

Golf de Saumur
Route des Mortins, St-Hilaire-St-Florent (4 km downstream from Saumur), T02 41 50 87 00, infos@golf-saumur.fr.

Golf Club d'Angers
Moulin de Pistrait, St-Jean-des-Mauvrets (15 km southest of Angers), T02 41 91 96 56, golfangers.com.

Golf Blue Green d'Avrillé
Chateau de la Perrière, Avrillé (6 km northwest of Angers), T02 41 69 22 50, bluegreen.com/avrille.

Heritage
La Mine Bleue
La Gatelière, Noyant-la-Gravoyère (42 km northwest of Angers), T02 41 94 39 69, laminebleue.com.
May-Sep daily 1000-1900. €12.50, €6.70 children (5-11), €35.50 family.
Explore the working environment of 19th-century slate miners by descending in a funicular to galleries 150 m below ground level, then take a miners' train to the seam. Sound and light effects add the final touch of atmosphere.

Transport

Angers is served by high-speed TGV rail services, the journey time being just 1 hour 35 minutes from Paris. There are also high-speed links to Nantes, Marseille and Lille, as well as local TER services throughout the Loire Valley. The journey time to Saumur is just 20 minutes; Tours a little over 1 hour. Saumur is served by Pays de la Loire TER services and is roughly mid-way between Blois and Nantes, each being within an hour or so. Tours and Orléans are on the same route.

In Angers eight bus services stop outside the railway station on place de la Gare, just 5 minutes from the city centre – an interactive information terminal in the station (available in English) will help you. A single ticket (sold on the bus) costs €1.20 and allows you unlimited travel for 1 hour. You must validate your ticket as soon as you start your journey. One-day tickets cost €3.50 or you can buy a book of 10 tickets at the bus station or at many cafés and *tabacs*.

Visitors to Saumur without a car can access the chateau using the local services 33 and 34, direction Hôpital. Route 1 follows the Loire to Turquant, Montsoreau and Fontevraud l'Abbaye – or you could go to Montreuil-Bellay on Route 4 (or Route 3 from the rail station). Tickets cost €1.35 for a single journey within 1 hour or €3.75 per day, and can be purchased at the Point d'Acceuil Agglobus at 19 rue Franklin Roosevelt, near the tourist office.

Rail travel in France can be a revelation.

Contents

The Nantais

A vibrant city – and gateway to the Loire Valley.

Introduction

The Loire has now widened considerably and is wisely held in check by raised *levées* (dykes), while river crossings are often impressive, long, causeway-like bridges striding across banks of sand and shingle. Here and there older farms perch on mounds which would have become small islands during past floods. Overlooking the river are cheerful villages whose cottages occasionally evoke the spirit of a bygone seaside promenade, and the former salt-trade port of St-Florent-le-Vieil, with its distinctive Benedictine Abbey. Further downstream, the chateau town of Ancenis opened a daring suspension bridge in the 19th century and built quays from which to ship its wines, before the railway rendered commercial river transport obsolete. Today, though, the local wine trade continues to flourish and the surrounding unspoilt landscapes offer trails designed to help you explore the area and observe wildlife on lakes and marshes. Ahead, beyond the viewpoint of Champtoceaux and the fishing port of La Patache, we finally reach Nantes – western gateway to the Loire Valley, and for centuries the most important seaport in France. Now Jules Verne's birthplace is rediscovering itself, has restored its Gothic cathedral and the Renaissance chateau of the Ducs de Bretagne, and is consistently voted best city in which to live in the whole of France.

Pastoral river idyll, Saint Florent-le-Vieil.

What to see in...

...one day
Make an early start with breakfast in Nantes' famous **La Cigale** brasserie. Stroll along nearby **rue Crébillon** then descend into the legendary **Passage Pommeraye**. Next, visit the **Château des Ducs de Bretagne** and its enthralling new museum and enjoy lunch in the courtyard restaurant. The immense Gothic **Cathédrale St-Pierre et St-Paul** is a short stroll away, after which you can climb the **Tour LU** to take in the view. Finally, head west to the **Ile de Nantes** to visit the fantastic **Machines de l'Ile** and ride the **Grand Eléphant**.

...a weekend or more
Visit Nantes' **Talensac daily market** and stock up on picnic fare before heading east beside the Loire's *rive gauche* to **Champtoceaux**, to see bird's-eye views of the river from the **Panorama de Champalud**, then follow the **Coulée de la Luce** woodland walk to the riverbank for a peaceful picnic lunch. Continue on to **Ancenis** to sample the local AOC wines at the **Maison des Vins d'Ancenis**. Dine on a floating *tapas* restaurant or return to Nantes to dine in the **Hangar à Bananes** on the Ile de Nantes.

Around Ancenis

As its long journey towards Nantes and the Atlantic Coast nears its end, the Loire flows through gentle, occasionally marshy landscapes, its progress apparently undisturbed by a succession of natural islands. There are few signs of the river's former importance as a navigable waterway but at St-Florent-le-Vieil you can still see the old quays built for the town's once-famous salt trade. Further downstream lies the chateau town of Ancenis, an important river crossing whose own quaysides once shipped wines from the local vineyards, until the coming of the railway ended the Loire's centuries-old role as the region's principal means of commercial and passenger transport. There's ample compensation, however, in the idyllic river scenery you can enjoy from the panoramic viewpoint near the former fortified town of Champtoceaux, which offers a peaceful woodland walk right down to the riverbank.

Essentials

⦿ Getting around Unless you're following the *Loire à Vélo* trail by bike, you'll really be better off using a car rather than relying on public transport. The train stations are away from the town centres and the bus services generally serve the needs of the local population rather than the tourist.

⦿ Train station Gare SNCF, rue de la Libération, Ancenis.

⦿ ATMs Around place Jeanne d'Arc, Ancenis.

⦿ Hospital Hôpital Robert, 160 rue Verger, Ancenis, T02 40 09 44 00.

⦿ Pharmacies Pharmacie de la Poste, 1 rue Georges Clemenceau, Ancenis.

⦿ Post offices 155 rue Aristide Briand, Ancenis.

⦿ Tourist information office Ancenis, 27 rue du Château, T02 40 83 07 44.

Around the region

Eglise Abbatiale, St-Florent-le-Vieil

*Esplanade, St-Florent-le-Vieil, T02 41 72 62 32
(tourist office), ville-saintflorentlevieil.fr.
All year 0900-1830. Free.*

It's said that the site of the town was first settled by
Viking invaders, who used it as a convenient base
from which to pillage vulnerable towns and
villages along the banks of the Loire. Such activity
ended when Comte d'Anjou Foulques Nerra
ordered the construction of a fortress here during
the 10th century. Little now remains, but later the
village found a new role as a port for the once-
important salt trade – the ancient-looking **Tour de
la Gabelle** overlooking the quayside helped
enforce *la gabelle*, a tax on the trade. During the
Revolution the Vendée Revolt began in St-Florent,
which resulted in mass executions and the village
being torched.

Just to the west of the town lies the
promontory of **Montglonne** (a scene recorded by
Turner in 1826) on which Florent, a former Roman
legionnaire and disciple of St-Martin of Tours,
preached the gospels during the fourth century.
Three centuries later St-Mauron founded a
Benedictine monastery, which suffered successive
attacks by Bretons, Normans and Vikings. The
monks fled to Tornus (Burgundy) before returning
to establish the important Abbaye de St-Florent le
Jeune in Saumur and later restored a presence
here. Much of the present abbey dates from the
17th-century reconstruction to repair the ravages
of time and the Wars of Religion which left their
mark on the main body of the abbey (1280-1311).

Unmistakable signs of the influence of the Renaissance.

Ancenis

This Breton town appears once to have been an island, judging by the Celtic ending of *'enis'* (isle). At some point the island became merely a hill when the river abandoned the northern detour – with or without man's intervention is unclear. Today the focus is an important river crossing via the 1950s **Pont Bretagne-Anjou** suspension bridge, whose even more slender predecessor was constructed as a toll-bridge in 1839 – the first such structure (after Nantes) to replace water-borne crossings of the Loire. Along the adjacent riverbanks are the 19th-century quays built to create a port which became redundant when the Angers-Nantes railway line opened in 1860. Overlooking the river is a forlorn 15th- and 16th-century **chateau** (currently closed for repair works) whose Renaissance logis carries François I's salamander emblem. Both stone and iron cannon-balls are embedded in the masonry of the outer bastions, which are now half-buried thanks to construction of the quays. Opposite the chateau is Rue des Tonneliers, whose elegant façades were created by the town's wealthy wine traders. Running parallel is Rue du Château (which becomes rue Général Leclerc) where a courtyard preserves an 18th-century Relais de Poste (mail coach stage). On the western outskirts of the town is the **Dolmen de Pierre Couvretière**, a megalith dating from the fourth century BC, while to the north is a vast area of marshland and lakes with various trails designed for exploring the area and observing wildlife. A leaflet is available from local tourist offices.

Champtoceaux

Known for centuries as Châteauceaux, this pleasant village poised on an escarpment high above the Loire possessed one of the river's most important fortresses, constructed around 988 by Comte d'Anjou Foulques Nerra. Its strategic position, squaring up to a fiercely independent Bretagne, saw it put repeatedly under siege. It was finally destroyed in 1420 as an act of vengeance by Jean V de Montfort, Duc de Bretagne, who had previously

Taste the local wines

Close to the riverbank, just downstream from the bridge, you can taste wines from both Muscadet Coteaux de la Loire and Coteaux d'Ancenis vineyards. *Maison des Vins d'Ancenis, 28 place du Millénaire, T02-40 96 14 92, maisondesvins-d-ancenis.com.* Apr-Oct Tue-Sat 0930-1230 and 1500-1830, Sun 1500-1830. Other times by appointment.

A centuries'-old vignoble.

been imprisoned in the chateau. All that now remains of a once-vast fortified citadel covering over 30 ha is a pair of **circular towers** which guarded entry to the walled town, and which are now the gateway to a pleasant wooded walk known as *la Coulée de la Luce*. The name comes from the Latin *'Lucus'* (sacred wood), suggesting a place for ritual ceremonies. The walk takes you to the riverbank, where you'll find the ruins of a water mill dating from the 13th century. Nearby is **La Patache**, a former port of some importance for fishing and river transport, while a little further upriver lies the **Ile Macrière**. You can enjoy a perfect overview of the river and the island from the Panorama de Champalud, accessible from gardens behind Champtoceaux's tourist office.

Nantes

Nantes has it all, and always did. It sits but a short distance from the Atlantic Coast on the very first point at which it was possible to cross the mighty Loire – all it took was bridging a tightly packed cluster of islands. Nantes not only did so, but went on to fill in the gaps and so create the vast Ile de Nantes which you see in the middle of the river today. Getting around the vibrant, forward-looking city is a snip thanks to a benchmark integrated transport system. As you begin to look around you'll see numerous signs of the city's pride in its illustrious past (as France's most important seaport), from the showpiece mansions of wealthy ship owners to the formidable fortress built by the powerful Dukes of Brittany and a soaring Gothic cathedral constructed from the same pale Loire Valley *tuffeau* stone as the great chateaux. It's a city with real soul and a spirit which gets to you and draws you in, and whose huge student population contributes to a lively café society and a sparkling nightlife. Far from being on the edge – or merely the gateway to the Loire Valley – Nantes really is quite something.

Former quayside mansions built by wealthy ship-owners on the Ile Feydeau.

Ile Feydeau maisons d'armateurs

Map: Nantes, p262.

Nantes, once the 'Venice of France', developed not only on the banks of the Loire but also on a series of islands in the river itself. The sites were understandably popular with ship owners, who could oversee proceedings at the quayside without leaving their sumptuous private residences. Inevitably, though, the combined weight of granite street-level masonry, topped with a further four storeys in limestone, proved too much for the minimal foundations. Soon the showpiece façades began sinking (as you can still see), only the buttressing effect of their terraced construction sparing them from total collapse. However, things were stabilized when the city began filling in the waterways. By the mid-19th century just a handful were left and now only the Loire and the River Erdre (part of which flows beneath the city in a tunnel) remain, leaving districts like the Ile Feydeau and a few 'Quai' signs as poignant reminders of Nantes' seafaring Golden Age. Today the Ile Feydeau is a treasure-trove of architecture dating from 1740-1780, many of the elaborate façades decorated with Neptune and other nautical figures. Many also feature stone balconies with swirling wrought-iron balustrades, all created at huge expense. You can see some of the best of them on quai Turenne and the streets behind, including place de la Petite Hollande.

Ile de Nantes

Map: Nantes, p262.

The 5-km-long Ile de Nantes was created from a group of smaller, mid-river islands and was once home to the city's commercial and naval docks. When the last shipyard closed in 1987 the site lay dormant while the city reflected on its future. The response was the breathtaking redevelopment plan which is currently transforming 337 ha by preserving and finding new uses for key buildings of historic importance, and then adding new housing, offices and a host of supporting facilities.

Essentials

❷ **Getting around** Transport in and around Nantes is via a fully integrated system. A one-hour ticket, valid on trams and buses costs €1.50, a book of 10 is €12, a 24-hour ticket is €4, a family (four person), 24-hour ticket is €6.50 is great value. The *Pass Nantes*, available from the tourist office, the airport and hotels (€18 for 24 hours, €28 for 48 hours and 36€ for 72 hours – reductions for families) entitles you to unlimited travel in and around Nantes and free admission to certain tourist sites. Nantes also has a self-service *bicloo* cycle hire service for short journeys.

❸ **Bus/tram station** The city transport network is run by Tan (T0810-444 444, tan.fr). There are several interchanges (*pôles d'échanges*) where you will find a range of bus services, a tram station, a TER rail station and sometimes a park-and-ride car park. 'Commerce' is the most central and a good place from which to begin exploring the city.

❹ **Train station** 27 boulevard de Stalingrad. From the north entrance, the station is just five minutes from the city centre by tram (or a 20-min walk). To the south of the station you can catch various bus services, including the Tan Air airport shuttle.

❺ **ATMs** Place du Commerce and nearby place Royale.

❻ **Hospital** Hôtel-Dieu, place Alexis Ricordeau, T02 40 08 33 33, chu-nantes.fr (with information in English) has an emergency department (*urgences*) at 9 Quai Moncousu.

❼ **Pharmacies** Pharmacie de Paris,17 rue Orléans, T02 40 48 64 48.

❽ **Post office** Poste Centrale, place Bretagne, Nantes.

❾ **Tourist information offices** 3 cours Olivier de Clisson, Nantes Feydeau, T02 72 64 04 79 or T0892-464 044 (€0.34 per min) in France, nantes-tourisme.com; 2 place St-Pierre, Nantes Cathédrale.

Mascaron nautical reference, Nantes.

Around the region

Cross the river by the Pont Anne de Bretagne and you'll enter a landscape dominated by **les grues Titan** – two huge cranes preserved from the naval dockyards. Other maritime survivors nearby include the early 19th-century former dockyard offices (**Ateliers et Chantiers de Nantes**) and a post-war banana-ripening store (**Hangar à Bananes**), now a minimally restored venue for restaurants, bars and clubs etc. Installed along the Quai des Antilles in front of it are **les Anneaux de Buren**, 18 large rings of red, green and blue neon sculpture which add a colourful glow to the old quayside at night. In brutal contrast is **Blockhaus DY10**, a vast German anti-aircraft emplacement built in reinforced concrete and completed in 1944 beside boulevard Léon Bureau. Fortunately, just across the road on the Prairie-au-Duc is a more uplifting landmark – Les Machines de l'Ile (see below).

Les Machines de l'Ile

Les Chantiers, bd Léon Bureau, T0810-12 12 25 (local call rate), lesmachines-nantes.fr. Jul-Aug daily 1000-2000, low season Tue or Wed-Sun 1400-1800 (check website for specific dates). Closed Jan to mid-Feb. €6.50, €5 under 18s, under 4s free. Disabled access (1 space available per ride). Map: Nantes, p262.

You've seen nothing like this. The former metalworking workshops of the naval dockyard no longer echo with the clamour of warship construction; instead they're now home to an extraordinary group of young workers who devote their creative talents to fabricating all manner of mechanical creatures in the spirit of Jules Verne, who was born just across the river. The buildings, covered by vast glass canopies, now have brightly

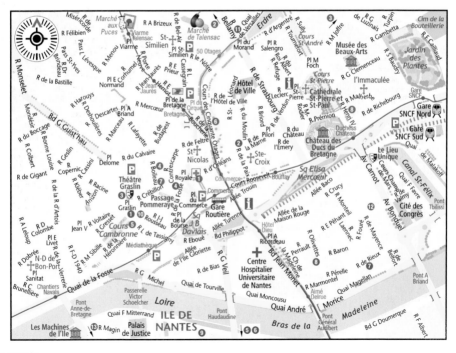

coloured façades, one of which sprouts a single 20-m-long branch of a tree constructed from skeletal steel tubing. It's a prototype built to test the structural qualities of the Arbre aux Hérons, a monumental steel tree destined to grow nearby (complete with hanging gardens and mechanical herons) in years to come. You can see a large-scale model of the finished thing inside the Galerie des Machines, along with other fantastic visions including a crab, a giant squid and a sea serpent. They're among the 27 sea creatures due to feature in **Les Mondes Marins**, a 25-m-high retro-style carousel whose various levels will depict the aquatic world (you'll even be able to control their movements). It's scheduled for completion in 2011. For now the highlight of the visit is a ride on **le Grand Eléphant**, a 12-m-high mechanical elephant (see page 264) which strides around the area outside the workshops, much to the amazement of

unsuspecting passers-by. After disembarking you can descend via walkways through a prototype branch of the similarly fantastic Heron Tree, to reach a souvenir shop and a bar.

The Grue Titan, a prominent survivor from the naval dockyards on the Ile de Nantes.

Nantes listings

Personal experience

Riding le Grand Eléphant

'Un billet pour voyager sur l'eléphant, s'il vous plaît…'

I can't believe that I've just said that. Africa is, after all, a long way away, as, I suspect, is the nearest circus. But I've heard that there's a giant elephant right here on the Ile de Nantes, something which sounds increasingly unlikely as I stare around the cavernous interior of what looks like a pair of giant greenhouses made from Meccano, with a giant tree sprouting from one of the multi-coloured façades. A minute or two later heads around me suddenly crane, mouths gape and eyes open wide in disbelief as a primal bellow echoes from the far end of the left-hand greenhouse. Sure enough, lumbering slowly towards us is an unmistakable elephantine outline on whose back, beneath a curious Victorian-looking canopy, sits a group of figures beaming down at us. Jules Verne would have approved. The beast keeps coming, growing steadily larger until I'm staring up at a giant, softly blinking eye which peers, rather unnervingly, straight back at me. After halting to let the riders dismount it's time to climb a couple of flights of steps, cross a gangway and take a ride myself. Once installed in – rather than on – the beast, it occurs to me that it's not everyday you get to see the inside of an elephant – especially when he (I think it's a 'he', although it's hard to tell from up here) happens to be constructed from tulipwood and leather around a skeletal framework of steel tubing. Curiosity aroused, I climb a spiral iron staircase, to see how the world looks from the back of a 12-m-high mechanical elephant.

'Very different', is the predictable answer. As soon as everyone's safely aboard we set off, after another trumpet-like bellow, on a gentle amble around the open spaces. If you've never ridden an elephant, real or mechanical, I can tell you that the expression 'lumbering gait' suddenly makes sense; as each massive foot meets the ground we sway from side to side, as if on safari. Onlookers, on the other hand, are rooted to the spot. As the elephant lumbers slowly onwards, he displays a mischievous side to his nature, turning his head and flexing his long trunk to spray water over anyone who happens to be within range. Passing motorists can't believe what they're seeing, and, if I'm honest, neither can I.

By now it's clear that our surreal journey isn't exactly going to be epic; 45 minutes won't get you

very far at an average speed of 'barely perceptible'. After passing the preserved offices and giant yellow crane of the long-departed naval dockyards we amble around the island to the rear entrance of the furthest of their former workshops. As we enter the cavernous interior the daylight is fading, and the greenhouse look replaced by an astonishing post-industrial scene, which finds shipbuilding replaced by the construction of *Les Machines de l'Ile* – fantastic mechanical versions of sea creatures. And the Great Elephant, of course. During the few minutes it takes to reach the far end of the vast hall I glimpse some of the industrious activity taking place in the adjoining halls in which he was 'born'. When we've finally ground to a halt where the journey began I descend to the belly of the beast and marvel at the complexity of his hydraulic circulatory system, before stepping back onto the gangway and heading back to earth. First, though, I head round to a viewing area overlooking the machine assembly area. The scene below resembles a vast sci-fi film set, with complex mechanisms being installed into an assortment of as-yet unidentifiable body parts. When I finally tear myself away the weirdness continues, my descent to the exit being through a giant tree branch (mechanical, of course) sprouting 20 m from the front of the workshops. It turns out to be a design prototype, and will form part of the immense Heron Tree that is destined to become the most fantastic of all the Ile's landmarks. And the marine creatures? You'll eventually see them for yourself in the similarly-scaled (and no doubt equally fantastic) Marine Worlds Carousel, which I, for one, can't wait to see.

The vast Palais Royal brought Renaissance refinement to a mighty fortress.

Château des Ducs de Bretagne & Musée d'Histoire Urbaine

4 place Marc-Elder, T0811-464 644 (local call rate), chateau-nantes.fr.
Open all year except 1 Jan, 1 May, 1 Nov, 25 Dec and Mon or Tue low season (check website for specific dates). Entry to the museum is €5, €3 18-26 years, children free. Entry to temporary exhibitions extra. Last admission 1 hr before closing. Audio guides in various languages are available for €3. It is free to stroll around the courtyard and the ramparts. Disabled access, including part of the ramparts. Map: Nantes, p262.

One of the largest, yet least-known of the Renaissance chateaux of the Loire sits partly on the Gallo-Roman walls of a town originally settled by the Namnètes people and summarily levelled in 1466 to build the mighty fortress you see today. It was begun by François II, the last duke of what he was determined would remain an independent Brittany. History decided otherwise, though, when his daughter Anne de Bretagne became Queen of France after marrying Charles VIII (and then Louis

XII). She was responsible for the completion of the present sombre, moated stronghold guarded by seven formidable artillery towers. Overlooking the vast inner courtyard lie the first **Ducal Palace** (*le Petit Gouvernement*) and its dramatically larger Renaissance replacement (*le Grand Gouvernement*). In 1598 it accommodated Henri IV during his visit to sign the Edict of Nantes (see page 28). Note the Classical style of the right-hand wing, reconstructed in 1681 by Louis XIV after fire damage in 1670. Above the doorway is a huge royal coat of arms. You can visit over 30 rooms in the beautifully restored chateau, which houses a ground-breaking museum revealing the history of the building, the city, the port and much more. In addition to a huge range of historical exhibits displayed with contemporary flair in atmospheric settings from basement to roof-spaces, you'll find enthralling multimedia simulations (which allow you to fly at will over the city during various historical periods) and virtual walk-throughs. When you can eventually tear yourself away, round off your visit in style by climbing to the sentry walk for a stroll which circumnavigates the entire site.

Cathédrale St-Pierre et St Paul

Place St Pierre, T0892-464 044 (local call rate).
Daily, no visits Sun am.
Map: Nantes, p262.

From a distance there's an almost English Perpendicular purity to this spectacular cathedral's sturdy towers, the French spirit only revealing itself in the intricately detailed Flamboyant Gothic western portals, and the curved eastern apse. The building's construction, which gradually replaced a previous Romanesque structure, spanned over four centuries, making the architectural unity truly remarkable – a quality which becomes more evident as the ongoing cleaning campaign reveals the dazzlingly pale *tuffeau* exterior stonework. Step inside and look to your left at the great timber doors, where an ancient-looking plaque records the laying of the first stone in April 1434, well after the great age of medieval cathedral construction in France. Not that things appear compromised;

the vaults (designed by Jacques Corbineau, architect of the Château de Brissac), soar to 37.5 m and the colourful decorative bosses adorning their crowns include the arms of Louis XIII, who funded this phase of construction in 1627-1628. Note also the tough granite bases of the *tuffeau* nave piers, the granite being used to withstand the loading and to resist ground humidity. Continue down the nave and in the right-hand transept you'll find the tomb of Duc de Bretagne François II and Marguerite de Foix. A dazzling Renaissance masterpiece in white marble, it was sculpted between 1502 and 1507 by Michel Colombe and now sits below what is claimed to be the tallest stained glass window in France. In the opposite transept is another finely sculptured figure, this time on the monument to General Juchault de la Moricière. A native of Nantes, he commanded a Papal army in an Italian campaign against Garibaldi in 1860 (marble for his grand monument was given by a grateful Pope Pius IX).

The chevet (apse) is a picture of Gothic architectural complexity.

Passage Pommeraye, Vieux Nantes & Tour LU

Map: Nantes, p262.

Among the more atmospheric landmarks of Old Nantes is the now-legendary **Passage Pommeraye**, a startling neoclassical extravaganza created in 1843 by visionary notaire Louis Pommeraye. The respected local solicitor dreamed of linking the port area with the upper city via a three-storey shopping arcade. The final design – bringing together cast iron and oak steps, Corinthian columns and allegorical statues, with an atrium-style canopy of glass and wrought iron – virtually bankrupted its developer and his backers, but the unique arcade remains one of the showpieces of Nantes, and featured in the film *Lola* (Jacques Demy, 1961). A short distance from the upper exit lies another atmospheric spot, the celebrated brasserie **La Cigale**, whose sizzling, perfectly preserved 1900s interior continues to attract those eager to dine in real style. There's more of it right outside, in the neclassical form of the **Théatre Graslin**, opened in 1788. For its sumptuous 18th-century interior we have to thank Emperor Napoléon Bonaparte, who authorized costly repairs after the structure had been ravaged by fire in 1796.

To see further recently rebuilt architecture follow rue Crébillon to **place Royal**, now showing no sign of its wartime devastation. Just beyond lies the **Eglise St-Nicolas**, whose 19th-century Gothic interior rivals the great medieval cathedrals (particularly when illuminated at nightfall, when the doors often remain open). All around lies the heart of Old Nantes, which is worth exploring well beyond the major artery of the **Cours des Cinquante Otages** (particularly if you're dining out).

Beyond the chateau lies another prominent landmark, the curious **Tour LU** – a belle époque tower from the former LU factory whose *Pétit Buerre Nantais* biscuits made Nantes world-famous. Climb to the top of the tower for a fine view of the city (open every afternoon, €2).

A stroll though the Passage Pommeraye.

Musée des Beaux-Arts

10 rue Georges Clémenceau, T02 51 17 45 00, nantes.fr.
Daily 1000-1800 (late opening Thu until 2000). Closed Tue and public holidays. €3.50, free under 18s and 1st Sun of each month from Sep-Jun.
Map: Nantes, p262.

The magnificent setting of this fine arts museum is a purpose-built late 19th-century neclassical structure. It houses a collection purchased by the city in 1801 and created by French diplomat and avid art collector François Cacault. The body of work (thousands of paintings and prints plus numerous sculptures) spanned western European art from the late 13th century to the early 19th century, and was mainly acquired during his travels in Italy. The museum's collections have since expanded to embrace the 20th century, with works by Raoul Dufy, Paul Signac and Claude Monet, plus Max Ernst, Vassily Kandinsky and Pablo Picasso. The acquisitions continue, and the museum is scheduled to close at some point during 2011 to enlarge its display spaces, add an auditorium and improve disabled access.

Sleeping

Le Mésangeau €€€
Drain (12 km south of Ancenis), T02 40 98 21 57, loire-mesangeau.com.
Wonderful 19th-century gentleman's residence in a 6-ha park with a selection of beautifully furnished rooms with ensuite bathrooms. You can also enjoy a candlelit dinner (reservation only, €35 per person) in the dining room. Free Wi-Fi and bicycles for loan.

Le Palais Briau €€€
Rue de la Madeleine, Varades, T02 40 83 45 00, palais-briau.com.

Magnificent Italian-style villa built in the mid-19th century by wealthy railway engineer François Briau. Beautifully restored by the present owners, the four rooms are individually styled with original furniture and sumptuous fabrics. Two of the rooms have views to the Loire and the abbey at St-Florent-le-Vieil.

Le Champalud Hotel Restaurant €€
1 place du Chanoine Bricard, Champtoceaux, T02 40 83 50 09, lechampalud.com.
Situated in the heart of the village next to the church (with bells), Le Champalud provides a comfortable stopover in well-equipped rooms just a few steps from views of the Loire. Its convenient restaurant serves local cuisine (closed Sun evenings Oct-Mar).

Hostellerie de la Gabelle €
12 quai de la Loire, St-Florent-le-Vieil, T02 41 72 50 19, lagabelle.com.
In a superb position on the banks of the Loire, La Gabelle is known for its gastronomic restaurant and river views. However, if you want to stay in the area, they also have plain but well-kept rooms with private bathrooms.

Hôtel de la Regate €€€
155 route de Gachet, T02 40 50 22 22, bestwestern.fr.
Map: Nantes, p262.
In a quiet situation near the banks of the river Erdre, this hotel has a contemporary style and an environmentally friendly ethos. Light and airy rooms have modern bathrooms and there's also a convenient restaurant.

Minimalist chic, Hôtel La Pérouse.

Unless you need to be near the exhibitions centre, though, there are better value hotels in the city centre.

Hôtel Graslin €€€
1 rue Piron, T02 40 69 72 91, hotel-graslin.com.
Map: Nantes, p262.
The Graslin retains some of its art deco elegance but (with rooms entirely redecorated in 2009) offers modern comforts in a superb city centre location. There is parking 100 m from the hotel (€2/night) for guests. Free Wi-Fi.

Hôtel La Pérouse €€€
3 allée Duquesne, T02 40 89 75 00, hotel-laperouse.fr.
Map: Nantes, p262.
Built in 1993, the hotel's contemporary architecture fits Nantes perfectly. The minimal interior, with furnishings by big-name designers, has won the hotel a listing among the 'Hip Hotels' of France. The hotel has a commitment to quality of service and the environment, offers free Wi-Fi and serves local produce in an exceptional buffet breakfast.

L'Hôtel €€€
6 rue Henri IV, T02 40 29 30 31, nanteshotel.com.
Map: Nantes, p262.
Located near the train station and just a few steps from the chateau and the cathedral, the hotel offers well-equipped,

modernized rooms. Some have a terrace overlooking the garden.

All Seasons Nantes Centre €€
3 rue Couedic, T02 40 35 74 50, accorhotels.com.
Map: Nantes, p262.
With rooms overlooking place Royale, this couldn't be better placed for city centre attractions and nightlife. Expect functional, well maintained rooms in this good-value chain hotel.

Hôtel des Colonies €€
5 rue du Chapeau Rouge, T02 40 48 79 76, hoteldescolonies.fr.
Map: Nantes, p262.
Tucked away in a side street, the hotel is close to Graslin and Place Royale. The contemporary rooms decorated in bright colours have quality bed linen and are available for occupation from 1400. The reception area doubles as a lively art gallery.

Hôtel Pommeraye €€
2 rue Boileau, T02 40 48 78 79, hotel-pommeraye.com.
Map: Nantes, p262.
Situated close to the entrance to Passage Pommeraye in the heart of the city, the Pommeraye has a subtly contemporary feel. Rooms are calm and have free Wi-Fi. Rooms overlooking the street are relatively quiet for a central location. The delicious buffet breakfast includes local produce and home-made conserves.

Self-catering
Un Coin Unique
Nantes, T06 64 20 31 09, uncoinchezsoi.net.
Map: Nantes, p262.
Centrally located self-catering apartments that you can rent for just one night if necessary. They all have different themes, such as the *Cabane du Capitaine Némo* – a tiny, centrally located house superbly fitted and furnished in contemporary style, yet strongly influenced by Jules Verne. Or how about *Villa Hamster* – complete with exercise wheel? If you wish, you can also take advantage of hotel service. Around €99 for a single night, from €58 a night for stays of 21 days or more.

ActLieu
Nantes, actlieu.com.
Map: Nantes, p262.
Stay in the heart of the city in one of Actlieu's chambre d'hôtes and you can choose to have hotel service with breakfast, or be independent and self-cater. Accommodation includes trendy loft apartment *Le Briseux* and a luxurious 1930s boat *Le D'Ô*. If you long for something uniquely chic, and you have deep pockets, this is for you. Prices only on enquiry.

Campsite
Camping du Petit Port
21 bd du Petit Port, T02 40 74 47 94, nge-nantes.fr/camping.

The site is open all year to welcome campers and caravans, and also has mobile homes for hire. Just 10 mins north of Nantes city centre by tram.

Around Nantes

Le Domaine d'Orvault €€€
Chemin des Marais du Cens, Orvault, T02 40 76 84 02, domaine-orvault.com.
Hotel in its own grounds with a restaurant, spa centre with pool and outdoor activities including mountain-bike hire. All rooms are spacious and well furnished, although you'll pay a little more for those with a private balcony. Access to the city centre is easy via the tramway (Line 2) from Orvault Grand Val.

Self-catering
Le Relais de la Rinière
Le Landreau (about 25 km southwest of Nantes), T02 40 06 41 44, riniere.com.
Price €220-450 per week depending on season, electricity, linen and towels extra.
Converted from former outbuildings and a bake-house, the accommodation comprises an open plan kitchen/dining area, ground floor double bedroom and a loft room suitable for children. It has its own private gardens and is located in the heart of the Muscadet wine area just 30 minutes from Nantes centre.

Eating & drinking

Around Ancenis

La Charbonnière €€€
Bd Joubert, T02 40 83 25 17,
restaurant-la-charbonniere.com.
Daily except Wed and Sun pm.
Closed Sat lunchtimes Oct-Mar.
Dine on the banks of the Loire
with panoramic views from a
lovely terrace in summer, or
near a cosy open fire in winter.
If you're looking for local dishes,
try the *Pays de la Loire* menu with
fish and meat choices at €32 or
€40. There's also an inspired
vegetarian menu created from
seasonal produce for €18.

La Bouche à Oreille €€
44 rue Aristide Briand,
T02 40 83 08 05, damien.
secheretclub-internet.fr.
Mon-Sat.
Two brothers run this bright and
clean town centre restaurant.
The food is traditional French
with some spicy influences.

L'Eau à la Bouche €
90 place Millénaire, T02 40 98
57 36, eau-a-la-bouche.com.
Tue-Sat 1130-1500 and
1830-2300, also Sun 1130-1500
Jul-Aug.
Tapas bar on a boat moored a
few steps from Ancenis'
suspension bridge. The modern
interior and smart seating on
an outside deck (perfect for
summer evenings) complement
an interesting menu of assorted
meat and fish dishes.

Nantes

Brasserie La Cigale €€€
4 place Graslin, T02 51 84 94 94,
lacigale.com.
Daily 0730-0030.
Map: Nantes, p262.
This classic belle époque
brasserie with its sumptuous
interiors is a Monument
Historique. Enter this period
jewel box at any time of day and
you'll find first-class service from
white-aproned waiters and a
classic brasserie menu. The fresh
seafood is especially good.

La Civelle €€€
21 quai Marcel Boissard,
Trentemoult (access by Navibus),
T02 40 75 46 60, lacivelle.com.
Mon-Fri 1200-1400 and
1930-2230.
Map: Nantes, p262.
On the banks of the Loire in
Trentemoult, this popular
restaurant with terrace and bar
has a welcoming ambiance with
warm lighting and dark leather
seats. Menus, featuring fresh fish
from the Loire and market
produce, change daily. Look out
for fresh Loire eels in a Provençal
sauce, followed perhaps by *tarte
tatin* with pears.

La Maison Baron Lefèvre €€€
33 rue de Rieux, T02 40 89 20 20.
Tue-Sat 1200-1400 and
1930-2300. Closed Aug.
Map: Nantes, p262.
The setting is an old
greengrocer's warehouse
fronted by an *épicerie*. The
restaurant at the rear has
smart loft-style decor with a
mezzanine floor. The menu is
modern and refined and there
is an excellent wine list.

L'Atelier d'Alain €€€
24 rue des Olivettes,
T02 40 84 38 66.
Closed Sat lunch and Sun.
Map: Nantes, p262.
You'll discover chef Alain Ruffault
in the very centre of this
restaurant creating his dishes in
view of the diners. He's certainly
passionate and creative but you'll
also share the heat and clamour
of the kitchen. One to try.

Le 1 €€€
1 rue Olympe de Gouge,
T02 40 08 28 00, leun.fr.
Daily 0900-2300.
Map: Nantes, p262.
This is La Cigale's contemporary
sibling. There's a large well-lit
dining area with cosy bench
seats and colourful armchairs,
an open kitchen and a large
mosaic bar. The lunchtime
Formule Express is good value
at less than €15, evening menus
are around €25, or you can graze
on tapas at the bar.

Le Square €€€
14 rue Jemmapes, T02 40 35
98 09, squarenantes.com.
Daily except Sun.
Map: Nantes, p262.
Fashionable restaurant with a
terrace beneath the maple trees

for summer evening shade. Chef Pascal Perou is passionate about incorporating fresh produce in his creative menu and the restaurant has its own organic *potager* growing forgotten varieties of vegetables bursting with flavour.

L'Océanide €€€
2 rue Paul Bellamy, T02 40 20 32 28, restaurant-oceanide.com.
Mon-Sat 1200-1400 and 1900-2130. Closed end Jul to mid-Aug.
Map: Nantes, p262.
You'll find a refined and welcoming interior here with warm wood panelling and white table cloths. The fish and seafood menu is embellished with fresh produce from the nearby Talansac market, the menu changing according to availability. The wine list is particularly notable for its selections from Nantais producers.

Crêperie Heb-Ken €€
5 rue de Guérande, T02 40 48 79 03.
Tue-Fri 1200-1400 and 1900-2230, Sat 1200-1500 and 1900-2300. Closed mid-Aug.
Map: Nantes, p262.
Authentic Breton crêperie just off place Royale with a truly enormous selection of savoury galettes and sweet crêpes best accompanied by Breton cider. All the ingredients are fresh and locally sourced where possible.

Look out for fresh fruit fillings and the local favourite: *caramel au buerre salé*.

Le Bistrot de l'écrivain €€
15 rue Jean Jacques Rousseau, T02 51 84 15 15, manoir-regate. com/bistrot_ecrivain.htm.
1200-1400 and 1930-2230 (2330 Thu-Sat), closed Sun.
Map: Nantes, p262.
A few steps from place Graslin is a small, simply decorated restaurant serving inventive and traditional French dishes at affordable prices. The menu of the week is around €17.50 and you can buy wine by the glass for €2.50.

Cafés & bars
Around the Théâtre Graslin, particularly rue Jean-Jacques Rousseau, place du Commerce and place Royale, are the main areas for bars and cafés but there are plenty of other interesting places to discover elsewhere around the city.

Café Cult
2 rue des Carmes, T02 40 47 18 49.
Closed Sun.
Map: Nantes, p262.
Charming half-timbered café-restaurant in the heart of Nantes with a lively terrace in summer. Favoured by locals and students during the day, the intimate interior is ideal for a romantic dinner.

Café Graslin
1 rue Racine, T02 40 69 81 79.
Mon-Sun 1600-0200.
Map: Nantes, p262.
Bar with a Breton ambiance, Celtic music and a jovial atmosphere. The owner has selected over 200 beers for you to try (nine of them on draught).

La Guinguette
20 quai Marcel Boissard, Trentemoult, T02 40 75 88 96, laguinguette.fr.
1100-0100. Closed Sun lunchtime, Mon pm and 1-8 Jan.
Map: Nantes, p262.
Situated on the left bank (you can cross on the river ferry) in the small port of Trentemoult, La Guingette has a reputation for great atmosphere and good food. The bar, dining rooms and terrace have views over the Loire and there are regular live music nights.

Hangar à Bananes
21 quai des Antilles, Ile de Nantes, hangarabananes.com.
Map: Nantes, p262.
Located at the extreme west of the Île de Nantes, the warehouse has been converted into a place to relax, with bars, restaurants, an art gallery and a nightclub. It's open all day, every day – summer lunchtimes are good for views from the terrace, and Friday and Saturday evenings are best for the nightlife.

Entertainment

Festivals

Culture Bar-Bars
T06 72 56 02 26, bar-bars.com.
A late November festival with music, poetry, theatre – just about anything is performed in over 100 cafés and bars in Nantes and Rezé.

Folle Journée
Cité de Congrés, T0892-705 205 (tickets, from 2 weeks prior to festival, €0.34/min), follejournee.fr.
An annual classical music festival held in late January. It consists of a series of orchestral concerts, each with a maximum 45-minute duration, featuring international artists and young musicians.

Rendez-vous de l'Erdre
Information T02 51 82 37 70, rendezvouserdre.com.
At the end of August the riverside quays in the heart of Nantes echo with jazz music and entertainment provided by artists from every continent. The events are free.

Nightlife

Le Floride
4 rue St-Domingue, T02 40 47 66 80, lefloride.free.fr.
Wed-Sun 2300-0500.
Entry €8 including a drink.
Franz Ferdinand, Red Hot Chilli Peppers, Pixies, Radiohead and Manu Chao feature on the playlist in this unconventional

Orgue de barbarie.

club attracting people looking for rock rather than disco. There's occasional live music and you can dance under the stars on the terrace (summer nights only). Reasonably priced drinks, even after 0200.

Le Lieu Unique
2 rue de la Biscuiterie, T02 40 12 14 34 (tickets), lelieuunique.com.
On Friday and Saturday nights (2230-0300) the bar turns into a club with live entertainment. There is also a full programme of theatre, dance, music and art exhibitions.

Le Marlowe
1 place St-Vincent, T02 40 48 47 65, le-marlowe-nantes.com.

Mon-Thu 2230-0400, Fri-Sat 2230-0500.
Party the night away in this converted church that's now a lively and friendly club with a road-movie Americana theme. A mix of both age groups and musical styles.

Le Zigidi Saloon
2 rue de l'Heronnière, T02 40 71 99 00, zigidi.com.
Tue-Sat 2000-0400.
For a late drink and music from the 1980s and '90s, head for Zigidi for comfortable seating and friendly conversation. Aimed at a 30-50 age-group, smart dress required.

Shopping

Antiques
Rue Jean Jaurès and place Viarme
Those looking for elusive bargains can browse the antique and *brocante* shops and art galleries. Five minutes walk from here, place Viarme hosts a weekly *marché aux puces* (flea market, Sat 0730-1300) and is where artists and craftsmen have their workshops.

Clothes
Rue Crébillon and Passage Pommeraye
The best shopping street in Nantes is rue Crébillon. In fact, local slang for 'to window-shop' is *'crébillonner'*. You'll find smart boutiques and designer labels as well as jewellers, leather goods, perfumeries and chic cafés.

There's also the famous Passage Pommeraye with its own selection of fine boutiques.

Galeries Lafayette
2 rue de la Marne,
T02 40 99 82 12.
Mon-Sat 0930-2000.
A department store which offers 10% discount to holders of a valid *Pass Nantes*.

Food & drink
Gautier-Debotté
9 rue de la Fosse, T02 40 48 23 19,
gautier-debotte.com.
Tue-Sat 0900-1915.
This is the most beautiful of four Gautier-Debotté shops in Nantes and is listed as a Monument Historique. It's truly a feast for the eyes and is a real jewel box full of tempting confectionery and chocolates.

Gourmandine
18 rue de Verdun, T02 40 47 58 31.
Here you'll find the famous *Rigolettes Nantaises* – fruit sweets with a soft centre, packaged in beautiful boxes and decorated in tins in all shapes and sizes. A perfect gift.

La Friande
12 rue Paul Bellamy,
T02 40 20 14 68.
Sells a selection of gifts and souvenirs including confectionery, LU biscuits, Guérande salt, jams and chocolates.

Marché de Talansac
Place de Talansac.
Tue-Sun 0800-1300.
Established in 1937, this is the oldest and biggest market in Nantes. On the busiest days there are an incredible number of fruit and vegetable stalls outside with fantastic seasonal displays, while indoors are dozens of butchers, cheese producers and bakers selling local and regional products.

Marché de la Petite Hollande
Place de la Petite Hollande.
Sat am.
Shop with the locals in this busy food market. You'll find fresh seafood, warm brioches and masses of colourful stalls.

A visionary shopping experience.

Activities & tours

Boat hire

Ruban Vert

Ile de Versailles, Nantes,
T02 51 81 04 24, rubanvert.fr.

Hire an electric boat (no licence required) and cruise the river at your own pace and in total silence. Various craft are available for just an hour or a whole day on the river.

Boat trips

La Luce

11 rue du Pont-Levis, Oudon,
T02 40 83 60 00,
loire-en-scene.fr.

An hour-long river trip with a commentary on the wildlife and heritage of this beautiful stretch of the Loire. Binoculars provided.

Les Bateaux Nantais

T02 40 14 51 14,
bateaux-nantais.fr.

River trips to discover the Loire and Erdre rivers, plus a choice of cruises combined with lunch or dinner on board. Bookings essential. Departure points vary.

The Loire's lower reaches remain navigable.

Transport

Marine & Loire Cruises
Quai Ernest Renaud, T02 40 69 40 40, marineetloire.fr.
Trips around the port of Nantes with a commentary on its history. You'll pass the Béghin Say sugar cane refinery, the Machines de l'Île's workshops and former ship-building yards. Booking essential.

City tours
Ecolud'
Office de Tourisme Ile Feydeau, T0892-464 044.
A fun and eco-friendly fleet of Segways is available for those longing to have a go (over 14s only). Tours leave every day, duration 1-2 hours.

Guided tours on foot
Office de Tourisme, T0892-464 044, nantes-tourisme.com.
Daily visits (weekends all year round) on a number of themes with an expert guide. Booking recommended. Alternatively, you can download a tour of Nantes onto your MP3 player from the website.

Cycling
Détours de Loire
Gare routiére, allée de la Maison Rouge, T02 40 48 75 37, locationdevelos.com.
Bike hire, self-guided tours and suggestions for outings around Nantes.

Gardens
Les Jardins des Plantes
Bd Stalingrad (opposite the rail station), T02 41 41 65 09, seve.nantes.fr.
Public gardens covering 7 ha and comprising rare plant collections, medicinal plants, camelias and extraordinary glasshouses (small entry fee). There are plenty of walks plus the *L'Orangerie* café – open in the afternoon with a terrace overlooking the park.

Parc du Grand-Blottereau
Bd Auguste Péneau, T02 40 41 65 09, seve.nantes.fr.
Vast gardens and a collection of tropical plants. You can join a guided visit of the greenhouses (small entry fee) and see exotics such as rice, cotton and coffee, as well as citrus and other food plants. It also hosts the *Folie des Plantes* open-air plant show and market, held in September.

Golf
Golf de l'Ile d'Or
La Varenne, T02 40 98 58 00, golfdenantesiledor.com.

Windmill
Le Moulin de l'Epinay
Rue de l'Evre, La Chapelle-St-Florent, T02 41 78 24 08, moulinepinay.com.
It was only in 1989 that the villagers decided to restore this ancient windmill. You can now visit it, see the remarkable results and buy freshly milled flour.

Nantes lies at the extreme west of the Loire Valley, but it is still possible to use the TER rail service (ter-sncf.com) to travel upstream. Nantes to Angers for instance (line 4), takes about 40 minutes, calling at Ancenis – just over an hour if it calls at all stations. It will cost around €14 for a single ticket. Alternatively, you can go to the coast and bathe at Pornic in just over an hour on the direct TER train (line 10), a single ticket costing about €10. You can take a bike free of charge on most TER services – look for the bike symbol on the timetable.

The city's tramway, a model of efficiency.

Contents

Practicalities

Freewheeling across the Pont-Canal de Briare.

Getting there

Air

From UK and Ireland

Nantes Atlantique airport receives **Ryanair** (ryanair. com) flights from Shannon, Dublin, Liverpool and East Midlands airports plus **Aer Arann** (aerarann. com) services from Cork. Ryanair also flies from Dublin and London Stansted to Tours Val de Loire airport. Alternatively, about an hour's drive south of Tours, Poitiers-Biard airport has seasonal flights from Edinburgh and London Stansted with Ryanair.

From North America

There are currently no regular direct flights to the Loire Valley region from North America except a weekly flight between Nantes and Quebec during the summer with **CorsairFly** (corsairfly.com). **Continental** (continental.com), **British Airways** (britishairways.com) and **Air France** (airfrance.com) all fly to Paris from New York. **Delta** (delta.com) flies to Paris from New York and Seattle, and **American Airlines** (aa.com) flies from Boston and Chicago, as well as New York. **Air Canada** (aircanada.com) flies direct to Paris from both Toronto and Vancouver. There are regular rail services from the Gare TGV at Roissy Charles de Gaulle airport to Tours (1hr 45 mins) and Nantes (3 hrs). An alternative would be to fly with **Aer Lingus** (aerlingus.com) from New York to Dublin then direct to Nantes Atlantique via **Ryanair** (ryanair.com).

Airport Information

Nantes Atlantique

T02 40 84 80 00, nantes.aeroport.fr.

Nantes Atlantique is close to the Grand-Lieu Exit (51) on the western Nantes ring road. The shuttle bus between the city centre (south entrance of Nantes central railway station) and the airport is operated by the **Tan** (T0810-444 444, tan.fr) city transport network. It departs roughly every 40 minutes Monday-Friday. There are fewer on Saturday and Sunday afternoons (on Sun mornings, take line 37 then change to line 3 at Neustrie). Tickets cost €7 one way, free if you have a valid **Pass Nantes** (see page 261). Taxis wait just outside the terminal building, with a dedicated area for disabled passengers to alight. Car hire offices and parking are directly in front of the terminal building and there is a fuel station at the entrance. Inside the terminal hall, you'll find a bureau de change and ATM, plus shops and a choice of places to eat.

Tours Val de Loire

T02 47 49 37 00, tours.aeroport.fr.

Tours' airport is 10 minutes from Exit 20 on the A10 autoroute and just 20 minutes from the city centre. There's a shuttle bus (information from Tours bus station T02 47 05 30 49) to Tours city centre which costs €5 one way. The buses leave from the airport 20 minutes after the arrival of flights and will take you to the bus station, adjacent to the rail station in the heart of the city. Return shuttles to the airport depart from the bus station two hours before flight departure times. Val de Loire is a small airport, with limited services, but you can get a snack in the restaurant and there's a shop which opens when flights are due. The car hire office is in the long-stay car park (only open when Ryanair flights are due).

Rail

Rail travel in France is quick and efficient with high speed TGV (*Train à Grande Vitesse*) services between major cities and modern sprinter TER (*Train Expresse Régional*) services on regional lines. All seats on TGV services must be booked in advance, which can be done at a station or online (voyages-sncf. com). For local services, you can purchase your ticket online or at the station. Travellers from the UK to France have frequent **Eurostar** (eurostar.com) services from London to Paris with onward TGV connections direct to Orléans (1 hr), Blois (1½ hrs), Amboise (2 hrs), Tours (1¼ hrs), Angers (1½ hrs) and Nantes (2 hrs). There are also three connections per day from Lille direct to Angers and Nantes (both via Paris). Fares from London to the Loire Valley start at around £79 per person for a standard class return via either Paris or Lille.

Road

From London to Tours, in the heart of the Loire Valley, is around a 700-km journey, with a drive time of just over seven hours (if you travel on autoroutes, in which case expect to pay about €20 in tolls). The National Centre for Traffic Information *Bison Futé* (bison-fute.equipement.gouv.fr) website offers drivers current information on all major routes in France including roadworks, accidents and hazardous weather conditions.

Eurotunnel (eurotunnel.co.uk) trains take just 35 minutes and have up to three crossings an hour at peak times. Fares cost from £53 per car for a single crossing or from £84 for a five-day return. The Eurotunnel has motorway access on both sides of the channel at Folkestone and Calais and with 30-minute check ins, can be a fast and easy alternative to the ferry (see below).

Bus/coach

Eurolines (T+44(0)8717-818177, eurolines.co.uk) coaches depart from London, Gillingham, Canterbury and Dover and serve a number of destinations in France, including Tours, Angers and Nantes. Journeys must be booked a minimum of three days in advance. Adult return fares from London to Tours cost around £98, or £108 to Nantes or Angers – youth and senior travellers get a small discount. Travelling on Friday or Sunday usually incurs a supplement. Journeys are generally overnight, departing late afternoon from London and arriving the following morning. You may have to change at Lille and Tours if travelling to Nantes.

Going green

The area is eminently accessible by rail from Paris and London, making it an attractive option for the environmentally conscious traveller. You can then pick up a hire car at major railway stations – or discover the Loire Valley by bike. The *Loire à Vélo* (loire-a-velo.fr) trail will soon offer 800 km of secure, signposted tracks along the Loire and its tributaries. There's also a network of bike hire and accommodation providers, who have signed up to the Accueil Vélo (Welcome Bike) scheme – all offer specially adapted services tailored to the requirements of cyclists.

Sea

The western ports of St Mâlo and Caen are the most convenient points of arrival to access the Loire Valley. **Brittany Ferries** (brittanyferries.com) has daily services from Portsmouth to St Mâlo (excluding Sat from Nov) with crossing times of around nine hours during the day and 10+ hours overnight; and up to four crossings a day from Portsmouth to Caen (between 3¾ and 7 hrs). St Mâlo is about 320 km from Tours (3½ hrs drive time) via Rennes and Le Mans; from Caen you can access the Loire Valley at Tours, 275 km (3 hrs) via Alençon and Le Mans. **Condor Ferries**' (condorferries.com) fast services from Weymouth (5¼ hrs) or Poole (4 hrs 35 mins) to St Mâlo are an attractive option, but scheduled stops in the Channel Islands can cause delays. **P&O Ferries** (poferries.com) and **SeaFrance** (seafrance.com) serve Calais from Dover (1½ hrs). Calais is 520 km from Tours (5 hrs). Other routes to consider are with **LD Lines** (ldlines.co.uk) who travel from Portsmouth to Le Havre and Dover to Boulogne, or **Transmanche Ferries** (transmancheferries.com) from Newhaven to Dieppe. LD Lines also serve Le Havre from Rosslare and you can travel from Cork to Roscoff with Brittany Ferries.

Getting around

Rail

Most local rail journeys within the Loire Valley are on **TER** trains (ter-sncf.com). Fast, comfortable and affordable, you don't need to make a reservation to travel on and bikes travel free (some restrictions apply during rush hours). See ter-sncf.fr for full rail timetables, service information and special offers.

It's possible to visit most of the major towns and some chateaux by train and there are regular services Monday-Saturday but not Sunday. Using Tours as an example, take the train east to Amboise (less than 20 mins), to Onzain for the Domaine de Chaumont and the Festival Gardens (about 30 mins), to Blois (about 40 mins) or Orléans (about 1 hr 20 mins). Fares largely depend on what time of day you travel; Tours–Blois, for instance, is less than €20 for a return ticket outside of peak times. Travel west from Tours, and you can visit Savonnières, Langeais (10 mins), Saumur (45 mins), Angers (1 hr 20 mins) and Nantes (1 hr 40 mins). Azay-le-Rideau is about 25 minutes away on the Tours–Chinon line and costs €10 return. Check before you travel on this line if you have a bike as some of these services are replaced by buses. Chenonceaux is about 25 minutes from Tours and costs €12 for a return ticket. For information about specific train stations see gares-en-mouvement.com.

Road

Car

Speed limits on French roads are 130 kph (autoroutes), 110 kph (dual carriageways, urban autoroutes), 90 kph (single carriageways) and 50 kph (villages and towns) unless stated otherwise. Speed limits drop by 110 kph on motorways and dual carriageways when it's raining. *Péage* autoroutes are toll roads. It is compulsory to carry a warning triangle and a reflective jacket when driving in France – the jacket must be in the car, not in the boot. The law is enforced by on-the-spot

Tip...

All train passengers must *composter* (validate) their ticket before boarding a train – simply insert the left-hand end of your ticket into one of the machines on the platform or in ticket-halls.

fines of between €90 and €135. For regulations and advice on driving in France visit theaa.com.

Unleaded (*sans plomb*) petrol (95 and 98 octane), diesel (sometimes labelled *gasoil* or *gazole*) and LPG are available. The SP95-E10 (unleaded 95 octane containing 10% ethanol) is now being sold throughout France. This fuel is not compatible with all vehicles, so check with the manufacturer before using it.

It's generally easy to find parking in smaller towns, often right in the centre (except on market days) and it is usually free. Blue-Zone parking is free, but you are required to display a parking disc which can be obtained from police stations, tourist offices and some shops. In larger towns and cities, street parking is often charged (*payant*) with ticket machines (*horodateurs*) nearby. Expect to pay around €1 an hour, and read information on the machine, as parking is usually free at lunchtimes and after 1830. Multi-storey car parks issue a ticket on entry and charge by the hour. Expect to pay €2-3 per hour, depending on the location.

Roads in France are still relatively quiet and relaxed touring on empty countryside roads is a pleasure. However, town centre traffic systems can be confusing – if in doubt just follow *Centre Ville* or *Office de Tourisme* signs and you'll reach the heart of any town.

Car hire

Airports at Tours and Nantes and the main rail stations of Orléans, Tours, Angers and Nantes all have car hire offices. It's best to reserve your vehicle before you travel and to confirm that the office will be open when you'll be arriving – at Tours airport, for example, offices only open just before and just after Ryanair flights are due. For the best deals try **Holiday Autos** (holidayautos.com), a discount hire company which works with major rental businesses. Not all companies operate in the Loire Valley, but you'll find **Europcar** (europcar. com), **Hertz** (hertz.co.uk) and **Avis** (avis.co.uk) present in most large towns.

Requirements for hiring a car may vary, but you must possess a driving licence which is valid in France. If your normal licence is in a different language from the country in which you're renting the vehicle, you may also need an international driving licence.

Be aware that there is normally an insurance excess of between €600 and €2500, which could find you paying a substantial amount for any damage, however minor. Purchase a Damage Excess Waiver for a few extra euros per day and you'll avoid such risks.

Bicycle

The region has hundreds of kilometres of well-signed, dedicated cycle routes and long distance trails, notably the *Loire à Vélo* (loireavelo.fr), the *Châteaux à Vélo* network (chateauxavelo.com) and part of the *Euro Vélo 6* (eurovelo6.org) that links the Atlantic with the Black Sea. There are bike hire shops throughout the region and companies such as **Détours de Loire** (T02 47 61 22 23, locationdevelos.com) offer baggage-carrying services, and can suggest itineraries of varying length and difficulty. They work with local agents, allowing cyclists to pick up and drop off bikes where they choose. Hire costs start from around €14 for a day to €59 per week.

Nantes' fully integrated transport system has transformed the way people move around the city and cyclists will appreciate well-defined cycle lanes. The city's bike rental scheme is called *Le Bicloo*. (bicloo.nantesmetropole.fr), with

conveniently placed stations from which you can take and deposit a bike. You'll need to go to one of 26 stations which take a bank card to sign up and get an access code. For short term use, you pay €1 then about €1 per hour (the first 30 mins are free). Orléans has a similar system called *Vélo+* (agglo-veloplus.fr, see page 108). Other towns have their own bike hire systems: the tourist office on place Kennedy in Angers (angersloiretourisme.com, T02 41 23 50 00) has a hire service, and Détours de Loire have a central hire shop at 35 rue Charles Gille in Tours.

Buses

The main tourist sites in the heart of the region are well served by bus services. From Blois, for example, **TLC** (T02 54 58 55 55, transports-du-loir-et-cher.com) offers a 'Circuit Châteaux' from April-September costing around €12. From Tours, services to the Château de Chenonceau and Amboise operate all year, whereas Azay-le-Rideau and Villandry are best served during school holidays. Saumur has good services throughout the year to outlying villages like Montsoreauand Montreuil-Bellay. Bus journeys generally cost between €1.10 and €1.35 for a single journey within one hour, so day tickets for €3-4 may be better value if you are planning a day out.

When staying in one of the cities, check to see if the local tourist pass offers free travel – the **Pass Nantes**, for example, starts at €14 for 24 hours and includes entry to 25 sites, plus all public transport (including, usefully, the airport shuttle). For occasional journeys in Orléans, Angers and Nantes, trams are much more frequent than buses and are simple to use. Buy a day/weekend ticket for the best value.

Key bus companies throughout the region are **Ulys** (ulys-loiret.com), **Fil Vert** (tourainefilvert.com), **Agglobus** (agglobus.fr), **COTRA** (cotra.fr) and **Tan** (tan.fr).

Directory

Customs & immigration

UK and EU citizens do not require a visa, but need a valid passport to enter France. You are required to carry some form of identification with you at all times in France. Travellers from outside the EU may need to obtain a standard tourist visa valid for up to 90 days.

Disabled travellers

Tourism sites in France have improved facilities for disabled visitors over recent years with the installation of ramps, dedicated car parking and toilets with wheelchair access. However, many historic buildings and town centres have uneven surfaces underfoot, lots of gravel and assorted street furniture which can pose difficulties for wheelchair users and blind or partially sighted visitors. The Ministry of Tourism has been working with the industry to develop the *Tourisme & Handicap* label to communicate reliable, consistent and objective information regarding accessibility of tourist sites (see tourisme-handicaps.org for detailed of attractions and accommodation with the Tourisme & Handicap label).

Emergencies

Ambulance T15; **Police** T17; **Fire Service** T18 (if calling from a landline). The European emergency number T112 can be dialled free from any phone, including mobiles and call boxes.

Etiquette

The French are a formal and very courteous society and it is normal to greet everyone you meet. *Bonjour* (*Bonsoir* during the evening), followed by *Monsieur*, *Madame*, or for a young single woman, *Madamoiselle* (pronounced '*Mam'selle*') will start you off on the right foot. When meeting someone for the first time people often shake hands. Even with people who you know, such as a waiter at your favourite restaurant, a greeting will start with a crisp handshake. A *bisou* (kiss on the cheek) is strictly for good friends and family. Always use the formal *vous* to say 'you' in French rather than the more intimate form *tu* which is normally reserved for friends and family. It is best to let the French decide when they do it, then return the compliment.

Health

EU citizens should obtain a **European Health Insurance Card** (ehic.org) before travelling to France. This entitles you to emergency medical treatment on the same terms as French nationals. If you develop a minor ailment while on holiday, pharmacists can give medical advice and recommend treatment. Outside normal opening hours, the address of the nearest duty pharmacy (*pharmacie de garde*) is displayed in other pharmacy windows. The out-of-hours number for a local doctor (*médecin généraliste*) may also be listed.

In a serious emergency, go to the accident and emergency department (*urgences*) at the nearest *Centre Hospitalier* (numbers listed in the Essentials boxes in each chapter) or call an ambulance (SAMU) by dialling T15.

Insurance

Comprehensive travel and medical insurance are strongly recommended, as the European Health Insurance Card (EHIC) does not cover medical repatriation, ongoing medical treatment or treatment considered to be non-urgent.

Money

The French unit of currency is the Euro. ATMs throughout France accept major credit and debit cards. Currency exchange is available in some banks, and at airports, train stations and bureaux de change. Most restaurants, shops, and tourist attractions accept major credit cards, although restaurants in smaller towns may only accept cash. Toll (*péage*) routes accept Visa, Mastercard and American Express cards but not Maestro or Visa Electron cards.

Police

There are three national police forces in France. The *Police nationale* operate mainly in urban areas and are distinguished by silver buttons on their uniforms. The *Gendarmerie nationale* are under the control of the Ministry of Defence and wear blue uniforms with gold buttons. They deal with serious crime on a national level. The *Douane* is a civilian customs service. Only these three services have the power of arrest. All police in France are armed.

Post

You can buy stamps (*timbres*) in post offices or over the counter in *tabacs*. A stamp for a postcard will cost around €0.60. Many post offices now have self-service stamp machines with instructions in several languages, including English.

Safety

Away from very large cities the crime rate in France is generally low. Think carefully, though, about where you park your car at night – and never leave valuables in your car, even briefly. In provincial towns and cities it is generally safe to walk where you please, although at night avoid wandering into unlit areas. Only carry small amounts of cash, and keep passport, credit cards and cash separate. Travelling on public transport in France is generally very safe. Never leave luggage unattended at bus or railway stations and always be alert to risk, especially late at night. If you are a victim of theft, report the crime to the police (*Gendarmerie*)

immediately as you will need their report (*constat de vol*) to claim on your insurance.

Telephone

French telephone numbers consist of 10 digits and always start with a zero. Area codes are incorporated into the number so the first two digits denote the region (02 in the Loire Valley), the second pair is the town, the third pair the district. To call France from abroad dial the international prefix 00 plus 33 (the country code) followed by the phone number required (drop the first 0). Search online for phone numbers using pagesblanches.fr (private numbers) or pagesjaunes.fr (business numbers). For France Télécom directory enquiries dial 118 712 (calls cost a min €1.12) or visit 118712.fr.

Time difference

France uses Central European Time, GMT+1.

Tipping

Most restaurants include service in their prices (*servis inclus* or *compris* is usually stated at the foot of the menu), so leaving extra for a tip is not necessary. Taxi drivers expect a small tip, usually 5-10% of the fare.

Voltage

France functions on a 230V mains supply. Plugs are the standard European two-pin variety.

Language

Basics

hello   bonjour
good evening   bonsoir
goodbye   au revoir/salut (polite/informal)
please   s'il vous plaît
thank you   merci
I'm sorry, excuse me   pardon, excusez-moi
yes   oui
no   non
how are you?
  comment allez-vous?/ça va? (polite/informal)
fine, thank you   bien, merci
one moment   un instant
how?   comment?
how much?   c'est combien?
when?   quand?
where is ...?   où est ...?
why?   pourquoi?
what?   quoi?
what's that?   qu'est-ce que c'est?
I don't understand   je ne comprends pas
I don't know   je ne sais pas
I don't speak French   je ne parle pas français
how do you say ... (in French)?
  comment dites-vous ... (en français)?
do you speak English?   est-ce que vous parlez
anglais? / parlez-vous anglais?
help!   au secours!
wait!   attendez!
stop!   arrêtez!

Numbers

one	un	17	dix-sept
two	deux	18	dix-huit
three	trois	19	dix-neuf
four	quatre	20	vingt
five	cinq	21	vingt-et-un
six	six	22	vingt-deux
seven	sept	30	trente
eight	huit	40	quarante
nine	neuf	50	cinquante
10	dix	60	soixante
11	onze	70	soixante-dix
12	douze	80	quatre-vingts
13	treize	90	quatre-vingt-dix
14	quatorze	100	cent
15	quinze	200	deux cents
16	seize	1000	mille

Shopping

this one/that one   celui-ci/celui-là
less   moins
more   plus
expensive   cher
cheap   pas cher/bon marché
how much is it?
  c'est combien? / combien est-ce que ça coûte?
can I have ...? (literally 'I would like)   je voudrais...

Travelling

one ticket for...   un billet pour...
single   un aller-simple
return   un aller-retour
airport   l'aéroport
bus stop   l'arrêt de bus
train   le train
car   la voiture
taxi   le taxi
is it far?   c'est loin?

Hotels

a single/double room
une chambre à une personne/deux personnes
a double bed   *un lit double/un grand lit*
bathroom   *la salle de bain*
shower   *la douche*
is there a (good) view?
est-ce qu'il y a une (belle) vue?
can I see the room?
est-ce que je peux voir la chambre?
when is breakfast?
le petit dejeuner est à quelle heure?
can I have the key?
est-ce que je peux avoir la clef?/La clef, s'il vous plaît

Time

morning   *le matin*
afternoon   *l'après-midi*
evening   *le soir*
night   *la nuit*
a day   *un jour*
a week   *une semaine*
a month   *un mois*
soon   *bientôt*
later   *plus tard*
what time is it?   *quelle heure est-il?*
today/tomorrow/yesterday
aujourd'hui/demain/hier

Ticket machine, Gare d'Orléans.

Months

January	*janvier*	February	*février*
March	*mars*	April	*avril*
May	*mai*	June	*juin*
July	*juillet*	August	*août*
September	*septembre*	October	*octobre*
November	*novembre*	December	*décembre*

Days

Monday	*lundi*	Tuesday	*mardi*
Wednesday	*mercredi*	Thursday	*jeudi*
Friday	*vendredi*	Saturday	*samedi*
Sunday	*dimanche*		

Index

Credits

Footprint credits

Project Editor: Alan Murphy
Picture editors: Rob Lunn, Emma Bryers
Layout & production: Emma Bryers
Maps: Gail Townsley
Editor: Sarah Thorowgood
Proofreader: Tamsin Stirk
Series design: Mytton Williams

Managing Director: Andy Riddle
Commercial Director: Patrick Dawson
Publisher: Alan Murphy
Publishing managers: Felicity Laughton, Jo Williams
Picture researchers: Kassia Gawronski, Rob Lunn
Marketing: Liz Harper, Hannah Bonnell
Sales: Jeremy Parr
Advertising: Renu Sibal
Finance & administration: Elizabeth Taylor

Print

Manufactured in India by Nutech
Pulp from sustainable forests

Every effort has been made to ensure that the facts in this guidebook are accurate. However, travellers should still obtain advice from consulates, airlines etc about travel and visa requirements before travelling. The authors and publishers cannot accept responsibility for any loss, injury or inconvenience however caused.

Publishing information

FootprintFrance Loire Valley
1st edition
© Footprint Handbooks Ltd
May 2010

ISBN 978-1-906098-93-3
CIP DATA: A catalogue record for this book is available from the British Library

® Footprint Handbooks and the Footprint mark are a registered trademark of Footprint Handbooks Ltd

Published by Footprint
6 Riverside Court
Lower Bristol Road
Bath BA2 3DZ, UK
T +44 (0)1225 469141
F +44 (0)1225 469461
footprinttravelguides.com

Distributed in North America by
Globe Pequot Press